PENGUIN BOOKS

WILLIE'S TIME

Charles Einstein has been a newspaperman, novelist, essayist, editor, columnist, screenwriter, and prizewinning short story author. Yet for all seasons, he prefers the baseball season: He is a lifetime member of the Baseball Writers' Association of America and a ranking historian of the game. He has put together six baseball anthologies, the most recent being *The New Baseball Reader*.

Willie's Time

A Memoir by

CHARLES EINSTEIN

PENGUIN BOOKS

PENGUIN BOOKS
Published by the Penguin Group
Viking Penguin, a division of Penguin Books USA Inc.,
375 Hudson Street, New York, New York 10014, U.S.A.
Penguin Books Ltd, 27 Wrights Lane, London W8 5TZ, England
Penguin Books Australia Ltd, Ringwood, Victoria, Australia
Penguin Books Canada Ltd, 10 Alcorn Avenue, Suite 300,
Toronto, Ontario, Canada M4V 3B2
Penguin Books (N.Z.) Ltd, 182–190 Wairau Road,
Auckland 10, New Zealand

Penguin Books Ltd, Registerd Offices:
Harmondsworth, Middlesex, England

First published in the United States of America by
J. B. Lippincott Company 1979
Published in Penguin Books 1992

1 3 5 7 9 10 8 6 4 2

Grateful acknowledgment is made for the following:

Excerpts in Parts One and Two from *How the Weather Was* by Roger Kahn. Copyright © 1973 by Roger Kahn. By permission of Harper & Row, Publishers, Inc.

Excerpts in Part Two from *A Day in the Bleachers* by Arnold Hano, published by T. Y. Crowell, New York, 1955. Reprinted with permission of the author.

Excerpts in Part Three from *A Thousand Days* by Arthur M. Schlesinger, Jr. Copyright © 1965 by Arthur M. Schlesinger, Jr. Reprinted by permission of Houghton Mifflin Company.

Excerpts in Part Four from *The Vantage Point* by Lyndon Baines Johnson. Copyright © 1971 by HEC Public Affairs Foundation. Reprinted by permission of Holt, Rinehart and Winston, Publishers.

Excerpts in Parts Three, Four, and Five from the book *Baseball Has Done It* by Jackie Robinson. Edited by Charles Dexter. Copyright © 1964 by Jack R. Robinson and Charles Dexter. Reprinted by permission of J. B. Lippincott Company.

THE LIBRARY OF CONGRESS HAS CATALOGUED THE HARDCOVER AS FOLLOWS:
Einstein, Charles.
Willie's time.
1. Mays, Willie, 1931– 2. Baseball players—
United States—Biography. I. Title.
GV865.M38E53
796.357'092'4
ISBN-0-397-01329-9 (hc.) 79–10097
ISBN 0 14 01.5840 5 (pbk.)

Printed in the United States of America

CONTENTS

Willie's
Time

PART ONE

HARRY

—◆◆◆—

The Exact Answer to the Most Critical Need

The CANVAS SACK HUNG LIMP from its standard like the body of a Cromwellian highwayman from his roadside gibbet. But this one flanked the single-track line of the Santa Fe Railroad at a place called Dana Point, where, ribboning down from Los Angeles through the adobe mission town of San Juan Capistrano three miles inland, the roadbed finally met the sea. At two minutes past four every afternoon, the southbound San Diegan swept through Dana Point at 58 miles per hour, and a scythelike claw reached out from the combination mail-and-baggage car and snatched the canvas bag into the train. In the same instant an empty sack was tossed trackside from the speeding U.S. Railway Post Office, for tomorrow's use. By the time the streamliner made its next coursing mail pickup, six miles farther south, at San Clemente, the Dana Point collection would be emptied, sorted, and pigeonholed for delivery. That was how the mail moved, nor could anyone recall when it had been different.

Music, please. A blues beat. *Hear the train a-callin'* (a youthful Dinah Shore had sung), *Hoo-eee!* But on the last Friday in May it never rained at Dana Point, and fewer and fewer trains, the San Diegan included, went *hoo-eee*, that lonesome signature in the night. American lore, it had been. (Passenger: "Why is this train ten minutes early?" Conductor: "It's yesterday's train.") The old *Chambers's Encyclopaedia*, giving figures for the year 1855, showed the United States even in those pre-transcontinental times with 19,247 miles of railroad lines, compared to 21,140 for all of Europe. (Passenger: "Can't you go any faster?" Conductor: "Yes, but I want to stay on the train.") But in 1951 the era of steam was phasing out, and in the stead of the *hoo-eee*, though still in the same code of rhythm as the train reached a whistle board before a grade crossing—one long, another long, one short, one last long: *oooh, oooh, ooh, ooooohhh*—now more and more came the impersonal blat of the diesel horn.

A baseball player named Willie Mays—Willie Howard Mays, actually, so named for William Howard Taft, President of the United States in 1912 when this Mays was born—could tell you about trains. *Oh, the boss man high with the TC&I.* TC&I: that was Tennessee Coal and Iron, the great subcorporation of United States Steel in its Fairfield works outside of Birmingham, Alabama. Mays worked there. Then in World War II, at the instigation of a fellow ballplayer who had already made the move, he traveled to Detroit and went into essential war work there, draft-deferred because of his job with the Kelsey-Hayes Wheel Company. But after the war he landed a job as a porter for the Pullman Company, manning the sleeping cars out of Detroit on the tracks of the old Wabash Cannonball. From the sound of the whistle in the night, he said, you could tell which engineer was driving the train. "He'd lay his hand on that rope and it was like an autograph."

His sleeping-car assignment had the advantage that it landed him time and again back with his family in Birmingham, and there his reputation as a ballplayer carried over. He had worked for the Spike and Bolt division at the TC&I mill, playing frequently for the company team, and that was fast baseball. A small, bouncy, Buddha-tummied figure, he was known as Kitty Kat, Kat for short, for his spring as an outfielder and the feline grace he showed in beating out a bunt. "I made it during the Depression," he has said. "I'd play for anybody who'd give you money. Because every time somebody come to get me to play baseball, I'd say, 'I can't go, man—I got something to do.' And he'd say, 'Come on, man, I'll give you $2.50.' Sometimes when things was bad you'd have to go for ten cent a game. And for that money you *learned* baseball. You know, I used to study the pitchers when I got on first base 'cause I could bunt my way on, and if I got to first base it was like getting a double. And to me, from second base to third base was much easier than from first to second."

His father, Walter Mays, was a sharecropper in Tuscaloosa,

but he was also a pitcher of distinguished reputation. "It went from him through me," Kat said, "and to the third generation, my own son. And they say the third generation is it. But it's not true we were rivals, my boy and me. Couple of times we played together on the Gray Sox. I played with them off and on till I was thirty-eight." The Gray Sox, a semi-pro team occasionally featuring Kitty Kat in the outfield and his adolescent son at second base, did their playing on a close-bordered football field at 63rd Street and Court F in Fairfield, where today its light poles still stand, brooding over a sea of weeds. A few blocks away is what's left of Fairfield Industrial High School, fire-bombed by segregationists to a Berlin state of free-standing concrete wall and blackened, rusted girders. This act of arson took place in 1970, the year the school was to be renamed for E. J. Oliver, a fundamentalist martinet who had retired after forty-three years as the school's principal. Kitty Kat's son, Willie, had gone to that school; so earlier had Kat's wife, a lithe girl named Anna Sattlewhite, who was, Oliver says today, "the type of young people you like to deal with, because she soon became knowledgeable about what the values were in life. We had the majority of our children trying to become someone, so we didn't worry about the five percent who weren't trying. At least they did not hinder the others."

But the year in focus here is 1951. The newsstand price of *The New York Times* had gone up from three cents to five. Rain pelted eastern Kansas, bringing a million acres under flood. The same food basket that cost $5 in 1939 now brought $11.97. In his castle at San Simeon, William Randolph Hearst had retired to his deathbed. In Chicago, the Wanzer Dairy phased out the last of its horse-drawn milk-delivery routes. And across the Pacific Coast Highway from the Santa Fe track at Dana Point, an ocean-side motel, beset by a glut of local produce, had begun to force salad onto its menu as a dish thrust upon the customer before, rather than with or after, the entree. The restaurant left it to the patron to choose his own salad dressing. French, Roquefort,

Thousand Island, went the bottled litany. That last was most intriguing, for—the way it was packaged—Thousand Island was for all intents and purposes the same as Russian dressing. The difference lay in the name, because Russian dressing had become un-American. A United States senator from Wisconsin, Joseph R. McCarthy, had seen to that.

McCarthy? By the enlightened standards of today, even to end a paragraph with him is to ennoble him, and the convenience is to regard McCarthyism as old hat, like the Southern railroad jokes. (Passenger to dining-car waiter: "Bring me a steak and a few kind words." Waiter, returning: "Here's your steak." Passenger: "What about the kind words?" Waiter: "Don't eat that steak.") But in 1951, McCarthy was no joke. A year earlier, assigned to deliver a partisan address to the Ohio County Women's Club of Wheeling, West Virginia, he had in the exercise of his greatest commodity, which was sloth, used a text already preached by a fellow Republican, a California congressman named Nixon, four days earlier at another site. The words were identical: "We are not just dealing with spies who get thirty pieces of silver to steal the blueprints of a new weapon. We are dealing with a far more sinister type of activity because it permits the enemy to guide and shape our policy." To this, McCarthy added:

"While I cannot take the time to name all the men in the State Department who have been named as members of the Communist Party and members of a spy ring, I have here in my hand a list of two hundred and five that were known to the Secretary of State as being members of the Communist Party and are still working and shaping the policy of the State Department."

"He may have been holding a laundry list, a shopping list, or an old Christmas card list" wrote historian William Manchester a generation later. He may also have been holding a B&O timetable. Whatever it was, his most apposite phrasing—*While I cannot take the time . . . I have here in my hand*—was to serve him expeditiously for most of what was left of his life. Even in his death from drink seven years later, by then exposed and even ridiculed, he had lost less ground than it is popular to suppose; the disciples hinted darkly that he had been poisoned. "He regarded himself as betrayed," wrote the columnist George Sokolsky. "He particularly felt that he was betrayed by Vice-President Nixon, whom he had always trusted."

But in the full flower of McCarthyism, in 1951, schoolchildren mailed dimes and quarters to him; their parents mailed dollars. If, as Manchester notes, the great anti-Communist crusader took the money and invested it in soybean futures, that certainly did not challenge his appeal. The noblest Republican of the day, Senator Robert A. Taft of Ohio, knew how to gauge the wind. "If one case doesn't work," he told McCarthy, "try another."

And in that atmosphere, you did not ask for Russian dressing. In the phobic scramble to more patriotic labels, the oldest established team in professional baseball, the Cincinnati Reds, even announced an official name change, from Reds to Redlegs. Mordant to report, that was just about the only divorce that didn't take, for the baseball public refused to accept the new name. "We were Reds before they were," Cincinnati sportswriter Tom Swope explained.

A-clickety-clack, a-echoin' back. Same music. Slow Pine Top left hand. The traditions in a nation barely two hundred years old are few enough, and the ones we have tend to get kicked around. Walter Mays, Kat's father, was a pitcher in Tuscaloosa before there was even a Pledge of Allegiance to the flag. (And a person born in 1915 would have had to learn three different versions of the Pledge by the time he was forty.) George Washington's birthday, once known to every schoolchild as February 22, now is Monday. And the pressure waxes constantly to junk "The Star-Spangled Banner," whose stirring opening lines, according to Albert Brooks, now go:

> As we stand here wait-*ing*
> For the ball game to start . . .

The ball game itself, meanwhile, is doing business at the same old stand. Dick Young said there was something uniquely American in hitting one out of the park. But if baseball thus defies the confinements of space, so also has it eliminated the barrier of time, for it has no clock. Its scoring is done by the team that doesn't have the ball. And the game comes with the springtime.

Captured Northerners taught the sport to their Confederate jailers in the Civil War prison camps, and nearly twelve decades later General Motors would float a prizewinning radio-TV commercial, a jingle that sang: "They go together, in the good old USA: baseball, hot dogs, apple pie, and Chevrolet." Chevrolets, of course, are subject to recall. But so, in the truer sense of the word, is baseball. My immigrant grandfather took my father to his first baseball game in 1910. In 1932, my father took me to my first game and chose the occasion to announce that he was a magician. "When I say stand up," he told me, "everybody here will stand up." He told the people to stand up and they did. Then in an even softer voice he told them to sit down. They did that too. In 1957 I took my oldest son to his first game and executed the same small miracle for him. Now he has a son and the same plan in store. No one knows where or when the custom of the seventh-inning stretch arose. It is like Turnip Day in Missouri. "The twenty-sixth of July, wet or dry, always sow turnips," Harry Truman explained to Merle Miller. The latter was interested in how one went about setting dates like that. "Your grandmother tells you," Mr. Truman said.

The singular and expansive influence of such tradition is a reason among others why there is no good purpose in comparing baseball to other sports. There is nothing hereditary about attendance at basketball games; nor does the father of the son of the son of the father go to the racetrack on that account. Football, which at essence is a manifestation of Scotch Presbyterian sex—ritual collision and involuntary outcry, once a week—is the captive of a grotesque format: if it snows, you play anyway, and when the New York football Giants won two of their first fourteen games, they awoke to the discovery that the season was over. (The 1951 New York baseball Giants started off the same way, but it was still only April, and they went on to win the pennant.) In soccer, the most advanced stadium design calls for a moat. Boxing is a manly art, and according to Leonard Koppett (who could cite the works of Ernest Hemingway in illustration), it is the only spectator sport other than baseball that can really be written about. But even there things can go wrong. "I was watching the fights on television," Rodney Dangerfield said, "and a hockey game broke out."

Comparisons can be made, to be sure, within the game of baseball itself, and between any one of its eras and any other. Ask the ordinary buff about such champions as Lenglen, Armour, Willard, and Shaw, and he might have trouble identifying them by sex, let alone sport. But baseball presents fewer of these difficulties. Because it has changed so little, and because it has the vastest statistical library of any game in history, its bygone days and heroes mingle consensually with the present. *Move over, Babe—Here comes Henry!* So rang a disc-jockey favorite in 1974, as Aaron zeroed in on Ruth's career home-run record. Babe, of course, was not about to move anywhere. His record had been set thirty-nine years earlier, and for the last twenty-six of those he was dead.

Paul Fisher said statistics were the earmark of a literate people, and Herbert Warren Wind, writing in the pages of *The New Yorker*, remarked that Ty Cobb's lifetime batting average could tell you more about him than "a long parade of adjectives." I would want to agree. When the record proclaims that the 1930 Phillies collected 1,783 hits, had eight players with batting averages of .313 or higher, with just three of them driving in a total of 389 runs among them, and finished dead last, 40 games behind the pennant winner, then it has taken just four numbers to describe the 1930 Phillies.

In fairness, it needs to be said that not everyone shares this enthusiasm for statistics, nor the private cabalistic enjoyment that may attach to them. Taping his thoughts for Jerome Holtzman's book *No Cheering in the Press Box*, veteran San Francisco sportswriter Abe Kemp said, "Statistics, I detest. They're the scourge of the American sports page. The fifteenth time he wiped his ass, the sixteenth time he rubbed his nose. You're writing a story and you say he's six foot seven, he's four foot two, or his earned run average is _____. That's a lot of crap. You disturb the continuity of the story. But that's all you get today."

———◆———

Away then from statistics, though they are bound to recur. Treat instead of the scene at New York's "21" restaurant. It was 1951, and the waiter brought the menu for Charlie Chaplin and his wife. There the salad did *not* come before the main course; today it is one of the few places where it still doesn't, for the contamination of the country by California, in more things than salad, is by now fairly complete. But twenty-one years later, at that same "21," the same waiter would serve Mr. and Mrs. Chaplin again, this time with tears for their homecoming. Always a British citizen, Chaplin was to leave in 1952 for a routine trip to Europe. When he did, the U.S. summarily canceled his re-entry permit. The exile was to last two decades. Meanwhile the American Legion declared it unpatriotic to watch his old movies.

But segue now to another British-born actor named Charles,

this one Charles Laughton, who made his mark in movies as Captain Bligh and Quasimodo, the hunchback of Notre Dame. They may have retired the milk wagon and its horse, yet in 1951 the world's fastest ocean liner, the S.S. *United States*, was still under construction. (Completed at a cost of $70 million, it would upon its maiden voyage the following year cross the Atlantic in a record 3 days, 10 hours, 40 minutes.) And if you applied for life insurance, you had to say how often you traveled by air. If it was frequently, they upped your premium.

Laughton had no such problem. Built off World War II bomber prototypes, two propeller-driven, four-engine aircraft, the Douglas DC-6 and the Lockheed Constellation, were now in regular coast-to-coast passenger service, the Sixes for United and American Airlines, the Connies with TWA. All made a mandatory pit stop at Chicago, using the diagonal runways. (They had to: Chicago's Midway airport was only one mile square, auto access and parking, terminal facilities, hangars, taxiways, and ramp space included.) The fastest (eastbound) scheduled time was just under twelve hours, and under a new pricing concept some of the planes were all-first-class, others all-coach. George Jessel liked the first-class overnight passage, which offered sleeping berths. "You'll wake me up at Newark," he said to the stewardess, upon boarding at Los Angeles' even-smaller two-runway airport at El Segundo, "and that'll be the whole thing altogether." No one—and that included both Jessel and the stewardess, whose union would later complain about it —had ever heard of jet lag.

But Charles Laughton went that one better. To judge from his conversation, he had never heard of airplanes. When he went into New York from the Coast, it was—*a-clickety-clack*—in the high style of the day: a bedroom on the Santa Fe's Super Chief from Los Angeles to Chicago and from there, graduating from the heights to the summit, a bedroom aboard the New York Central's Twentieth Century Limited, from Chicago's granite La Salle Street station into Grand Central Terminal at 42nd

Street and Park Avenue. They painted that train an under-stated, soot-resisting gray. Rolling south out of La Salle Street, it made its mandatory second Chicago passenger pickup at the Englewood–63rd Street station, then droned its swift sixteen-hour trip through Gary, Elkhart, Toledo, Cleveland, Erie, Buffalo, Rochester, Syracuse, Albany. (In the post-midnight run from Buffalo to Albany, looking out the right-hand window from the train, you could see successive sweeping spears of light, the beacons that stabbed the night to show the way for airplanes overhead as they matched the route of the Erie Canal.) And after Albany, there was one more stop for the Twentieth Century, at a little-known place called Harmon, New York, where its giant locomotive was replaced by a workhorse Westinghouse electric, the EP-3 "flat-bottom," which looked like a square-built mole and flourished as one as it burrowed underground at 97th Street for the final 2½-mile run to the raised concrete platforms of Grand Central.

Considerations such as these did not preoccupy the Beverly Hills travel agent who booked Laughton's transportation. He had other and more pressing curiosities to deal with. Clients who flew daytime from the Coast to New York, for example, now included some who insisted they be seated on the left side of the aircraft. That was the side away from the sun, and the request made some sense. Laughton on the other hand made no sense at all. Indifferent to his bedroom location aboard the Super Chief, he still insisted that his Twentieth Century bedroom be on the right-hand side of the *train*. Worse than that, he demanded also that the Pullman porter awaken him at Albany, which on the Century's run would be just past five o'clock in the morning, with a full three hours still left before arrival in New York.

The travel agent shrugged. Maybe Laughton was slow to dress, but nobody wants to be awakened in Albany, let alone on the right-hand side of a train passing through. Nevertheless the accommodation was always made, and when the porter's rap on the door at Albany brought him awake, Laughton would snuffle into consciousness, then begin to smile in anticipation. Ten minutes later, there would be another knock, and an extension of porter's arm would hand in a glass of orange juice—cold, freshly squeezed. (With two years' lead time and a saturation commercial jingle sung on radio by Bing Crosby, a frozen concentrate called Minute Maid was making powerful inroads, and the time was not that far distant when a teenager could be born and raised in an orange grove without ever having tasted a fresh orange. The New York Central Railroad swore that before the Twentieth Century Limited ever served processed juice, the train would go out of business. The train did. So did the railroad.)

Now, though, for actor Laughton the next step was to raise the window shade and lie back in his berth simply to watch and wait. The wait was not a long one. There would be morning twilight, and then the dawn, and outside the window of the train the mists began to swirl and to lift slowly, almost thoughtfully, from the surface of the great sleeping river. One could liken it to the development process of a Polaroid photograph (but at that time Polaroid was only two years old, like Minute Maid, and came in black-and-white only), with progressive formation of background and detail. Then the sunlight struck the western shore of the Hudson and the unbroken forested upsweep of the Rip Van Winkle country beyond. It was Baedeker who called the Hudson "grander and more inspiring than the Rhine," and as the Twentieth Century glided down the eastern bank, this was the vista he had in mind. Mile after mile, the steeper rises pressing closer to the shoreline now, to the gray battlements of West Point, their narrow panes prismatic, names like High Tor, Stony Point, and Storm King, the looming shoulder of Bear Mountain, the sudden stark scape of the Jersey Palisades. Always the same, yet never the same with weather and time of year. "And that is why I always have the porter wake me at Albany," said Laughton in the pages of *Life* magazine, "for to me that view across the Hudson from my train window is more glorious and moving than any other I know of."

That same right-hand window on the Century could have afforded Laughton another view across another river. For the train had made its arching left turn at Spuyten Duyvil (great phrase of the old Dutch Bronx), and the river on his right was no longer the broad Hudson but the narrow Harlem, the risings across the water not the Catskills but the apartment buildings of Washington Heights. It is a point in trivia that the route of the Twentieth Century ran within sight of no fewer than four major league ball parks: Comiskey Park on Chicago's South Side, Municipal Stadium on the lakefront in downtown Cleveland, Yankee Stadium on the Bronx side of the Harlem, the Polo Grounds on the Manhattan. Of that last park, one got but the barest glimpse; but the view was extraordinary, nevertheless, for it did what baseball does: it suspended time. All you could see of the Polo Grounds was a sign—eight freestanding letters —atop the center-field clubhouse and office complex, and to see even that you had to fix through the gingerbread cupolas and lacy ironwork of an el station that seemed designed for some Alice Faye set on the back lot at 20th Century–Fox. Yet if the looks of the el station turned back the clock, the lettering on the sign went even farther back. It showed the flared filigreed capitals of the nineteenth century, to which the "N" and the "Y" were particularly suited. That was how the sign began. NY GIANTS, it said.

Rivers and signs. On this Friday, May 25, 1951, another man also looked to his right out of the train window on another journey. This train, a Pennsy drawn by one of the legendary GG-1 electrics with the short-time output of 8,500 hp, began at the Pennsylvania Station in New York, shortly before noon, headed for Washington. It carried a passenger who would debark at the 30th Street station in Philadelphia. He was newly arrived from Minneapolis this morning; now, after the briefest of New York stopovers, en route to Philadelphia, to play with the New York Giants in tonight's game at Shibe Park there against the Phillies. The young man—he had turned twenty years of age just this same month—stared out of the right-hand window of the train as it crossed the Delaware at Trenton, from New Jersey into Pennsylvania. A hundred yards to the north was a vehicular bridge bearing the sign TRENTON MAKES—THE WORLD TAKES. The young man—he was Willie Howard Mays, Jr., Kitty Kat's boy—had crossed and recrossed that vehicular bridge time and again the previous summer, but riding on top of it then, rather than viewing it as now from the railroad bridge, he had never noticed the sign before.

A year ago he might have attracted attention for the fact that his was the only black face aboard the team bus of the Trenton club of the Class-B Interstate League, but there was no such singularity aboard the train, nor about Mays himself. He was not a large individual, and one would have to look more than once to realize that his hands were outsize and, missing the usual inward taper of wrist, seemed to connect directly to the fore- arm. ("My God, look at those hands!" the company doctor who delivered him had exclaimed. That was in Westfield, Alabama, a town which today no longer exists, plowed under to become a part of the Fairfield steelworks. The community was all black; the services, across the entire spectrum from police to medical [other than its schools], were all white. According to the going rule, the doctor was paid $15 for the delivery. If it had been a girl, the price would have been $10.)

More remarkable than himself, upon that Pennsylvania Rail- road trip in 1951, were Mays's impedimenta. He wore sports clothes and a plaid, many-colored touring cap whose style went out with the Scottish golf tournaments of the twenties. To match this he carried a golf bag—it was a going-away present to him from the citizens of Minneapolis. His only other carry-on luggage was a small canvas tote bag containing a fielder's glove, spiked shoes, and a jock strap. Inside the golf bag were two 34-ounce, 35-inch Adirondack baseball bats. Going into his first major league game, at Philadelphia that night, he would be playing center field, as he had played it with the Birmingham Black Barons of the Negro American League in 1948 and 1949; then in the Giant organization with Trenton in 1950; then with his promotion to Minneapolis of the Class-AAA American Association—the next stop short of the big leagues—in the early weeks of the 1951 season.

The position played was important. That same year, 1951, Chuck Connors, later become the television actor and star of the "Rifleman" series, was in major league baseball and sought to buy some furniture on time. He was with the Cubs, and the application for credit wanted to know the name of his employer. *The Wrigley Company*, said Connors. Position held? Connors pondered for a time, then put down: *first base*.

But Willie Mays was a center fielder, and there can be something special to that. Philip Roth had a feel for it in the pages of *Portnoy's Complaint*:

> Thank God for center field! Doctor, you can't imagine how truly glorious it is out there, so alone in all that space . . . Do you know baseball at all? Because center field is like some observation post, a kind of control tower, where you are able to see everything and everyone, to understand what's happening the instant it happens, not only by the sound of the struck bat, but by the spark of movement that goes through the infielders in the first second that the ball comes flying at them; and once it gets beyond them, "It's mine," you call, "it's mine," and then after it you go. Oh, how unlike my home it is to be in center field, where no one will appropriate unto himself anything that I say is *mine!* . . . Back I go, "*I* got it, *I* got it—" back easily and gracefully toward that wire fence, moving practically in slow motion, and then that delicious DiMaggio sensation of grabbing it like something heaven-sent over one shoulder. . . . Oh, the unruffled nonchalance of that game! There's not a movement that I don't know still down in the tissue of my muscles and the joints between my bones. . . . One knew exactly, and down to the smallest particular, how a center fielder should conduct himself. . . . Oh, to be a center fielder, a center fielder—and nothing more!

Mays the Minneapolis center fielder was revered. In six short weeks of the American Association season that far, they talked of nothing but him: the way he caught, the way he threw, the way he ran, the way he hit. At Borchert Field in Milwaukee, rather than repair a hole in the outfield wall that a Mays line drive had put there, they painted a sacrosanct white circle around it, much in the manner that Chicago consecrated the Great Fire.

Still, when Leo Durocher, manager of the parent New York Giants, phoned him to say they were bringing him up to the bigs, Mays demurred.

"I can't hit the pitching up there," he said.

"What are you hitting for Minneapolis?" Durocher asked.

".477," Mays said.

The Durocher silence that followed was untypical. So was his meekness of tone when he found his voice. The question was almost plaintive: "Do you think you can hit .2fucking70 for me?"

To violate the Abe Kemp caveat, Mays was five-foot-ten and weighed 170 pounds. Would one compare him with Joe Di-Maggio, six-foot-two, 193? Or by any stretch to Babe Ruth, six-foot-two, 215? No, it is stressed here again that Mays was not a large man. (Years later, however, in the course of an annual physical examination at San Francisco's Mount Zion Hospital, he would come to the attention of Dr. Herman Uhley, a distinguished heart specialist. Uhley at the time was pioneering the newest thing in diagnostic machinery, a vectorcardiograph, which produced cardiograms in three dimensions instead of two, and he tried it out on Willie. To make it work, two rubber suction cups had to be attached to the patient's back, their adhesion made possible by the subcutaneous layer of fat all humans have. All humans except Mays. Time and again Uhley would place the cups; time and again they popped off. "He didn't have any fat," the defeated physician explained. "His back was all muscle. His *back!*")

And there was little change with the passage of time. According to the New York Mets, with whom Mays ended his playing career in 1973, he had in the course of twenty-three years gained ten pounds in weight. (The Mets also showed him gaining one inch in height, due perhaps to the Mays penchant for going eleven feet up an eight-foot outfield wall to haul down enemy drives, much in the manner that Laughton's Quasimodo leaped for his bell rope to summon the faithful to prayer.)

Mays was a player who took good care of himself. Unlike Ruth or DiMaggio, he neither drank nor smoked, excepting the obligatory goblet of congratulatory champagne on four pennant-winning occasions, in Willie's case separated one from another by increasingly healthful intervals of three, eight, and eleven years. He had scattered moments of injury and exhaustion, and was afflicted by sinus trouble and the summer colds that can plague people who travel for a living. Thoroughbred-strung, he would at scattered times resort to a pill to induce sleep, and toward the end he discovered Vick's NyQuil, which was 50 proof and a nostrum in clear favor with teetotalers. But where Ruth with his stomachaches or DiMaggio with his heel spur were acceptable for weeks of inactivity, a one-day rest for Mays brought headlines and angry fan reaction. This can be understood: people brought their families hundreds of miles just to see him play.

It was Archibald MacLeish who said that historians control the reputations of statesmen. But, as Herb Wind suggested, the record book is there to control the reputations of ballplayers. The book says Mays set a major league record for the number of consecutive seasons in which he played 150 games or more, and his all-time mark of 7,095 putouts by an outfielder is one that will not be surpassed in our time. The inescapable notion underwritten by those figures is that Willie came to play. By common consent, his was the most electrifying presence the game had known since the heyday of Babe Ruth. By far less common consent, the case can be made that history will call Willie's time the true golden age of baseball.

Such an assertion flies directly in the face of the prevalent dictum that the game is no longer the innocent, joyful, and incorruptible exercise our fathers and grandfathers knew it to be. But that in turn is a wildly defective conceit, doing mischief to the game if not to the grandfathers. The salary demands of today, so often cited as proof that the players of our time think more of money than of baseball, in fact command less attention then they did in generations past, when Ruth and DiMaggio both were subject to merciless booing by the home fans for holding out for more money. Today, ball clubs no longer pay the traveling expenses for sportswriters covering their teams. In contrast, Maury Allen's book *Where Have You Gone, Joe DiMaggio?* points out that, in DiMaggio's time,

> Most sportswriters had a natural allegiance to the club management. Ballplayers came and went, but the clubs continued to subsidize their earnings, entertain them with free meals and lavish parties, and flatter their egos. A baseball writer had status, the kind of status no other reporter on the paper could acquire. The sportswriters would not jeopardize that by siding with a player in a contract dispute. And club owners were close to many publishers. There had been too many examples of sportswriters attacking a club in print and finding themselves the next day writing obituaries. So the writers fed the resentment against DiMaggio.
>
> Having no other recourse (the free-agent clause in a baseball player's contract having been ruled inviolate by the United States Supreme Court on three separate occasions), DiMaggio signed in late April 1938. He began working out alone in Yankee Stadium while the team went on the road. He had accepted his twenty-five-thousand-dollar contract grudgingly. The public accepted him grudgingly. When he made his first appearance, Di-Maggio was booed. Only twenty-three years old, he had demanded more money than many industrialists were making, and he was looked upon as a figure of greed.

In baseball's clean past, there was the case of William Wansley, who, on the night of Wednesday, September 27, 1865, was given $100 by a New York gambler named Kane McLoughlin to make sure Wansley's team, the Mutuals, lost the next day's game to the Eckfords. Aboard the Hoboken ferry en route to the game, Wansley, who was a catcher for the Mutuals, gave $30 each to Ed Duffy, the Mutual third baseman, and Tom Devyr, the shortstop, to make sure the fix worked. It did. The Eckfords won, 23 to 11. Wansley went 0 for 5 and had six passed balls.

In 1882, an umpire named Richard Higham was fixed. Part of the evidence that exposed him was a letter he had written:

FRIEND TODD:

I just got word we leave for the east on the 3 P.M. train, so I will not have a chance to see you. If you don't hear from me, play the Providence Tuesday, and if I want you to play the Detroits Wednesday I will telegraph you in this way, "Buy all the lumber you can." If you do not hear from me, don't play the Detroits but buy Providence sure, that is in the first game. I think this will do for the Eastern series. I will write you from Boston. You can write me any time in care of the Detroit BB Club, and it will be all right. You will see by the book I gave you the other day what city I will be in.

Yours truly,

DICK

Eight Chicago players brought about the notorious Black Sox scandal of 1920 for throwing the previous year's World Series to the Cincinnati Reds, a series the Sox nearly won anyway. And in 1946 a scandal arose in the Blue Ridge league surrounding fix money to a manager who was also the pitcher and whose team *did* win anyway.

But baseball's ruling class was stigmatized also in these affairs, for the penury which so often brought them on. Marshall Hunt remembered the club owners of the twenties: "They wore Brooks Brothers suits and had rather round stomachs. They got into the barber shop every day. Their shoes were shined. They lived in nice houses. They drove good cars." As far back as 1880, the New York *Mercury* had urged the players to "rise up in their manhood and rebel." This the players did, forming a Brotherhood whose manifesto decried their being "bought, sold or exchanged, as though they were sheep instead of American citizens." The success of the Brotherhood may be measured by a startling similarity of expression in a 1978 *Christian Science Monitor* article by player agent Bob Woolf: "As late as 1964 when I began advising athletes on legal matters, they were treated as chattels and routinely exploited by club owners. The players in those days were grossly underpaid and had no rights or bargaining power."

Memories of baseball's upstanding past tend also to ignore personal habits. From the Sweet Caporal trading cards of the 1880s to the Camel ads of the 1940s, ballplayers were paid to huckster cigarettes. (The outfield area used by relief pitchers actually got its name—bullpen—from the Bull Durham tobacco signs adorning the adjacent fences.) Booze had its equally honored place. The most commonplace fine levied against players was for drunkenness, and in 1903 the Cincinnati *Enquirer* printed the following advice to batsmen:

Whenever a ball looks like this:

0

0

0

Take a chance on the middle one.

Paul Waner, a Hall of Famer who was wont to take a chance on the middle one from time to time, once hit a double, slid into second, picked himself up, dusted himself off, turned to the second baseman, and said, "How did I get here?" (Nevertheless, he recorded 3,152 hits over a twenty-year career that began in 1926, a year also remembered for its World Series, when Grover Cleveland Alexander of the Cardinals came on in relief to strike out Tony Lazzeri of the Yankees with the bases loaded. So was Alexander, and his manager, Rogers Hornsby, knew it. "Years later," baseball writer John Drebinger of *The New York Times* recalled, "Hornsby and I were fanning around and he says to me, 'Hey, remember when I brought in Alex? Do you remember whether he took any warm-up pitches when he got to the mound?' I said I couldn't remember because I was too busy banging on the typewriter. 'Well,' he said, 'he never did. I was out there when he came in and I said, "How are you, kid?" and he said, "Okay, but no warm-up pitches. That would be the give-away." ' ")

One might also select from the past the notable case of an extraordinary turn-of-the-century pitcher named Arthur "Bugs" Raymond, who occasionally walked to and from the pitcher's mound on his hands and once was seen traveling comatose through the streets of Charleston, South Carolina, in a wheelbarrow piloted by the bemused manager of the Charleston Sea Gulls. In his first season with the New York Giants, Raymond won 18 games, but his manager, John J. McGraw, became convinced his new-found ace was smuggling alcohol into the ball park and assigned a private detective named Fuller to shadow him. Raymond took the surveillance in stride. "This is my keeper," he would say, by way of introducing the detective to his friends. "I'm full but he's Fuller." Eventually they had a falling out, and Fuller punched Raymond in the eye. Raymond complained to McGraw. McGraw punched him in the other eye.

Even gluttony was celebrated, as in L. H. Addington's structured limerick:

> The Dodgers have Del Bissonette.
> No meal has he ever missed yet.
> The question that rises
> Is one that surprises:
> Who paid for all Del Bissonette?

By now such allusions have all but vanished. The only relevant tale I know of in recent years may be more of a political statement than one of appetite. It involves the Giants, during Willie's time, and goes to a scene in their clubhouse directly following a defeat in a game they had pretty much kicked away. Their infuriated manager, Alvin Dark, took one look at the customary spread of post-game cold cuts set out on a central table and with a single slap of his hand swept them away, then launched a tirade at his players. All the time he was shouting, his right fielder, Felipe Alou, was on his hands and knees, eating the food off the floor.

When one reflects upon the overall picture, then, it would seem that any remembrances of baseball past which make the old game somehow more innocent than today's—and more appealing on that account—can only be the product of nostalgic overlay. Bubble gum cards have long since replaced cigarette cards. Today's players don't even womanize as much as yesterday's. They don't have to. The women manize.

———◆———

I first met Willie Mays on a day in June, 1951, at the Polo Grounds. I was down on the field before the game, and somebody introduced us, and Mays said in a high voice, "Say hey," then turned and laughed at something else, and that was it. Say Hey was to become his trademark. He used it to cover the fact that it was put upon him to greet far more people than he could ever remember by name, but it achieved a life of its own that seemed to breathe the infectious feel of his name itself. A time or two I've wondered what it would have been like if, all other things being the same, his name had been, say, Leon Dunleavy, who said, "How do you do?" Was it some preternatural stroke that it would be Willie Mays and Say Hey? If so, the proprietor himself came to resent it. "The Say Hey Kid digs in at the plate," Giant broadcaster Russ Hodges would intone automatically when Willie came up to bat, and he was still intoning it the year Mays turned forty. But neither Hodges nor any of

Willie's friends and peers would use the phrase to his face.

Yet when Mays in his forties discovered that you could get personalized license plates from the State of California, displaying up to six letters or numbers of your own choice, one guess which six characters he chose for his Cadillac Seville. ("Sometimes," his wife, Mae, told Jack Klugman in a television interview, "I turn to him and ask, 'Will the real Willie Mays please stand up?' ") In truth, Mays put in for SAY HEY as his license plate on something resembling a commuter schedule. He would park his car at a restaurant, emerge two hours later, and find the plates gone. No respectable souvenir hunter was going to miss that one.

But my first encounter with him is remembered not so much for what he said, which was minimal, as for the way he laughed, which went maximal and beyond. Over the years one would hear it—aboard an airplane, in a crowded room, floating free to the farthest cranny of a ball park's open space—as one might a cry from some perch of camouflaged splendor in a tropical rain forest. To Branch Rickey, who brought Jackie Robinson to the majors as the first Negro player in 1947, it was more than laughter. Here is an acolytic passage from Rickey's book *The American Diamond,* published in 1964:

> The memory of Willie as a rookie propelling the ball in one electric flash off the Polo Grounds scoreboard on the face of the upper deck in left field for a home run is a cherished image. The ball got up there so fast it was incredible. Like a pistol shot it would crash off the tin and fall to the grass below. He would still have the knob of the bat in his huge hand and be but leaning in the direction of first base.
>
> The fans watch their favorite hitters come to the plate, enjoying their every mannerism and facial expression, their every move in the batter's box. You know it's Mays for there will be a tremendous roar in Candlestick Park or anywhere around the league and Willie will smile in the sunshine and adjust his cap. He'll miss one and spin full around, he'll foul one off, he'll take a couple, and when the second pitch is close he'll freeze for a

moment and wait for the call. He'll dig in and the pitcher will breeze one close and Willie will duck, and you won't forget the look in his eye. Then he'll laugh at the catcher's remark and you will think he is eighteen. Then he'll step in and set himself for the three-and-two pitch and suddenly this loose, ebullient boy is a serious, intent hitter and the ball is there and Mays swings. Hit!

Willie Mays' true greatness is his equal strength hitting, running, and throwing and the intensity with which he executes every play. He is the only player to steal thirty bases and hit thirty home runs in a season. His single catch and throw in 1954 changed that World Series, and his throw to Westrum on August 15, 1951, to get Billy Cox at the plate began a miracle ending to his rookie year. He slid into Bruce Edwards in Ebbets Field one day and Edwards said Mays was the strongest man ever to hit him. If there was a machine to measure each swing of a bat it would be proven that Mays swings with more power and bat speed, pitch for pitch, than any other player.

Strength, Rickey emphasized. Interesting word for a five-foot-ten 170-pounder. But Rickey thought he knew why: "The secret weapon . . . is the frivolity in his bloodstream. . . . Willie Mays has doubled his strength with laughter."

A baseball man named Charlie Metro once told me about a routine scouting assignment that took him to Houston on a day when the Giants were playing the old Houston Colt .45s. (An outlander might have difficulty with such strange names for teams, but baseball does not cater particularly to the foreign trade. The story is told of the German whose maiden trip to the United States landed him at Boston's Logan Airport, where his first move was to consult with a reservations clerk about his continuing passage. *"Mein Herr,"* the German said by way of greeting, *"was sagst Du?"* The clerk regarded him sadly. "They lose," he said; "8 to 5.") In Metro's case, he chose an early inning of an uneventful game to fix his binoculars momentarily on Mays in center field. "And that's all I did for the rest of the game," Metro said. "I watched Willie. Watched him standing there, because he wasn't standing there. He was always moving. With all my experience, I never knew there was a dimension to the game like that. He had me like a bird transfixed by a snake."

The mere fact of the Mays presence has been remarked by many. In the second game of the 1962 World Series at Candlestick Park, Clete Boyer of the Yankees hit a sharp line drive to right-center field. "As the ball left the bat," he recollected, "I said to myself two things. The first thing I said was, 'Hello, double!' The second thing I said was, 'Oh, shit, *he's* out there.'" The box score of the game registers the putout and confirms the second thought.

The fans picked up on the presence too. In a book about the Broadway theater called *The Season*, award-winning novelist and screenwriter William Goldman found it pertinent to talk about the first time he sat in the stands as a spectator and watched Willie play:

> I fell in love with him that afternoon. And watching him then, I realized unconsciously that it was about time he arrived on my horizon, because during all those years of being bored by baseball, of sitting in bleacher seats for pitchers' battles, or dying with the heat while the manager brought in some slow reliever, I'd been waiting for Willie.
>
> He was what it was all about. He was the reason. In my head, there was a notion of the way things ought to happen, but never quite do. Not until Willie came along. And then I could finally sit there and say to myself, Oh, sure, *that's it*.

Another fan tribute comes from a cartoonist who gained syndication just a few months before Mays came to the major leagues. Only eight newspapers were carrying the cartoon strip at the time. No one was certain it would catch on, for it took an unorthodox approach: it would refer to adults by name but never depict them. Children and animals were all it would ever show. Even worse was the title the syndicate assigned to it, because it had nothing to do with anything. A generation later, though, the cartoonist, Charles Schulz, was reminiscing. "It's kind of fun now and then," he said on television, "to use the names of real people in my comic strip, *Peanuts*. And after looking over about twenty-five years' accumulation of strips, I discovered that I used the name Willie Mays more than any other individual. I suppose it's because, to me, Willie Mays has always symbolized perfection."

So testimonials may be obtained from participants on the one hand and observers on the other, and on occasion the viewpoints can actually coalesce, as in the case of Charlie Metro. I myself had a mild shot at that role during the Giants' spring training at Phoenix in 1962 when the team trainer, Doc Bowman, suggested I sweat out a hangover by umpiring an intra-squad game at first base. Fans got in free for those games, and the comments from the too-close seats in that crackerbox park at Central and Mohave were not always kind. "Hey, Epstein," I heard, "quit pickin' your nose!" But I was out to make a job of it, and when Mays, entering the game in the fifth inning, hung a two-base hit off the boards in center field, it was my automatic function to see whether he touched first base en route. He did. He hit the base so hard it kicked up a cloud of lime dust, and to this day there is frozen in my mind's eye that swirl of white dust, the nostrils flared, the eyes in their concentration gone to deepest black in the syndrome of fight-or-flight. On one level I can handle it: we were both trying. ("We all try," said the Rick-/Bogart of *Casablanca* to the Laszlo/Henreid. "You succeed.") But I was trying within the singular commitment to excise the gin from the pores. Why was Mays trying? What was he to the Hecuba of that silly intra-squad game, or the Hecuba to him? But there he rocketed past me at first base; a decade later, still doing the same thing, he brought this appraisal from Roger Angell:

Candlestick's classic pastime—and the best entertainment in baseball this year—is watching Willie Mays. Now just turned forty, and beginning his twenty-first year in the majors, he is hitting better than he has hit at any time in the past six or seven seasons, and playing the game with enormous visible pleasure. Veteran curators in the press box like to expound upon various

Maysian specialties—the defensive gem, the basket catch, the looped throw, the hitched swing, and so forth. My favorite is his base-running. He may have lost a half-second or so in getting down to first base, but I doubt whether Willie Davis or Ralph Garr or any of the other new flashes can beat Mays from first to third, or can accelerate just as he does, with his whole body suddenly seeming to sink lower when, taking his turn at first and intently following the distant ball and outfielder, he suddenly sees his chance. Watching him this year, seeing him drift across a base and then sink into full speed, I noticed all at once how much he resembles a marvelous skier in midturn down some steep pitch of fast powder. *Nobody* like him.

I might have asked Mays what his precise thoughts were as he rounded first in that meaningless game in Phoenix, and well he might have supplied an answer. But I had a bad history with that kind of question. The old International News Service, for whom I was working as a sports and feature writer in New York when Mays first came to the Giants, once sent me out to interview the Flying Zacchini. I asked that circus star what it felt like to be shot out of a cannon three times a day. "It's like anything else," he said.

The headquarters of the INS in New York may have been the last of the great newsrooms. The staff included the only man who ever got a medical discharge from the French Foreign Legion, as well as a one-armed copy boy who, when, harassed, would cry out, "For Christ's sake, I've only got two hands." We also had Les Conklin, believed to be the only person ever to be thrown out of Bickford's, the all-night cafeteria at Lexington and 45th. (Conklin, who wrote the overnight baseball roundup in those days, gained his revenge a short time later when Vern Bickford, then with the Boston Braves, pitched a one-hitter. "Bickford," Conklin's roundup began, "is still serving up the smallest portions.") And dear to memory is the occasion when sports editor Lawton Carver phoned in and said, "Give me Einstein," meaning to dictate his next-day column to me. The switchboard operator was new and did not know I worked there, but she did have a list of private phone numbers of celebrities. Accordingly she made the connection, the answering party picked up the phone, and Carver dictated his column about the Chicago Cubs to Prof. Albert Einstein. I found out about it the next day when Carver came in to the office. "You were drunk last night, you son of a bitch," he said to me.

The breaking news story of the greatest consequence in the spring of 1951 involved a former occasional patron of Toots Shor's restaurant on West 52nd Street. "He could handle a belt," Shor told Maury Allen. "I think he drank bourbon. He always had some friends with him. Never bothered anybody. I don't think anybody ever knew who the hell he was in those days, you know, just a little guy with glasses."

Shortly before midnight on April 10, 1951, the little guy with glasses learned that one of his newly made decisions had leaked out and would be printed in the Chicago *Tribune* the following morning. "Oh, no," the little guy with glasses said. "If that gets out the son of a bitch will quit on me. He's not quitting on me. I'm firing him." Accordingly, he immediately had a news release prepared. It was issued to the press at one o'clock in the morning of Wednesday, April 11:

> With deep regret I have concluded that General of the Army Douglas MacArthur is unable to give his wholehearted support to the policies of the United States Government and of the United Nations in matters pertaining to his official duties. In view of the specific responsibilities imposed upon me by the Constitution of the United States and the added responsibility which has been entrusted to me by the United Nations, I have decided that I must make a change of command in the Far East. I have, therefore, relieved General MacArthur of his commands. . . .

Nearly a dozen years later, a panel of distinguished historians, asked to index all U.S. Presidents in order of greatness, would place Harry Truman in ninth place (the "near-great" category), directly behind Theodore Roosevelt and James K. Polk. Dwight Eisenhower, Truman's immediate successor, came in 28th. In the years since the poll was taken, no detectable sentiment has arisen to improve Eisenhower's standing, but a ground swell gathered almost instantly to advance Truman's. The panel's choice of the top three—Lincoln, Washington, and Franklin Roosevelt—was beyond dispute. But many people, including John F. Kennedy, who was President at the time the poll came out, wondered why Woodrow Wilson would be ranked fourth when he had failed in one objective after another. Arthur M. Schlesinger, Jr., pointed out that the panel consisted of professors, and Wilson was the only professor to achieve the Presidency. "It seemed evident," Schlesinger wrote, "that [Kennedy's] measure of presidential success was concrete achievement; thus people who educated the nation without necessarily accomplishing their particular purposes rated, in his judgment, below those, like Polk and Truman, who accomplished their purposes without necessarily bringing the nation along with them. The best, of course, were those who did both." Truman did not have that second satisfaction. (Nor would have Lincoln, Washington, or FDR if their administrations had survived the transition to peacetime from active state of war.) He had his moments, but the public reaction to his impressive list of accomplishments was not always salutory.

Leave it to Harry himself to compound that problem. In 1952, Bob Considine of the INS had the privilege of introducing Truman to a dinner at the Overseas Press Club. "President Truman," Considine said, "will be remembered by the future historian as the Chief Executive who had more difficult decisions to make than most of the others combined. He faced and overcame with courageous decisions more crises than confronted Washington or Lincoln, Wilson or FDR. Six readily come to mind:

"He had to make the agonizing decision to drop the atomic

bombs on Hiroshima and Nagasaki, which killed tens of thousands and opened the Atomic Age.

"He set in motion, with a firm decision, the wheels of the greatest humanitarian effort in history, the Marshall Plan.

"He proposed and implemented the Point Four program that revitalized the industrial complexes and economic security of friend and foe.

"He drew the line in Greece and Turkey and told the Communists on that side of the world they must not cross it.

"He stopped Communist aggression on the other side of the world by making a stand in Korea.

"And he re-established civilian control over the military by firing the most popular military figure in modern history, Douglas MacArthur.

"And now, ladies and gentlemen, here he is—President Harry S. Truman!"

The little guy with glasses got to his feet smiling, moved to the microphone, beamed at Considine, and said, "Thank you, Eric Sevareid." Truman's daughter, Margaret, seated hard by, pulled at his coattail. There was a whispered consultation. Truman nodded and returned to the microphone. "Forgive me," he said, "for making a natural mistake. I got two fat reporters mixed up."

Within a couple of weeks, MacArthur's dismissal had begun to recede from the headlines, and on the sports side, the following month, we had a new hero-apparent to deal with. The New York Giants were bringing up a rookie from the Minneapolis Millers named Willie Mays. The news did not exactly cast Mays instantly into the Hall of Fame, but a truly curious side story came with it. In an odd, perhaps unprecedented, step, the owner of the Giants, Horace Stoneham, had placed an ad in the Minneapolis papers apologizing to the home folks for taking Willie away. Since Mays was more popular in Minneapolis than MacArthur, and President Stoneham of the Giants less so than President Truman of the United States, some expression was called for, and the advertisement took it up:

We appreciate his worth to the Millers, but in all fairness, Mays himself must be a factor in these considerations. Merit must be recognized. On the records of his performance since the American Association season started, Mays is entitled to his promotion, and the chance to prove that he can play major league baseball. It would be most unfair to deprive him of the opportunity he earned with his play.

We honestly admit, too, that this player's exceptional talents are the exact answer to the Giants' most critical need.

The Giants in 1951 started off winning their first game, losing their second, winning their third, then losing the next eleven straight. (MacArthur was witness to one of those in a celebrity visit to the Polo Grounds a few days after his arrival in New York.) They had done somewhat better after that—it would have been difficult to do worse—but on May 25, the day Mays joined them in Philadelphia, they still were in the second division. Atop the standings, the hated Brooklyn Dodgers—the first edition of the team Roger Kahn would call the Boys of Summer —had a two-game lead over the St. Louis Cardinals. Pittsburgh was in last place, but in those days Pittsburgh was always in last place. "The trouble with these guys," outfielder Sid Gordon said after being traded to the Pirates, "is that after you've been with them a couple of weeks you start to play like them."

In the case of the Giants, however, what was most lacking was not talent on the hoof but the manager's patience. Flamboyant and intense under the best of circumstances, Leo Durocher had insisted that owner Stoneham let him remake the club in his own image. "Back up the truck," was the way Durocher phrased it in getting Stoneham to trade front-line players for the likes of the second base–shortstop combination of Eddie Stanky and Alvin Dark. "What I want is my kind of team." His kind of team having proved it could lose eleven straight, the manager's thoughts had taken a natural turn toward the possibility of further improvement. And there was no doubt in his mind that Mays would be it. (Little doubt in Stoneham's mind either, judging by that ad in the paper: *this player's exceptional talents are the exact answer to the Giants' most critical need.*)

Against the Phillies in his first game as a Giant, The Exact Answer went 0 for 5 at the plate. In the field, he ran into teammate Monte Irvin, and what should have been a fly ball went instead for a double. In any other paper, the story run in *The New York Times* next morning would have been a model in sarcasm: "Inspired by the presence of their flashy rookie star, Willie Mays, the Giants rallied for five runs in the eighth inning. . . ."

But they won the game. Next day they won again. Mays? 0 for 3. The day after, they won a third time, to sweep the Philadelphia series. Mays? 0 for 4. "This boy can take us all the way!" Durocher enthused to columnist Tom Meany as they boarded the train at the North Philadelphia station for the trip back to New York.

Meany nodded. "Some day," he said, "he may even get a hit." But he found himself weirdly in agreement with the manager. From somewhere in the noisy passenger car came that high sudden peal of laughter. The Giants, sullen at worst, uncommunicative at best, had through some alchemy become a relaxed band of merry men. Willing fingers shot out to goose trainer Bowman as he threaded his way down the aisle. There was a chorus of "It's Howdy Doody Time." And doubtless it had much to do with the three-game sweep of the defending league-champion Phillies.

But some writers who were with the club swore afterward that the euphoria had set in the moment Willie joined the team. ("He is Rousseau's Natural Man," wrote Gilbert Millstein in *The New York Times*. Said rival manager Charley Grimm, "He can help a team just by riding on a bus with them.")

It still would be nice, as Tom Meany had seemed to suggest, if sooner or later Mays got a hit. His next chance would be at the Polo Grounds, the night of Monday, May 28, against Warren Spahn and the Boston Braves, and a goodly crowd turned out to watch.

Spahn, already established as the bell cow of the Boston staff, was into a career that in the end would see him win more games than Dizzy Dean *pitched*. His career with the Braves is memorable to many people for many reasons. (For Spahn, among other things, it was for the time the financially strapped Braves management talked him out of tapping their coffers for a new nose, his old one having been broken by an enemy line drive in a spring training game. "They told me it would make me look more distinguished leaving it as is," Spahn said.) Tonight, the princely lefthander sighted crookedly on Mays as the youthful outfielder came to bat with two out and no one on base in the bottom of the first inning. Reasoning that Durocher had counseled the anxious Willie not to chase the first pitch—something he had begun doing in Philadelphia—Spahn decided to throw a fast ball past him for an introductory strike.

Up in the radio booth, it was Russ Hodges's custom to seal a Giant home run with his own pet line: "Tell it Bye-Bye Baby!" The Spahn pitch rode in and Mays swung at it, and in this instance all Hodges had time to say was "Good-bye!" In one flashpoint the ball disappeared into the night over the left-field roof at the Polo Grounds. At the last it was still traveling up. "You know," Hodges said afterward, "if that's the only home run he ever hits, they'll still talk about it." Understandably he did not foresee that in his lifetime he would describe more than 600 additional Mays home runs. (When Hodges died twenty years later Mays was still hitting them.)

In the clubhouse after the game, Spahn was asked what kind of pitch he had thrown to Willie. "For the first 60 feet it was a hell of a pitch," he said. Durocher was less philosophical. "I never saw a fucking ball get out of a fucking ball park so fucking fast in my fucking life," he reasoned. "He swings, and bang, it's clearing the fucking roof and still going up." ("The ball came down in Elmira," Lefty Gomez subsequently reported. "I know. I was managing there at the time.")

Durocher's language, as reported here, is not designed to enflame. His habit was to employ vulgarity as verbal punctuation more than anything else, nor did he enjoy particularly high ranking in that field. By more or less common consent, the foulest mouth in baseball belonged to its most upright symbol of rectitude, the game's first commissioner: Judge Kenesaw Mountain Landis. "I never heard words like that in my life," Happy Chandler, Landis's immediate successor as commissioner, told me. And Ford Frick, who succeeded Chandler, gave Jerry Holtzman a tame example of the Landis vocabulary, in which the judge was discussing nothing more arresting than his golf game. "He said, 'I bitched my drive, boogered my mashie, I fucked up my approach shot.' I don't remember the whole sequence. But he just kept using words, every one of them worse than the one before."

———◆———

For more than twenty-one years Alonzo Fields served the White House as chief butler and maître d'hôtel. That meant from Hoover to Eisenhower, with FDR and Truman in between, and there was no doubt which of them he preferred. Harry and Bess Truman, he wrote in his book, *My 21 Years at the White House*, started off "with a sense of human understanding and appreciation which never waned during the eight years to follow." The Fields book makes the added point that "the Trumans did not care for elaborate meals." In the same breath it makes a somewhat more subtle point: "Neither did the Roosevelts; but, unlike the Roosevelts, the Trumans demanded better-cooked food, for Mrs. Truman is a very good cook and she knew and appreciated good cooking."

And when she had to, Bess Truman could make her move. It was up to her to select the menus during the Washington visit in 1951 of Princess Elizabeth of England and the Duke of Edinburgh. Dinner the first night was at 8 P.M. for twenty-two guests, with a hundred more invited to the reception afterward, and one would not care to say the six-course meal was governed by poke roots:

BLUE POINTS ON HALF SHELL
COCKTAIL SAUCE, LEMON WEDGES
CRACKERS

SHERRY:

CLEAR SOUP WITH MARROW BALLS
CELERY HEARTS   ASSORTED OLIVES
MELBA TOAST

WHITE WINE:

LOBSTER THERMIDOR
PARSLEYED SLICED TOMATOES AND CUCUMBERS
WHOLE WHEAT BREAD SANDWICHES

RED WINE:

ROAST FILLET BEEF
WINE ESSENCE
WATERMELON PICKLES
BROILED MUSHROOMS
FRENCH FRIED POTATOE BALLS
ASPARAGUS HOLLANDAISE

CHAMPAGNE:

GREEN SALAD WITH ARTICHOKE HEARTS
BAKED OLD MISSOURI HAM
HERB FRENCH DRESSING
CORN STICKS

VANILLA ICE CREAM MELON MOLDS
BRANDIED MACAROONS
ANGEL FOOD CAKE

At eight o'clock the following morning, Princess Elizabeth had a cup of coffee and a glass of orange juice, and an hour later the royal party enjoyed a breakfast consisting of melon, orange juice, scrambled eggs, bacon and sausages, toast, hot biscuits and marmalade, and tea. "I seated Her Royal Highness and the others," maître d' Fields wrote, "and they had nearly finished their melon when in rushed the Duke, saying, 'I'm afraid I am a little late.' He was in his shirt sleeves with his collar open and he grabbed a seat before anyone could seat him. The Princess did not stop eating her melon."

It is not recorded whether either of the royal pair stopped long enough to ask what was for lunch, but they would find out soon enough:

OLD FASHIONEDS
MARTINIS
ORANGE JUICE
TOMATO JUICE

CANAPÉS

HONEYDEW MELON
SEMINOLE

SPARKLING
BURGUNDY:

SMOTHERED PHEASANT
CURRANT JELLY
BREAD SAUCE
FRIED SAMP
BROCCOLI WITH LEMON DRAWN BUTTER
BAKED STUFFED TOMATOES
ROLLS

GREEN SALAD ROQUEFORT CHEESE BOWL
RADISH GARNISH
FRENCH DRESSING
TOASTED TRISCUITS

STANLEY CREAM MOLDS
SPONGE DROPS

NUTS   FRUITS   CANDIES   DEMI-TASSE
    CIGARS   CIGARETTES   LIQUEURS

The evidence is here of Mrs. Truman's correct touch in serving the salad after, rather than before, the main course, and this was true for any White House function for any guest, including General Dwight D. Eisenhower when he returned to the United States in triumph following V-E Day in 1945. (He got turkey, succotash, molded fruit salad, and chocolate ice cream, which is much how Les Conklin dined at Bickford's, but the fact is that by and large Harry Truman did not have much use for generals. "I fired MacArthur because he wouldn't respect the authority of the President," he said. "That's the answer to that. I didn't fire him because he was a dumb son of a bitch, although he was, but that's not against the law for generals. If it was, half to three quarters of them would be in jail." Truman remembered also the time Eisenhower asked him who was chief of staff in the White House: "I held my temper. I said to him, 'The President of the United States is his own chief of staff.' But he just could *not* understand that.")

A quarter of a century from their first visit, as Queen and Prince Consort, Elizabeth and Philip would return to the White House, this time in celebration of the American Bicentennial in 1976. This time Mr. and Mrs. Willie Mays would be among the invited guests, at a reception broadcast nationally on television. A note can be made that television's capacity to beam a program live from one coast to the other had just come into being in 1951. Only three years earlier the *Saturday Evening Post* had carried a three-part article entitled "Television: Boom or Bubble?" But the capability was there to take a signal previously limited to the horizon and boost it farther via microwave relay and coaxial cable. In anticipation of this, CBS and NBC led the rush to line up local stations for their networks. The word "simulcast" came into being; it meant any program, like "Arthur Godfrey and His Friends," that was broadcast simultaneously on TV and radio. Essentially it was a holding action for the latter medium, which could not compete with the flight of audience—and its own talent—to television. "The safest place to be in the event of atomic attack is the RCA Building," Goodman Ace said in 1951. "No radioactivity."

The two ingredients that ensured television's commercial success both were expropriated entire from radio. One of them went back to 1931, with the discovery that if instead of telling listeners it was six o'clock you said, "It's six o'clock B-U-L-O-V-A, Bulova Watch Time," Bulova would pay for it; and in that instant was born the financial largesse of the station break. The other occurred March 24, 1936, with the well-received network debut of "Major Bowes and His Original Amateur Hour," which proved the entertainment potential of a spectrum of programs—amateur shows, quiz shows, game shows, talk shows, phone-in shows—whose guests happily performed for next to nothing, if not nothing itself. This combination of the profit on dead time and the saving on live talent was the benefactor of television at its beginnings. It still is today. Sophisticated advances in technology have had no noticeable effect on these truisms. By the 1970s it was routinely feasible for a TV station in Honolulu to pick up Walter Cronkite and the "CBS Evening News" by satellite. Given the time difference between New York and Hawaii, what was just as feasible —and far cheaper, considering the time charges for corporate-owned satellites—was to have a copy of the show taped in Los Angeles and placed aboard the next commercial flight to the Islands, for showing there at 8 P.M. local time. (The International News Service, in 1951, had a measurable number of clients who received the daily news report not by teletype but by bus.)

In one of the reminiscent news specials that plagued television's 1977–78 season the same way south-of-the-border musicals infested the movie theaters of the forties, CBS showed its prized anchor antecessor Edward R. Murrow presiding over the first coast-to-coast cable link-up in mid-November, 1951. In the narrowest sense of both coasts transmitting pictures on the same show, that might have been so, but as Bill Manchester has noted, the first live nationwide telecast was President Truman's address at the Japanese Peace Treaty Conference in San Francisco over two months earlier, on September 4. That one was beamed to ninety-four stations and doubtless made up in novelty appeal what it lacked in box office, although the figure for its total number of viewers—40 million—creates the suspicion that whoever issues the ratings nowadays must also have been in charge of them then. A heavy majority of American homes still did not have television ("We used to go next door to the neighbors' to watch wrestling," comedian Jack Carter said, "until they got a TV set"), and the alternate viewing site, the neighborhood pub, opted more for the cleavage of Dagmar and Faye Emerson than for any tonal Truman allegretto declaring finis to a war six years after it had ended.

But the Truman speech from San Francisco did presage the availability of a coast-to-coast audience for the next event, which would be the 1951 World Series, beginning the first week in October; a matter extra-felicitous for television's purposes, since it would be an all–New York Series, already the mother location of the best transmitting skills and facilities. It was an even more marvelous stroke that nobody knew whom the Yankees, champion-apparent of the American League, would be playing. In the National League there might have to be a best-of-three playoff between the Dodgers and Giants, and if so, that would be shown on nationwide TV too. The sudden prospect of this double bonanza—a playoff *and* a World Series, back to back—touched off the wildest set-buying spree in all of television's history, before or after. In some cities, the sale of TV sets actually exceeded the sale of radios, even though the latter's totals included the radios in automobiles, at the height of their new-model-year production, not to mention such specialties as clock radios and consoles that offered radio, TV, and phonograph all in one (Your Complete Home Entertainment Center, the manufacturers labeled it, but there were few takers: the malfunction of the smallest vacuum tube in the works could queer the whole machine).

And so a good part of the nation not only heard but saw what came next. Twenty years later, an Associated Press poll would record it as the most dramatic moment in sports history. The coincidence of television's sudden new outreach had its part to play in that, surely. But it could stand rightfully on its own merit. "Now it is done," the unflappable Red Smith would say of it in his column in the New York *Herald Tribune* the following morning. "Now the story ends. And there is no way to tell it. The art of fiction is dead. Reality has strangled invention. Only the utterly impossible, the inexpressibly fantastic, can ever be plausible again."

Smith's column painted what was for me an indelible picture, for the fact is that I too was there, seated in the same press section, yet never saw it for myself. He was writing about the immediate aftermath of the final game of the 1951 National League playoff:

Down on the green and white and earth-brown geometry of the playing field, a drunk tries to break through the ranks of ushers marshaled along the foul lines to keep profane feet off the diamond. The ushers thrust him back and he lunges at them, struggling in the clutch of two or three men. He breaks free, and four or five tackle him. He shakes them off, bursts through the line, runs head-on into a special park cop, who brings him down with a flying tackle.

Here comes a whole platoon of ushers. They lift the man and haul him, twisting and kicking, back across the first-base line. Again he shakes loose and crashes the line. He is through. He is away, weaving out toward center field, where cheering thousands are jammed beneath the windows of the Giants' clubhouse.

At heart, our man is a Giant, too. He never gave up.

From center field comes burst upon burst of cheering. Pennants are waving, uplifted fists are brandished, hats are flying. Again and again the dark clubhouse windows blaze with the light of photographers' flash bulbs. Here comes that same drunk out of the mob, back across the green turf to the infield. Coattails flying, he runs the bases, slides into third. Nobody bothers him now.

On August 11 the Giants had lost to the Phillies 4–0 while the Dodgers were beating Boston 8–1 in the first game of a double-header. The Giants were in second place behind Brooklyn in the standings by then, but their advancement seemed little other than academic, since at that precise point they trailed the Dodgers by 13½ games. From that point, too, the Dodgers had only 49 games to play to complete their regular 154-game schedule, and they were to win 26 of them.

For the Giants, meanwhile, their position on August 11 was if anything even worse than their 13½-game deficit in the standings would indicate, for they had actually lost 16 games more than the Dodgers and had even fewer games—only 44—left to play.

What happened was that they won 37 of those 44 games, a percentage performance of .841—the most astonishing seven-week stretch run ever recorded. I recall that several of us in the press marquee during the U.S. tennis championships at Forest Hills drew frowns and stares from umpires and players for our animated chatter as the baseball results came in; and when I went to the Polo Grounds the night of September 26 to cover the fourth bloodied featherweight title bout between Sandy

Saddler and Willie Pep, even single-minded fight fans were clamoring for the ball scores. That night the Giants moved to within one game of the Dodgers. "They're closing the Brooklyn Bridge—at both ends," Howard Sigmand wrote as his lead for the INS baseball roundup.

By Saturday, September 29, the two teams were tied for the lead. Both won their games that day, and the Giants won again at Boston on Sunday in the final game on their schedule. At Philadelphia, the Dodgers were losing, but they managed to tie the score, and then Jackie Robinson won it for them single-handedly, first with a game-saving nab of a line drive in the 12th inning, then with a home run in the 14th. The Giants were homebound from Boston on the train when they got the news.

The first playoff game would be held at Ebbets Field in Brooklyn the following afternoon, and Sigmand, Pat Robinson, and I drove there in my car. The only conversation I recall came when we went past a Brooklyn synagogue during a break in high holy days services and noticed the congregants informally clustered in the late-morning sunshine outside the temple. Robinson, a columnist of the old school who tended to reduce his speech to sporting terms, was intrigued by the yarmulkas that covered the worshipers' heads; though the sight was not totally unfamiliar to him, he had never realized they came in colors as well as in black. "What do the white ones stand for?" he asked. "The home team," Sigmand told him.

If not here in Brooklyn, then certainly among the populace at large, the Giants had to be the sentimental favorite in the playoffs, for the way they had come from behind in the role of hopeless underdog in the closing weeks of the season. But seven weeks is a long time, and suddenly it was the Dodgers who had come from behind with their own underdog theatrics at Philadelphia the day before, and one could sense something of the feel of the final episode of a Flash Gordon serial ending with the hero no better off than hanging from one more cliff and the audience admonished to come back next Saturday for the *real* finale, with Ming the Merciless now no worse than even money.

The Giants won that first playoff game, 3 to 1, and now needed to win only one game in their own Polo Grounds to sew it up. So they lost the second game 10 to 0. "What happened?" manager Durocher was asked afterward. "We got the shit kicked out of us," he explained. "Does anybody else have a bright question?"

The day of the third and final game, Wednesday, October 3, was gray and gloomy, with the lights being turned on as early as the third inning. No one in any event could plan ahead for the third game—the "if" game—of a playoff that itself was unexpected. So it was not surprising that the attendance at that game was 34,320, barely 60 percent of the Polo Grounds' capacity. But I think bad theater had something to do with it too. On the Giant side, Flash Gordon well might have overstayed his welcome; on the Dodger, Ming's 14-inning miracle at Philadelphia Sunday had failed in the re-creation of the day before: if you have to win to stay alive, it's overkill to do it 10–0. And if you wanted a hot ticket, it was there for the scalping for tomorrow's World Series opener at Yankee Stadium regardless of who won today.

The INS staff covering the final playoff game occupied seven places in the expanded press section—the upper grandstand behind home plate—including a spot for Benny-the-puncher, a non-Runyon character with a Runyonesque name, who was our teletype operator. I sat beside him, handling the running story for afternoon papers and radio. In this day's case, I had to file two update leads in short succession, one for the seventh inning when the Giants tied the score at 1–1, the next after the top of the eighth when the Dodgers scored three times to take a 4–1 advantage. Now I put some fresh copy paper into my typewriter (as did Bob Considine beside me, doing the morning-paper lead), and we both began to work out our stories on the Dodger victory. I don't know what his read like. Mine was terrible.

Going into the last of the ninth, it was still 4–1. Alvin Dark led off for the Giants and singled on the ground through the right side. Don Mueller did the same thing.

Considine and I stopped typing.

Monte Irvin came up and pop-fouled out to the right side. He brought his bat down in disgust, so vehemently that he broke it. Now it was Whitey Lockman's turn, and he sliced a double past Cox at third. On the hit, Dark scored. There was a play on Mueller at third, but he beat it with a slide—a slide so intense he sprained his ankle and had to be removed from the field on a stretcher. There was an interlude for that, an interlude in which the Dodgers changed pitchers, replacing Don Newcombe with Ralph Branca. But now the score was 4–2 with one out, the tying runs in scoring position, and Bobby Thomson coming to bat.

I turned to Benny-the-puncher and said, "If he hits a home run we'll flash and dictate." There was no prescience in what I said. The flat fact was that for the first time the winning run was at the plate, and if he hit it out, there would be no time for me to roll new paper into the typewriter and confect a substitute lead.

But at INS headquarters downtown, obviously all things had come to a stop. At the Polo Grounds, while Mueller was being replaced by pinch runner Clint Hartung and Newcombe by Branca, three bells sounded on Benny's machine, the signal for a message. I looked over Benny's shoulder. CE/BP the incoming said, TRUNK YRS. PGR/HN. The CE stood for my initials, the BP for ball park, our call letters. PGR was Philip G. Reed, the managing editor, and HN the call letters for INS New York. TRUNK YRS meant simply that all other flow on the trunk wires of the International News Service had been held up, to await the outcome of this inning. It was also Phil's way of telling me that, like

Jack Geiger, he couldn't fit in the TV room because too many others were there ahead of him. I remember wondering idly what would happen if the Giants tied the score and the game went to extra innings. Then it occurred to me this was the reason for Reed's message: the trunk lines would stay clear for our bulletin update at the end of nine innings.

But it meant too that in Chicago, the relay point for INS to the South, Southwest, and Pacific Coast, fifteen teletype machines had come to a halt, with bureau manager Jerry Healey prowling the interior of their horseshoe configuration, ready to shout a flash if it came. In San Francisco, Jack Hanley would do the same for the Coast wire and the radio transmission links to the far Pacific and Hawaii. The company manual said no verbal flashes were permitted. But the shortest flash in INS history, WASHN—FDR DEAD, had been a verbally communicated flash and beat the UP by thirty seconds and the AP by two minutes. The sales department knew what side that bread was buttered on.

Now Ralph Branca, taking the mound, threw a called strike past Thomson. Sitting there without premonition, I watched Thomson swing at the next pitch, and out it tracked toward the left-field stands. At first my eyes followed the ball, but then they went to Andy Pafko, the Dodger left fielder. His behind was plastered against the wall, and he was looking up. But his hands were at his sides. I said, "Flash, Benny."

Roger Kahn would recall the moment, in his book *How the Weather Was:*

> Then the ball was gone, under the overhanging scoreboard, over the high wall, gone deep into the seats in lower left, 320 feet from home plate. For seconds, which seemed like minutes, the crowd sat dumb. Then came the roar. It was a roar matched all across the country, wherever people sat at radio or television sets, a roar of delight, a roar of horror, but mostly a roar of utter shock. It was a moment when all the country roared and when an office worker in a tall building

on Wall Street, hearing a cry rise all about her, wondered if war had been declared. . . .

In left, Pafko stood stunned. Then he started to walk slowly toward the clubhouse, telling himself over and over: "It can't be." Most of the Dodgers were walking before Thomson reached second base. Jackie Robinson held his ground. He wanted to make sure that Thomson touched all bases before conceding that the Giants had won, 5–4, before conceding that the pennant race was over.

Clyde Sukeforth gathered gear in the [Dodger] bullpen, and nearby Carl Erskine turned to Clem Labine. "That's the first time I've seen a big fat wallet go flying into the seats," Erskine said.

It is the simplest measure of an epochal event that people want to tell you, either then or years later, where they were at the time it happened. This was true of Pearl Harbor, and of the deaths of Franklin Roosevelt and John Kennedy; and all three of those were unexpected. It was true too of such expected events as the first landing on the moon and the resignation of President Nixon. But Bobby Thomson's "home run heard round the world" would surpass either of those categories because it delivered in both: it was totally unexpected, and yet the audience already was in place.

At the Polo Grounds I had no feel of how fast I reacted. Jack Geiger told me later that in the office the flash bells on the ball park teletype actually started ringing before the roar from the television room. Ordinarily that would be hard to believe, but in this case it may well have been so, for the fact was that in losing track of the ball I had trained on Pafko instead, and he knew it was gone before anybody.

The actual wording of the flash I sent was by prearrangement no more than cosmetic fail-safe. GIANTS WIN PENNANT, it went. BEAT DODGERS 5–4. In the INS headquarters, Carver had already prepared two dummy flashes. GIANTS WIN, said one; DODGERS WIN, said the other—the comma in each case to be followed by the final score. "Barry Faris was standing in front of me, watching the teletype," Geiger said. "To his dying day he never trusted a television set." Faris was the editor in chief of INS. He said, "Four bells. Flash." At the filing table, Phil Reed said to the operators, "Four bells. Make it five to four."

In Chicago, Jerry Healey read it aloud off the eastern trunk. Nine teletypes banged out four bells, then GIANTS WIN, 5–4, then twelve more bells in three sets of four. A flash in the Chicago bureau, where I had sojourned as midwest sports editor from December, 1945, through July, 1949, was fun city, with the bells making a shooting gallery out of the newsroom there.

Now I had my head implanted over Benny's shoulder at the Polo Grounds, dictating my bulletin lead. He was seated on the aisle, so just as I leaned in over one of his shoulders, all sorts of passersby were leaning over the other. They were fans, nothing more or less, but obviously they held a lively interest in the communicative arts, and some of them, inevitably, were critics. Thus, as I dictated my version of the game into Benny's right ear, a succession of strangers were dictating theirs into his left. Quickly as I could, I filled in the details of the final inning, then went to a pickup line into my previous running story, then turned to my right. Considine's first take was ready. I handed it to Benny, who placed it gratefully on the platen of his teletype machine. From here on in he could punch from written copy. Any intervals in between takes of Considine's story could be filled by material from our returning clubhouse reporters. The steady flow of the ballpark report was assured.

And at that point, for the first time, I sat back, relaxed, and looked up. Aside from a scraggly group still congregated at the base of the clubhouse steps in deepest center field, the arena was bare. All this while, Paul Allerup, the INS news editor, had been seated silently behind me. He had no role in our departmental coverage of this story, nor had he attempted to exercise any. But the editor in him was too ingrained to still him forever, even on his day off, and now he leaned forward and touched my shoulder. "So long as you've cleaned up your lead," he said, "why not do a sidebar on what it was like after he hit the homer?"

The idea made all kinds of sense, though my reaction to it might have been a shade impolite. For in the instant of Allerup's suggestion, it came to me that I didn't *know* what it was like after Thomson hit the homer. I never even saw him leave home plate, let alone the jubilant kangaroo circle of the bases and the final leap into the wild cascade of his joy-maddened teammates. I didn't see Eddie Stanky eject like a test sled from the Giant dugout to third base, where Durocher was coaching, to nail the manager with a flying tackle. (There was more than celebration to that move: Stanky wanted to immobilize the suddenly crazed pilot for fear he might try to kiss Thomson or otherwise interfere with his progress on the base paths.) I heard later that the lower stands emptied their hysterical human contents onto the field like the death of a waterfall, but I didn't see it. I didn't see the Giants hoist Thomson to their shoulders in the triumphant surge to their clubhouse, or the Long March of the Dodgers to theirs. Surely I had sense of the moment for what it was and the place it would own in history, but all the coin of it, the touches that others like Red Smith would supply, I had missed completely. And if 34,320 people were at the Polo Grounds the day Thomson hit the homer, I have the accumulated sensation over the years of having spoken with 68,640 people who remember being there—all of them with far more vivid memories of the occasion than the ones I came away with.

Our report from the Dodger clubhouse did include, of course, full quotes from Dodger manager Charley Dressen on his ninth-inning strategy. In the first playoff game at Ebbets Field, the Giants' margin of victory had been a two-run homer by Thomson off Branca. Why not then issue an intentional walk to Thomson this time—first base was open—and take a chance with what Red Smith called "the dead-end kids" toward the bottom of the Giant batting order? Dressen's reply was ritualistic: in the rigid baseball thinking of the time, one did not intentionally put the winning run on base.

It is one thing to measure this decision in hindsight, but it takes no second guess to report that it set extremely well with the man who followed Thomson in the Giant batting order, a thoroughly frightened twenty-year-old named Willie Mays. Even as Thomson swung and connected, Mays's flash reaction was that the ball would be caught, though deep enough to get the run in from third, bringing him to bat with two out and the tying run still on second base.

Hank Greenberg, the Detroit Tigers' Hall of Fame first baseman, said that a great hitter becomes great only when he *wants* to be the man at bat in the key situation, and in the mid-1960s a poll of managers conducted by *Sport* magazine would rate Willie Mays on a plane apart as the finest clutch hitter in the game. (In 1962, on his final at-bat in the regular season, the league playoff, and the World Series, and with all three of those games in jeopardy, Mays had produced a home run, a single, and a double. To say this is neither to overstate his reputation nor to overendorse it on that sole account. As magnificent a hitter as Ted Williams was systematically savaged by the press for his failure to produce in similar end-season, playoff, and Series situations, and what was fair for Willie could nonetheless have been what was unfair to Ted.) But if Mays was to acquire that special zest for being the man the game depended on, he did not yet have it as a rookie in 1951. He had played in all 121 Giant games since he joined the club in late May. His batting average had been .274, a shade better than the .2fucking70 Durocher had conjured, though it was under .200 for the stretch run in September, and in all was not sufficiently intimidating to command what pitcher-author Jim Brosnan a decade later would call the pitchers' brooding respect at the mention of Willie's name. (The brooding was honestly come by. Long after his retirement, computer-driven statisticians of the eighties were still transfixing pitchers with Maysian data, like the discovery that he had hit more home runs in extra innings (22) than any other player in history, and the revelation by the Society for American Baseball Research that he was the only man to have homered at least once in every inning up to and including the 16th.)

What does seem logical is that Mays would have had more to lose than gain from having to come to bat in the ninth inning of the final playoff game. Success would only have gilded the reputation that was to see him named Rookie of the Year; failure not only would tarnish it, but do so in full view of a nationwide TV audience. In the event, he viewed Thomson's home run from the on-deck circle, and post-game films would reveal him stationed at the plate like an usher at a rock concert holding back the rush for the box office, lest the rest of the Giants engulf Thomson before he touched home.

That moment to one side, there is no question that Mays's award as Rookie of the Year was honestly come by. At the plate, having gone 12 times without a hit before his home run off Spahn, he would now go hitless another 13 straight times. "What's he hitting—.039?" humorist Jack E. Leonard said. "I had that for breakfast." But from that point Willie was to break out and go on a summer-long tear. On one road swing late in June, Mays hit a three-run homer in the tenth inning at Chicago, went on a ten-game hitting streak, totaled four home runs and 16 runs batted in for the trip. In a stretch of eight days late in July, Mays collected six hits—hardly an overpowering figure in and of itself, but worth remarking nonetheless for the fact that all six were homers. For the season as a whole, he would hit 20 home runs, but when Durocher said later, "He carried the whole team on his back," the manager obviously had other things as well in mind. There was, for example, the "break" Mays got in center field on a batted ball—the sixth sense that actually puts some fielders into motion *before* the hitter makes contact. There is no teaching this: some have it, some don't.

DiMaggio had it; his brother Vince, also a center fielder, even more than Joe. Casey Stengel said Willie Mays had more of it than anyone with the possible exception of Red Murray, an early-century Giant right fielder who once made a game-saving catch in total darkness: just as the hitter swung, a suddenly gathered Allegheny storm plunged the Pittsburgh ball park into midnight black; then a flash of lightning silhouetted Murray's leaping catch against the wall. (Tom Meany wrote that for some years thereafter, the Giants while traveling would stage a version of instant replay, with somebody dousing the lights in the parlor car while someone else struck a match to reveal Murray posed in the tableau of his Pittsburgh catch.)

On the bases in 1951, Mays stole only seven times. That number would increase dramatically in years to come, yet even in his first year Mays was a dramatic base*runner*. (Joe DiMaggio never stole seven bases in a season in his major league lifetime, yet he too was highly credentialed as a baserunner. Like the 1951 Giants, the Yankees of his era eschewed the steal in favor of the long ball. But the key moment in the Yankees' '51 league campaign came in a critical September game against Cleveland at Yankee Stadium before a crowd of 68,000, with the score tied in the ninth, DiMaggio on third, and Phil Rizzuto, then the game's most accomplished bunter, at the plate. The combination of Rizzuto's special talent and DiMaggio's skill as a runner made the game-winning squeeze play foreordained. "Tell me," DiMaggio said idly to Al Rosen, the Cleveland third baseman. "Do you think he's going to bunt?" "I'll be the most surprised Jew in the place if he doesn't," Rosen responded. In the outcome, Rosen was not surprised.

(One observes withal that in 1971, at the age of forty, Mays would steal 23 bases, placing him among the top eight in that category in the National League that year. The '71 figure takes added significance for the fact that he was caught stealing only three times. The other seven leaders, with their average age of twenty-seven [the optimal age in an athlete's life, according to the Helms Foundation], were a 77-percent shot to make it when they took off to steal a base. When the old man took a whack at it, he was an 89-percent shot.)

As he would twenty years later, Mays picked his base-stealing spots in 1951. True that he may have stolen only seven bases all that year, but two of them came in Boston on the season's next-to-last day, when he walked, stole second, stole third, and came home on a ground out, giving the Giants their winning run without benefit of a hit. (Like father, like son; remember Kitty Kat: "If I got to first base it was like getting a double. And to me, from second base to third base was much easier than from first to second." His son in years to come would develop this formula in ways not even Kat had envisioned.)

And with his arm in center field, Willie was Willie. It was something truly new for all who experienced it. There was, for example, the throw he made to get Billy Cox at the plate in the August 15 game Branch Rickey alluded to. Rickey was not alone in the astonishment he registered over that play. *Time* magazine referred to it simply as The Throw. And Dodger manager Dressen had no substantive comment to make. "When he does it again," he said, "I'll believe it." (Come to think of it, that probably *was* a substantive comment.)

The situation for that one was that the Dodgers and Giants were tied, 1–1, with Brooklyn threatening, having the speedy Cox on third with only one out in the top of the eighth. Now Carl Furillo put up the hit that would score Cox from third, a fly ball to medium-deep right-center. Center fielder Mays overtook it with a sprinting catch, and Cox, tagged up at third, broke for the plate, and there was no way Mays or any other human of record was going to throw him out. Willie threw with his right hand but his bodily momentum was to his left. For him to try a throw in that state would resemble an actor in *The Boys in the Band* dancing toward offstage while waving to the audi-

61

ence with his retreating hand, and with just about that much baseball effect.

Mays, however, had a different idea. In the act of catching the ball he came down hard on his left foot, spun counterclockwise with his back to the infield, came out of the spin with a low, humming throw—"It wasn't a throw," first baseman Lockman said afterward, "it was a *pitch*"—and it came in to the plate on the fly at what catcher Wes Westrum estimated as "85 miles an hour—minimum." The startled Westrum caught it, then turned to confront the equally startled Cox, who said, "Oh, shit, no," and didn't even bother to slide.

In years to come, Mays would make so many astounding throws that his colleagues gave up on trying to rate them. "When they hit it to him," Bill Rigney (Durocher's successor as manager) would explain to his tyro infielders at the start of spring training, "please go to a base. Don't confuse the issue by asking me why. Just *be* there." Daniel M. Daniel, a sportswriter who himself was elected to baseball's Hall of Fame in 1973, first started covering the game in 1909. He saw them all, including his coverage of the Yankees during the entirety of Joe Di-Maggio's career. "Willie Mays," he stated flatly, "has the greatest throwing arm I ever saw." There is a place in the record book for the player who can "hit for the cycle"—single, double, triple, home run—in a single game. In a game at Los Angeles in May of 1966, Willie Mays *threw* for the cycle! In the record, his throws from the outfield got one runner at home, another at third, another at first. He had a fourth man at second, but Giant second baseman Tito Fuentes, his back turned to the incoming runner, swung the wrong way and missed the tag. "Mays threw so many base runners out he may lead the entire Giant infield in assists," Jim Murray wrote in the next morning's Los Angeles *Times*. "He should play in handcuffs to even things up a bit." Of the Mays throw from center that caught Willie Davis at third, Murray estimated 100 mph.

You ran at your own peril against Willie's arm, sometimes not even realizing yourself what he was doing to you. More than once, not even his own team picked up on it. (Shades of Rigney.) Sometimes, his own manager didn't. (Shades of Clyde King, who was managing the Giants in 1969 one day when Mays fielded a single in center field and overthrew the cutoff man in a vain attempt to get a runner going from first to third on the hit; on the sequence, the hitter moved up to second base. Herman Franks, who had preceded King as Giant manager, was sitting next to me in the press box. "Look at him," he said of Willie. "He's managing in place of King. He wanted that hitter to move up to second base so first base would be open. Now they'll walk the next hitter on purpose. Then they'll get the next guy out and have the guy after him having to lead off the next inning. That's the way Willie's got it planned.")

On another occasion, with Hank Aaron on first base, the batter hit a deep shot to right-center. Willie caught it with his back turned, then wheeled and threw. Aaron had already passed second base, and in his frantic attempt to return to first, he had to be a probable out for a double play. But Mays didn't throw to first. Instead, he threw to second, where the ineffable Fuentes received the ball and now had to confront the problem of what to do with it. Mays helped him out. From deepest right-center, he jabbed his forefinger straight down. With this cue, Fuentes stamped on second base, then looked to the umpire. It was an appeal play. "You're out, Henry," the umpire said to Aaron. "You didn't retouch second on your way back to first." In the moment of his decision, Mays had transformed a probable double play out at first into a sure double play out at second. Yet how did he *know* Aaron had missed second on his way back? He himself was turned away from the action at the time. To Mays, the mystery was no mystery. "I know the way he runs," he said.

An occasion can be cited too when Willie Mays actually struck out on purpose. Here again no true mystery attached to the action. (We shall encounter later in these pages a Dodger batsman doing the same thing, for a separate but equally strategic reason.) Willie's case came in the first inning of a game at the old ball park in St. Louis, and he swung and missed in order to see the same pitch later in the game when it might count for something. He did and it did. The pitcher was Curt Simmons of the Cardinals, and having established his out pitch with Mays in the first inning, he tried it again in the eighth, this time with the Cardinals leading 1–0 and a Giant runner on base. Willie hit it over the right-field roof and the Giants won, 2–1.

He would in fact wait, if he had to, not innings but years. In 1954, Harvey Haddix of the St. Louis club fed him a change-up at the Polo Grounds, and Mays hit the thing in excess of 500 feet, upstairs in the deepest reach of the grandstand to left of center, where the stand curved to abut the bleachers. As time went by after that, Haddix made it evident Mays was not about to see that pitch again. And he didn't—not for five years, till the point in 1959 when Haddix, now in the employ of the Pittsburgh Pirates, decided to invoke the one-upmanship that theoretically is always on the pitcher's side (he knows what the pitch will be; the batter doesn't). In the eighth inning of a tight game at Forbes Field, on July 18, 1959, Haddix let Willie see his change-up for the first time since July 27, 1954. Mays cracked it on a rising line over the left-field fence.

Surely education is there to nourish instinct. The rookie Mays of 1951, in slavish imitation of his idols DiMaggio and Williams, wore his uniform pants long. It took a Durocher to point out that this made him artificially tall, in the sense that to an umpire's eyes it lowered Willie's knees, thus enlarging his strike zone. Yet, just as certainly, neither Durocher nor anyone else could change that laugh, or the "Say hey!" or the Willie Mays who whiled the post-game hours away playing stickball with the kids in the street outside his Harlem rooming house. In that game, played with a handball and a broomstick, the fenders of parked cars served as touch points to represent first and third base; manhole covers, called "sewers" by the participants, served as home, second, and the delineation of outfield distance.

On August 30, 1951, having hit two home runs against the Pirates in a must game at the Polo Grounds that afternoon, Mays changed into T-shirt and slacks and with Mrs. Goosby, his landlady, looking on disapprovingly from a brownstone window, took her broomstick and hit one for five sewers.

There was an ebullience there that no one could, or would want to, touch. It carried over to Willie's return at season's end to his home in Birmingham. On impulse, the first place he went was to the Woolworth store downtown, where his Aunt Ernestine worked at the lunch counter. He saw her before she saw him; her back was turned as he slid onto the stool.

"Hey, gal," he piped. "How about a glass of water?"

She responded reflexively and filled a glass, then turned and saw who it was. The surprise was in all ways complete. She set the water down in front of him and said, "Junior, you drink this fast and then you get out of here. It's my job if you don't." She looked fearfully around. "You know colored can't sit down at the counter in here."

PART TWO

IKE

The Only Man Who Could Have
Caught It Hit It

If THE 1951 SEASON MARKED THE BEGINNING of an era for one man, so it was the end for another. Meeting for the first time and clasping hands for the photographers before the opening game of the '51 World Series at Yankee Stadium were the rival center fielders, Mays and Joe DiMaggio. Though the official announcement would not come until December, the latter would play out the six games it took the Yankees to beat the Giants in the Series, giving way to a pinch runner at third base in the eighth inning of the final game, and trotting to the dugout to the almost reverent applause of 70,000 fans who sensed the end. "I used to watch him and it was agony for him just getting in and out of a taxicab," his teammate Phil Rizzuto told Maury Allen; and another Yankee, Jerry Coleman, said, "You could see that he didn't have it any more. He had one throw a game from the outfield, and he didn't have the snap in his bat like he did before." A friend who learned of DiMaggio's decision to retire asked him why. "Because I don't want them to remember me struggling," DiMaggio said. He was thirty-six.

But already flanking him in right field in the final game of the 1951 Series was the rookie heir-apparent to the Yankee spot in center, a switch-hitting nineteen-year-old from Spavinaw, Oklahoma, named Mickey Mantle. The contrast when the two teams changed sides between half innings produced a sight totally new to organized baseball. With the injury to right fielder Don Mueller on his slide into third in the ninth inning of the playoff finale, his place in the World Series lineup was taken by Henry Thompson, a part-time infielder who had been in the majors for a brief spell (27 games, "a cup of coffee" as baseball lingo had it) with the St. Louis Browns in 1947, then was hired by the Giants in 1949. In this, Giant-owner Stoneham was quietly delivering his own follow-up to the action of Branch Rickey, who signed Jackie Robinson in 1945 and brought him to the majors at the outset of the 1947 season. Rickey's understandable fixation was that the first Negro in the major leagues (Robinson actually was not the first, but he was the first in this century not to pass as white, Cuban, or whatever) must be an athlete of such caliber that he could not fail. Stoneham's move, in its way even more daring than Rickey's, in those days, was to give Thompson the truest status of equality: like any white player, he could bomb out his first time around and yet rate another chance.

(The time frame here is that of our own postwar era. Dr. Harold Seymour, in volume one of his distinguished history *Baseball,* records the notable if brief playing careers of the black players Moses Fleetwood Walker, Weldy Walker, William Higgins, George Stovey, Bud Fowler, James Jackson, and Frank Grant in the majors and high minors of the late nineteenth century. But, adds Seymour, "It is a well-known historical paradox that, as the Civil War receded, Jim Crowism in America became more pronounced. Southern caste attitudes spread increasingly to the North and West, much to the alarm of liberals and reformers. This blight included professional baseball in its contagious advance. White players objected to the 'colored element.' Even the redoubtable [Cap] Anson refused to go through with an exhibition game against Newark if Fleet Walker and George Stovey played. So by the late 1880's the major leagues erected a solid, though unofficial, dam against Negroes, shutting off completely the tiny trickle which had previously flowed through.")

There was Thompson, then, in right field for the Giants in the 1951 Series, and Mays in center, and Monte Irvin in left—an all-black outfield in Yankee Stadium, whose management would not hire even the first black Yankee player until 1955.

Mays in that 1951 World Series collected four hits, all of them singles, and Thompson only two of the same, but their compatriot in left field lashed out eleven hits in six games, and as the action unfolded an anonymous quatrain, its authorship ascribed to a veteran Chicago writer, was circulated in the press box:

Willie Mays is in a daze
And Thompson's lost his vigor,
But Irvin whacks for all the blacks—
It's great to be a nigger.

In this connection, I have a memory of the afternoon of October 5, 1962, when I was standing in the hallway that separates the home and visiting teams' dressing rooms at Candlestick Park in San Francisco. Once again the occasion was a World Series between the Giants and the Yankees. That day's game had just ended, and as the players came in from the field my eye fell on Mays and Mantle as they entered together, immersed in private conversation of the sort two consummate, tired professionals will have at the end of a day's work. There was no sensation that one was black, the other white. The only visible difference between them lay in the tools of their trade: Mays, having been in the field when the game ended, had what Mantle did not have —a pair of flip-up sunglasses dipping like a lower lip from the visor of his cap.

So it may be that not many people today—few if any under the age of forty—can remember what it was like *not* to see blacks in organized baseball. Today, in fact, some socioeconomic note has been taken of a new pendular cycle, characterized by the 1978 Rochester team of the International League, where the only black on the roster was the manager! In truth, though no precise figures are available, the probability is strong that fewer blacks make their living from professional baseball today than at any previous time in this century. Part of this may be ascribed to the theory, espoused by Julian Bond and others, that white America in the seventies had moved toward a "this-far-and-no-farther" stance toward Negro advancement, a standpoint codified by the Supreme Court's Bakke decision and a landmark tax-relief victory in California for property owners rather than renters. Another factor was the elongation of football and basketball seasons: those being the two college sports that offer the most attractive scholarships, an all-around black athlete like a Vida Blue (or for that matter a Jackie Robinson in his own day) no longer can accept the college emolument and still have time to develop and display his baseball potential. The chief irony, however, dates back to the coming of Robinson to the majors, which established that a Negro could make it; and the coming of Mays, which established that a *young* Negro could make it. In this signal victory for integration, an insufficiently noticed side effect took its counter toll on one of what at the time were the only two thriving Negro industries: newspapers and black baseball. Robinson's departure could be tolerated—he was one of many seasoned performers. Satchel Paige's departure for the majors in 1948 was harder to take—but he was a curio, whispered to be nearly fifty years of age. With the signing of the teenage Mays, however, it was like the opening of a freeway bypassing the old road through town. Easily the youngest black player signed so far by white organized baseball, Mays symbolized the route fresh talent would take. Within two years of his joining the Giants, the two great Negro baseball leagues collapsed.

(Perhaps this is a place to record a further piece of irony, which is the way Horace Stoneham's Giant scouts infested Latin America at the same time they prowled the Negro leagues. Players like Juan Marichal, Orlando Cepeda, Ruben Gomez, the three outfielding Alou brothers, and Manny Mota came to the Giants in this manner. Stoneham himself checked out a future Giant shortstop named José Pagan during winter-league play in Puerto Rico when Pagan was only fourteen years old. And from the Giants' chief Caribbean scout, Alex Pompez, there came a major recommendation to sign a young Cuban pitcher he had seen and who, Pompez felt, was definitely major league material. Negotiations were attempted, but the twenty-three-year-old right-hander, whose name was Fidel Castro, appeared to have some other ideas about his future.)

Upon his induction into the Black Athletes Hall of Fame,

during the inaugural banquet of that organization at New York's Americana Hotel in March of 1974—white waiters serving prime rib to formally attired black diners—Willie Mays said:

"This award means a great deal to me, because the time that I broke into baseball, I was like a young Jackie Robinson. I broke into the Interstate League. I was at it by myself, and I had a lot of hardship that no one knows about. I don't like to speak about it because I was very ashamed of it. I've been told, 'Willie, you don't care about your people.' But that's a lie. The suffering that I received in the last, I would say, twenty-three years, I couldn't talk about because it was inside of me. I had to hold it. But this award here again tells me that the young blacks have a hell of a chance. This award here tells me again that we are getting together. As one man said, it may take a little while, but we're coming."

Discrimination having been for all practical purposes the same for all, different black athletes would nonetheless respond to it in different public ways, in a range from Muslim firebrand to Uncle Tom (each inevitably accusing the other of betraying the cause). For his heavyweight title fight against Muhammad Ali at Madison Square Garden the night of March 8, 1971, an event witnessed by a live worldwide television audience estimated at 300 million, the dark-skinned Joe Frazier found himself not only cast as the white hope against the lighter-skinned Ali but at the same time taunting him in the clinches by the slave name of Clay. Jesse Owens, four-time gold medalist at the Berlin Olympics in 1936, would spend the balance of his life advertising his memory of the master-race Nazi opponent who offered him cordial advice in the broad jump. And Satchel Paige, possibly the greatest pitcher who ever lived, had his own private reaction when the St. Louis Browns offered him a contract for the 1952 season. The manager of the Browns that year was Rogers Hornsby, possibly the greatest hitter who ever lived, and an outspoken racist to boot.

Paige put through a phone call to Browns owner Bill Veeck.

"Mr. Veeck," he said, "I'm not sure I should sign to play for this man, because in his eyes I'm nothing more or less than a no-good nigger son of a bitch."

"No, no, no," Veeck remonstrated. "That may have been true once, but what you don't realize is the way times have changed. This is the big league, and it's 1952, and I've talked with Hornsby. There won't be any problem."

Accordingly, Paige signed, but in the course of a springtime exhibition tour as the Browns barnstormed their way back toward St. Louis, he missed the team bus to the ball park for a game in Oklahoma City, could not find a taxicab that would accept him as a passenger, and finally had to walk to the park, arriving there with the game already in progress. In short order, he now put through another long-distance call to the team's owner. "Mr. Veeck," he said, "you remember what it was I said I was in the eyes of this man? Well, that is what I is. He just told me."

Mays made a special round trip from Florida to attend the banquet of the Black Athletes Hall of Fame. Among his fellow inductees, Ali, Paige, and Owens had in common that they failed to show up, though Owens did send his wife. Master of ceremonies Bill Cosby handled the matter through superb direction from the dais. "This is our first dinner and we missed a whole lot of people," he told the audience. "It should have been the whatever, the 117th dinner . . . but wasn't nobody giving us no dinners in 1923. And I've noticed quite a few athletes out in the audience who will soon be in the Hall of Fame, not because they're good but because they're black." The black audience, and the few whites among them, rocked with the same shared laughter. Then Cosby zeroed in on Mays:

"Willie will never realize what he did to barbershops, because dudes in barbershops be arguing about Mays, and Lord, to be black, and play baseball for the Giants, and do something wrong . . . why, you let the whole race down! If you walk down the street after dropping a fly ball and letting in an important run, dudes on the corner don't even want to talk to you. That's how important you are, that they will ignore you the day after you blow it, and let you know it. Say, man, I had 75 cent bet on you. You lost my money, man. So there's a lot of heavy loads you gotta carry when you one of the first people out there."

Do something wrong, you let the whole race down. . . . That's how important you are. . . . So there's a lot of heavy loads you gotta carry when you one of the first people out there.

Roger Kahn has recorded an episode that took place in 1954, when the New York and Cleveland clubs, both training in Arizona, were booked for an exhibition game at Las Vegas. Playing there was all right, but the Giants did not plan to stay overnight:

The Stoneham regime is paternalistic, and the idea of a troop of young ball players abroad among the gamblers and the bosoms of Vegas was disturbing. The team would play its game with the Indians. The players would be guests for dinner at one of the big hotels. They would watch a show and seek as much trouble as they could find up until 11 P.M. Then a bus would take them to the airport for a flight to Los Angeles, where two other exhibitions were scheduled. We wouldn't get much rest.

It was a gray, raw afternoon in Vegas, and Bob Feller pitched for the Indians. Sal Maglie opposed him. My scorebook is lost, but I believe the Giants won by one run. Afterward we wrote our stories and took a bus to the hotel that had invited us all. We ate well, and I caught up with Willie in the hotel theater, where Robert Merrill, the baritone, was to sing. As I joined Willie's table, Merrill began *"Vesti la giubba,"* the aria from *Pagliacci* in which Canio, the clown, sings of having to make people laugh, although his own heart is breaking.

Merrill gave it full voice and all his passions. When he was done, Willie turned to me amid the cheering. "You know," he said, "that's a nice song."

An hour later, he was in a gambling room, standing quietly amid a group of people close to a dice table. Monte Irvin and Whitey Lockman were fighting a ten-cent one-armed bandit. Sal Maglie, glowering like a movie Mafioso, was losing a steady fifty cents a game at blackjack. I walked over to Willie. "How you doing?"

"Oh," Willie said, "I'm just learnin' the game." We both grinned.

I moved on. A stocky gruff man grabbed me by the arm. "Hey," he said. "Wait a minute."

I shook my arm free.

"That guy a friend of yours?" said the man. He pointed to Mays.

"I know him."

"Well, get him the hell away from the dice tables."

"What?"

"You heard me. We don't want him mixing with the white guests."

"Do you know who he is?"

"Yeah, I know who he is, and get that nigger away from the white guests."

If there was a good answer, except for the obvious short answer, I didn't come up with it. Very quickly I was appalled, unnerved and angry. What unnerved me was the small, significant bulge on the man's left hip.

"Do you know that boy just got out of the Army?" I said.

"That don't mean nothing. I was in the Army myself."

"You bastards invited him down to your hotel."

"Who you calling a bastard?"

We were shouting and Garry Schumacher, the Giants' publicity director, suddenly loomed large and put a hand on my shoulder. "What's the trouble?" Garry said.

"This guy," the tough began.

"I asked him," Garry said, nodding at me.

I had a sensible moment. "No trouble, Guv," I said to Garry. I took my wallet out of a hip pocket and withdrew the press card. "This joker has just given me one helluva story for the Sunday New York *Herald Tribune.*"

The hood retreated. I walked over to Irvin and told him what was happening. Lockman listened briefly and then, taking the conversation to be personal, stepped back. "Maybe Willie and I'll get on the bus," Irvin said. It was his way, to avoid confrontations, but he was also worried lest Willie be shocked or hurt.

Now a hotel vice president appeared, with a girl, hard-faced, trimly built, dark-haired. He asked if "my assistant and I can buy you a drink."

We went to the bar and the man explained that he had nothing against a Negro like Irvin or Mays playing one-armed bandits. It was just that the dice table was a somewhat different thing. As far as he, the vice president, was concerned, Negroes were as good as anybody, but he had to consider the wishes of the customers. That was business.

"We're really in the South here," said the brunette.

"I thought the South was Alabama, Georgia, Texas."

"That's it," the brunette said. "We get a lot of customers from Texas." She glanced at the bartender, and I had another drink. "We're really a very liberal place," the girl said, "even though we are in the South. We not only book Lena Horne to sing here, but when she does, we let her live on the grounds. We're the only hotel that liberal." She leaned toward me, a hard, handsome woman, working.

"Why did you invite him if you were going to shit on him?" I said. I got up and joined Monte and Will in the bus.

Later, Irvin asked me not to write the story. He said he didn't know if it was a good idea to make Willie, at twenty-two, the center of a racial storm. That was Monte's way and the Giants' way and Willie's way, and you had to respect it, even if dissenting. I never did write the story until now.

The late Garry Schumacher would confirm Kahn's account, adding that he recalled an agreement, quite logical in view of baseball's wish not to place ballplayers in a gambling environment, that no Giant, black or white, would be seen in the casino. He also remembers Monte Irvin's part in cooling the thing, though Schumacher believed, not against common sense, that Mays would have liked to get into the dice game, not just loiter alongside. Mays himself is vague in the recollection of this incident. No undue suspicion can attach thereto. There was the Mays who repudiated the Say Hey label, yet putting in for that same label on his license plates. There was the late-career Mays responding to Roger Kahn:

KAHN: You want to manage?
MAYS: Yeah. I think I'd like to.
KAHN: What about handling pitchers? Could you do that?

MAYS: You're a manager, man, you get to
hire help.

And the same Mays, at about the same time, responding to Jack Klugman's same question for television:

KLUGMAN: How do you feel about managing a
ball club?
MAYS: I don't think I even want to manage. Let's put it this way—you're
just lonely, by yourself.

"The man is a complex individual," Willie's wife, Mae, has said. "Most people thought of him as being very . . . just baseball. He'd go out, hit the ball, come home, and watch TV. That's what they thought. And that was so erroneous. The man is really very deep."

There was another episode in Las Vegas, and Willie was not present for this one. A public impression has gained favor that Jimmy the Greek sets the prevailing Nevada odds on various events, but in fact the betting line has originated mainly with a transplanted New Yorker named Bob Martin, who a decade ago took over the Churchill Downs Race Book betting parlor on the Las Vegas Strip. In so doing, Martin instituted some adroit novations, such as setting his clocks five minutes ahead and creating a loser's raffle, by which holders of losing tickets could collect anyway at day's end. The clock stunt was to preclude rip-offs on the part of any signal-activated patrons of Martin's betting parlors who might place their horse wagers after post time but before the result of the race came in. The establishment of a consolation drawing for bettors who deposited their losing tickets in a handy drum not only paid for itself in the savings on after-hours janitorial help but kept the floor clean all day long.

It was, however, in setting the betting odds for the final day of the 1971 baseball season that Martin encountered one of his finest moments of inspiration. The Giants, needing a victory at San Diego that night to clinch the western division title of the National League, more than made up in pitching what they yielded to the disadvantage of being the visiting team, for they were going with Juan Marichal, who at that moment had a spectacular career percentage of .667, with 220 wins and 110 losses. (Carl Hubbell was in the Hall of Fame with .622, Cy Young with .617, Walter Johnson with .599.) Beyond that, the news now reached Martin that Willie Mays, who in his forty-first year already had played 135 games and come to bat more than 400 times, had cast aside rumored injury and fatigue and was a definite starter for this evening's encounter. The presence of Marichal was sufficient to make the Giants the favorite in Martin's book, but the added presence of Mays pumping with pennant adrenaline was more than Martin wished to contemplate. As a result, the odds he set on the game were no odds. He simply took the game off the board and refused to take bets on it, reasoning not inexpertly that no one in his right mind would back San Diego.

The right minds had it. In the third inning Mays put a double off the center-field fence, and the question now for the Padres was how to pitch to Dave Kingman. If they threw him a fast ball he might hit it. If they threw him anything slower, Mays would steal third. A hasty conference concluded that Kingman must be the lesser evil; he got a fast ball. Mays stole third anyway. Or nearly so: he was within three strides of the bag when Kingman's bat came around and sent the ball into the left-field bleachers. It was a graphic extension of Murphy's Law: when one of two bad things may happen, they both happen. The Giants went on to win 5–1.

What it comes down to is that Bill Cosby was being funny only north-northwest when he talked about the burden on Willie Mays. When Jackie Robinson came to the majors, his fellow blacks rooted for him from the depths of their being, and if he had a bad day, at least there was always tomorrow. But from

Mays, Cosby's barbershop dudes expected even more. As they would for Jackie, so just as deeply would they root for Willie. But the notion of tomorrow was not always so agreeable. Not when they were betting their money today. *Why, you let the whole race down!*

———◆———

A less elegant, and less legal, bookmaking service than Bob Martin's in Las Vegas was offered to staffers at the old International News Service in New York by a printer named Charley Rizzo, whose office was his right pants pocket. Like Martin's, the Rizzo operation was not confined to horses. ("He'll also take dog racing," Davis J. Walsh told me. "In a pinch, cats.") My memory tells me that the first signed piece I did after going to work for the International News Service in 1945 was a letter to the Hon. Saul Streit, Judge of the General Sessions, written on the best INS stationery and attesting from lifelong first-hand knowledge to the upright character of defendant Charles Rizzo, whom I had just then met. "Why don't you write the letter?" I asked sports editor Carver. "I can't," he said. "I wrote last month's."

Carver was embattled, and as time went by he did not take kindly to my increased use for non-sports reporting. He failed to share the cityside brand of humor that mandated someone with the by-line of Einstein to cover the annual St. Patrick's Day parade, and his complaining was at least equally intense the day he discovered I had been made archaeological editor and taken off the sports desk to witness the arrival of a South American freighter whose cargo contained a crated Peruvian mummy. "Fuck the mummy!" Carver cried to Phil Reed across the newsroom, to the enlightenment of a new copy girl whose job at INS was an extension of her work-study curriculum at Bard College.

(She subsequently was graduated with honors in what we all assumed was journalism, but it turned out she was majoring in abnormal psychology.)

In 1952 my defection from the sports side included a full two weeks, while as the newly anointed medical editor I might cover a seven-city swing under the aegis of the American Cancer Society, devoted to going public with the newest breakthroughs in prevention, treatment, and cure. The novelist Gerald Green, at that time an INS deskman, called that assignment the worst piece of miscasting since Herbert Marshall played the halfbreed in *Duel in the Sun,* but the assignment of a nonmedical writer to a medical story was in its way due and proper. That year the government was spending $18 million—in percentage, .00029 of the federal budget—for basic research in *all* fields of medicine. The allowance for plant and animal diseases was considerably higher. The country as a whole in 1952 spent $26 million on playing cards and $254 million on chewing gum. The most arresting development in the food and drug field that year came with the final decision that margarine could be colored yellow the same as butter.

In Chicago I was detached from the cancer tour and put on rewrite to cover the Wisconsin primary. And the tour brought me to Washington the night the President of the United States delivered an announcement to a Jefferson-Jackson Day dinner of 5,300 Democrats. "I shall not be a candidate for re-election," Harry Truman said. "I have served my country long and I think efficiently and honestly. I shall not accept a renomination. I do not feel that it is my duty to spend another four years in the White House."

In volume two of his *Memoirs,* Truman says he first registered this decision in a memorandum which he locked away on April 16, 1950. On that date, the 22nd Amendment to the Constitution, limiting a President's time in office, was en route to ratification. The amendment was worded specifically not to apply to the incumbent at time of passage, but Truman had something of the sense of it anyway, in that 1950 memorandum to himself:

> I am not a candidate for nomination by the Democratic Convention.
>
> My first election to public office took place in November, 1922. I served two years in the armed forces in World War I, ten years in the Senate, two months and twenty days as Vice-President and President of the Senate. I have been in public office well over thirty years, having been President of the United States almost two complete terms.
>
> Washington, Jefferson, Monroe, Madison, Andrew Jackson, and Woodrow Wilson, as well as Calvin Coolidge, stood by the precedent of two terms. Only Grant, Theodore Roosevelt, and F.D.R. made the attempt to break that precedent. F.D.R. succeeded.
>
> In my opinion eight years as President is enough and sometimes too much for any man to serve in that capacity.
>
> There is a lure in power. It can get into a man's blood just as gambling and lust for money have been known to do.
>
> This is a Republic. The greatest in the history of the world. I want this country to continue as a Republic. Cincinnatus and Washington pointed the way. When Rome forgot Cincinnatus, its downfall began. When we forget the examples of such men as Washington, Jefferson, and Andrew Jackson, all of whom could have had a continuation in office, then will we start down the road to dictatorship and ruin. I know I could be elected again and continue to break the old precedent as it was broken by F.D.R. It should not be done. That precedent should continue not by a Constitutional amendment, but by custom based on the honor of the man in office.
>
> Therefore, to re-establish that custom, although by a quibble I could say I've only had one term, I am not a candidate and will not accept the nomination for another term.

A more direct inkling of this privately held intention was gained by Alonzo Fields, chief butler at the White House, in overhearing the President remark that he intended to walk out of that building, not be carried out. And Truman himself told some newspapermen, in offhand early conversation, that he would be known as a former President, not an ex-President. No automatic clue in that, of course, but he did dwell on the distinction. Incumbents Martin Van Buren, Benjamin Harrison, William Howard Taft, and Herbert Hoover were, he said, all of them *ex,* since each had been voted out by the public. All others were *former.* Which of the two prefixes Richard Nixon would have earned in Truman's book cannot be known for certain, since he died with Nixon still in office, but an educated guess is not impossible. In a campaign speech at Texarkana on October 2, 1952, Nixon called Truman a traitor. The President never replied in kind. Goddamn lying son of a bitch, he did say, but that was a quantum jump short of traitor, and when actor James Whitmore recreated such salty phrasing in *Give 'Em Hell, Harry!* audiences from one coast to the other rocked with cheering and laughter. Nixon's resignation came in fact at the apogee of a wave of public affection for the former President, a swell of admiration which commenced in Truman's years in retirement and one in which Nixon, who did not have a poor opinion of himself as a political realist, was not the last to join. By the 1976 campaign, it became a matter of daily fascination to Truman's Democratic Party descendants to see which of the two Republican candidates, Ford for President or Dole for Vice-President, would praise Truman more.

Indeed, there was a letter that went forward toward the end of Truman's Presidency to Leonard Finder, then publisher of the Manchester, New Hampshire, *Union Leader,* which said, "The necessary and wise subordination of the military to civil power will be best sustained when life-long professional soldiers abstain from seeking high political office."

That view would have been characteristic of Truman at almost any time, but he didn't write the letter. It was signed instead by Dwight D. Eisenhower. Finder had placed Eisenhower's name in the New Hampshire primary. "I could not accept nomination even under the remote circumstances that it would be tendered me," Eisenhower wrote.

Harry and Ike did have one pro-military view in common: both of them venerated George C. Marshall, the five-star general who guided U.S. strategy in World War II and later became Truman's Secretary of State and father in name of the Marshall Plan for the revitalization of postwar Europe. Neither in fact nor effect would Nixon step over the ultimate line and hint that Marshall, like Truman, was a traitor, but others, including Wisconsin's Senator McCarthy, were less troubled by the practicality of restraint, and their denunciations of Marshall enraged Truman and Eisenhower alike. During the vilification coming at the height of the 1952 campaign, in which Eisenhower had by the remotest chance been tendered and accepted the Republican nomination, the opportunity arose for Ike to defend Marshall in a major political address at Milwaukee, the largest city in McCarthy's home state. In his book *The Ordeal of Power,* Emmet John Hughes, Eisenhower's chief speech writer, recalled Ike's reaction to that prospect:

> The major event of the 1952 campaign involving Senator Joseph McCarthy revealed still more of the man who was Eisenhower and the President he would be.
> . . . Suddenly, in our discussion of the Milwaukee speech, he leaned forward, bristling with excited indignation, and said: "Listen, couldn't we make this an occasion for me to pay a personal tribute to Marshall—right in McCarthy's back yard?" I was more than mildly enthusiastic.

The result of Hughes's more-than-mild enthusiasm was to assign these ringing words to Ike:

> Let me be quite specific. I know that charges of disloyalty have, in the past, been leveled against General George C. Marshall. I have been privileged for thirty-five years to know General Marshall personally. I know him, as a man and as a soldier, to be dedicated with singular selflessness and the profoundest patriotism to the service of America. And this episode is a sobering lesson in the way freedom must *not* defend itself.

So much for the gut paragraph of Ike's Milwaukee speech. The only thing amiss was that he never delivered it. McCarthyite pols, spotting the Marshall passage in the prepared text, talked him out of it. Eisenhower, according to Hughes, could exhibit "a faculty for holding his peace—for 'letting the dust settle.' . . . The years ahead would often suggest that no great political leader, in the nation or in the world, could surpass the Republican President-to-be in determined practice of this precept."

But President-to-be he was. If any doubt attached to the outcome of the 1952 election after sixteen years of Democratic rule, speech writer Hughes resolved it by planting Ike's late-campaign pledge that, if elected, he would go to Korea. A nation weary of attrition and stalemate ate that one up. Eisenhower won by a landslide over Adlai Stevenson, and in his telegram of congratulation to the winner, Harry Truman offered him the use of the Presidential plane "if you still desire to go to Korea." (Merle Miller, in his book *Plain Speaking,* draws a piece of cogent contrast between the Truman and Nixon presidencies. "Can you imagine," he wrote, "a member of his Cabinet seriously telling a committee of the U.S. Senate that he had *shielded* Harry from the truth?") Whatever its recommendations, circumspectness was never a hallmark of Truman policy, and the interregnum following Eisenhower's election in 1952 was marked by no especial warmth. Truman's book *Mr. Citizen* gives this record of the drive from the White House to the Capitol for Ike's inauguration:

> The journey in the parade down Pennsylvania Avenue was quite restrained—as far as the occupants of the Presidential car were concerned. We began our trip in silence. Then the President-elect volunteered to inform me: "I did not attend your inauguration in 1948 out of consideration for you, because if I had been present I would have drawn attention away from you."
> I was quick to reply: "You were not here in 1948 because I did not send for you. But if I *had* sent for you, you would have come."
> The rest of the journey continued in silence.

That night the Trumans left Washington and went home to Independence, Missouri. "We were amazed," Truman's daughter, Margaret, would write in her book *Harry S. Truman,* "by the mob scene in Union Station. At least 5,000 people were in the concourse, shouting and cheering. It was like the 1944 and 1948 conventions. The police had to form a flying wedge to get us aboard the train." The crowd struck up a thunderously spontaneous chorus of "Auld Lang Syne." People waved and wept. In the first two weeks following his return to 219 North Delaware Street in Independence, Truman received more than 70,-000 letters from well-wishers. Somebody asked him about his future plans. "I'd like to buy a car," he replied.

Music, please. Not a blues beat this time. No slow, Pine Top left hand. In inexorable evolution, first Stan Kenton, then Dizzy Gillespie, each experimenting almost timidly at first with new musical forms made possible by postwar technology in sound amplification, each recognizing radio's new dependence on phonograph records to replace the live talent lost to television, were testing a raucous sound. Mary Ford had a vocal of "How High the Moon" that sounded like five Mary Fords singing at once. It was: the process of tape overlay now was everywhere available. Plugged into an electrical outlet, a single guitar provided the decibel level of a sextet; boosted by advanced sound systems, a sextet could warp the rafters at Madison Square Garden. American troops fighting on the forbidding slopes and crags of Korea persisted in hopes of being rotated on furlough to Tokyo for rest and recreation—R&R, they called it. Stateside, a group called Bill Haley and the Comets brought a second definition to those initials. Ask any pop-music fancier what R&R stood for and he would tell you: rock 'n' roll. True musicians of the quality of Kenton and Gillespie stood back, appalled and ignored, as a new generation of musical entertainers took command. "People used to go to concerts to appreciate mastery," Robert Morley, the British actor, commented sourly. "Now they do it to appreciate themselves. They go away sated with the conviction—quite accurate in the majority of cases—that whatever was done on the stage, they can do better at home." The success of one rock star after another was based less on the musicianship of the artist than on the fable of the Emperor's New Clothes: make enough noise and you could get away with anything. Even the eminent fell into careless ways. Sir Thomas Beecham, newly arrived from London to perform as guest conductor with the Pittsburgh Symphony, cut short an afternoon rehearsal with the announcement that he saw no need to go over so familiar a standard as the Brahms Second. "But maestro," a youthful horn player protested as Beecham departed the podium, "I have never played this piece." "You'll love it," Sir Thomas assured him.

But if the concert-goer could entertain himself with the same instrument at home, so also at home could he be entertained by others. By the end of 1952, the United States had a total of 186 television stations and 27.6 million sets (an audience of 40 million for that Truman speech sixteen months earlier?). Coffee sold for 90 cents a pound. The turnstiles of the New York subway system now accepted not coins but tokens, available at the change windows at 15 cents a pop. Near the Eniwetok atoll in the Pacific, the United States detonated the first H-bomb; back at the army's Aberdeen Proving Ground in Maryland a first-generation computer was installed, of the unwieldy size then in initial manufacture by IBM and Sperry-Rand, and in due course a resident scientist named Roger Baldwin and three of his associates determined to put the machine to the ultimate test. Their findings, eventually published in September, 1956, by the *Journal of the American Statistical Association*, showed that with correct strategy the blackjack player had the edge over the house. To some people, like inmates of the Nevada penitentiary at Carson City, imprisoned in a jurisdiction where gambling was not only legal but viewed as a salutary form of convict recreation, this discovery did not exactly come as red-hot news. But it gained respectability for its publication as a scientific paper and widespread attention through an ensuing book by Edward O. Thorp, a C.L.E. Moore instructor at the Massachusetts Institute of Technology and a fellow of the Edinburgh Mathematical Society, called *Beat the Dealer*. Almost overnight, blackjack became the most popular casino game in the world, and some of the better players found themselves being barred with distressing regularity from the tables in Las Vegas, Havana, Nice, London, and Macao. In Nevada this led to some lawsuits, but the paradox of a man's being able to buy a book on blackjack strategy at the news counter in a hotel-casino, then being thrown out of the place if he tried to apply it, left Nevada judges for some reason singularly unmoved.

Overall, it was a caution what computers could do, not to mention what people believed they could do. In the mind-set of some liberal thinkers, the electronic calculators even lay behind the upsurge in juvenile delinquency, and the increase in the crime rate generally, which as early as 1952 had made unsafe the streets of half a hundred cities. The dogma of the Libs was to view this not as evidence of heightened criminal activity but proof instead that the authorities, with the help of the new technology, simply were keeping better records. This line of thinking may have bemused the New York Fire Department, whose total of false alarms, using the same number of pull boxes serving the same number of people, had more than doubled in ten years. It hardly reassured the lovers who in fear of their lives had deserted their nighttime bench space along Riverside Drive in New York and in Jackson Park in Chicago. As early as '52 (with computerized record keeping, in point of fact, only in its very infancy) the nation as a whole was experiencing 20 murders, 600 automobile thefts, and 3,300 larcenies every twenty-four hours.

There was one bright spot: the country had just gone through its first year without a lynching since 1882. This too may not have been altogether reassuring. In Shreveport, Louisiana, player-manager Piper Davis of the Birmingham Black Barons, performing for an all-black team against an all-white team in a post-season game, heard the epithet "alligator bait" hurled at him from the white section of the stands. Davis had encountered a racial slur or three in his time, but this one was new to him. He turned to teammate Ed Steele and said, "What's alligator bait?" "You," Steele explained.

But the first winds of change were stirring in the Confederacy, and baseball was the reason. Birmingham's notorious commissioner of public safety, Bull Connor, himself a former baseball broadcaster whose trademark in describing a home run for the white Birmingham Barons of the Southern Association was a sonorous "Going . . . going . . . gone!" would not permit black and white players to intermingle in games at Rickwood Park (a marvelous, prototypical Class AA ballyard which still stands today like a repented Don Juan, handsome but unused). The unrepentant Connor, who a decade later would turn fire hoses and dogs on peaceful civil rights marchers, personified the reason why Birmingham would fall behind in the economic development of the New South. Elsewhere, in places like Shreveport, Atlanta, Memphis, and New Orleans, dollar-wise promoters eyed the prospective barnstorming appearances of such major leaguers as Robinson, Campanella, Doby, and Newcombe, added the 2 and 2 of overflow gate and concession receipts, and got a sweetly desegregated 4.

Integration on the ball field took an even further step in such Virginia cities as Richmond and Norfolk, with the regular appearance of blacks and whites on the same *team.* The club involved was an army team from Camp Eustis, led in 1952 and 1953 by a draftee named Willie Mays. The Eustis post commander had in him, like many of his ilk, a bit of the Captain Holmes in *From Here to Eternity,* and he heaped pride and perquisites on the youthful center fielder and his teammates, who thus would augment not just their free time but their incomes with their traveling play. Over the twenty-one months of his hitch Mays would play in some 180 baseball games (in one of which he stole a base with his team in front 14–0)—and that is not to mention his starring role in the off-season with the post basketball team.

None of this sat particularly well with Giant manager Leo Durocher. To him, stealing a base with a 14–0 lead was to court injury for no decent reason. And when the news reached him that Mays had sprained an ankle in the course of a basketball game, the New York manager went ape. Already, with less than a single full season of major league play behind him, a Mays mythology had sprung into being, and the chief care and feeding of the myth belonged to Durocher. One element in the myth was a statistical nicety: the Giants were in fifth place when Mays first joined them in 1951, and went on to win the pennant . . . when he left them for the army in May of '52, they were in first place and did not go on to win the pennant . . . and, without him for the entirety of the 1953 season, they wound up fifth once more. Obviously they missed Mays, but Durocher's regret may have been a shade on the fulsome side. An opposing batsman's most uncatchable line drive up the power alley would invoke a scornful "Willie would've had it" from Leo in the Giant dugout. (Following Mays's return in 1954, when he won the batting championship, Durocher would introduce fellow Giant Don Mueller to post-season gatherings as "the man who lost the hitting title to Willie Mays.")

But the obvious display of Durocher favoritism lost Mays no popularity with his teammates and probably didn't cost Durocher any either, since it is doubtful he had all that much to begin with. ("That was a horseshit pitch you threw," he once said to righthander Bobo Newsom. "It was a good pitch," Newsom protested. "Ask the catcher." "Fuck the catcher," Durocher responded. "I'm the manager and I say it was a horseshit pitch.")

The absence of diplomacy would not, however, affect his reputation as a manager, save possibly on occasion to support it. Durocher managed in the major leagues off and on from the late thirties to the early seventies, and at last glance the number of men who played for him and then went on to manage in the majors in their own right had reached something like fifteen. Durocher's baseball sense was superbly honed; even in his legendary battles with umpires he was right more often than not.

He was right, come to think of it, the day at the Polo Grounds when he became the only manager ever to be thrown out of a game before the game even began. This one had its roots in a play the previous day when, with two out, a Dodger runner on third, and Carl Furillo at bat with a count of 3-and-2, the man on third tried to steal home on the ensuing pitch and was out at the plate to end the half inning.

Giant manager Durocher obviously had no protest to make over that call. His interest awakened, however, when the Dodgers sent the same Furillo up to bat as their lead-off man the following inning. Out of the dugout came Leo.

"What's he doing up here?" he asked plate umpire Larry Goetz.

"He was still at bat when the last inning ended, that's what," Goetz said. "So he gets to hit again."

"But what about that last pitch we threw him?"

"What about it?"

"What'd you call it?"

"Manager," Goetz said, "I didn't call it anything. Didn't have to. Last out of the inning was on the runner sliding in."

"But it was still a *pitch!*" Durocher cried. "Whether you called it or not. And it could only have been one of two things—strike three or ball four. Either way, his time at bat is over."

"Wrong," Goetz said. "It's nothing if I don't call it." He bent over to apply his whisk broom to home plate.

The Socratic method having failed, Durocher turned to a different form of logical conclusion: "You can go fuck yourself in the head."

Goetz looked up. "And you can go fuck yourself in the shower."

Durocher's fury, less over his being ejected than over the arbiter's evident miscall, simmered overnight, and when he went out to home plate just before the following day's game to present the Giant lineup to the umpires, his gaze fell reflectively on Goetz. "Just say you were wrong yesterday, pus-head," Durocher said to him. "That's all I want to hear."

"I didn't have to listen to it yesterday," Goetz replied, "and I don't have to listen to it today. Bye-bye, manager. You're out of here."

———————

It has to be said that 1954 was an extraordinary year—for Willie Mays, for the Giants, for baseball, and for the country as a whole. The Korean War had ended. (Just before it did, Gen. Mark Clark promised political asylum and a $100,000 reward to any Communist pilot who delivered a MIG-15 intact. A North Korean pilot did so and inquired about the reward. "What reward?" he was asked.) At home the nation was attuned to the good life. Certain amenities came and went, like the machines that for a time graced every shoe store, designed to fluoroscope the feet encased in new shoes. What resulted was not only a better fit but bone damage, and the alarmed shoe industry abandoned the new equipment. But other stores would flourish in the new climate, particularly the toy stores and expectant-mother emporia, and each of those had their spin-offs. For the toy stores, it was the accompaniment they gave to the practice of psychology for the young. They would not sell you modeling clay—it was messy and stuck to things. Instead, they sold you a product called elastic plastic, and its recipient was referred to inevitably, in Steckelian overtone, as "the child." The mother-

and-baby shops sold their customer lists to photographers, diaper services, druggists, and the manufacturers of strained vegetables and infant cereals. In the heady outgrowth of the postwar baby boom, the new breed of retailer now inhabited a shopping mall built around a supermarket, but adult needs were not ignored. The frozen food section now featured a brand new product called a TV dinner.

My enjoyment of those times was rich. There was a ball game on television every day of the season, and I was in the process of selling the same short story to three different magazines. The piece was based on one game during the college basketball "fix" scandals of a couple of years before, a game in which it turned out *both* teams were fixed, each by a different syndicate. The people at *Collier's* liked it and bought it, but then remembered that each year they picked an all-American college basketball team, a theme in conflict with mine. So in accordance with custom they returned the piece to me and let me keep the money. Shortly the story sold again, this time to *Sports Illustrated*, then building up an inventory of material prior to coming into publication. But the editors there now decided the magazine ought not to print any fiction, so once again I got the story back. In time, it sold again, to *Escapade*, which then folded. I got the thing back in the mail a third time. I guess I still have it here somewhere.

It was in that year of 1954—May 17 was the date—that the Chief Justice of the Supreme Court of the United States read aloud the majority decision in the case of Brown v. Board of Education. (Majority decision? Technically there was no majority: without opposition or cavil, the Court's vote was a unanimous 9 to 0.) In William Manchester's subsequent summary:

> Negroes still did not exist as people for mainstream America. In popular entertainment they were more like pets. Stepin Fetchit, Hattie McDaniel, Butterfly McQueen, and Eddie Anderson— these were good for the nudge and the guffaw but they weren't looked upon as human beings. If Hollywood wanted to portray

human feelings in a man with a black face, it put burnt cork on the face of somebody like Al Jolson. Black America was unnoticed by white America. "I am an invisible man," cried the hero of Ralph Ellison's 1953 novel. ". . . I am invisible, understand, simply because other people refuse to see me. I can hear you say, 'What a horrible, irresponsible bastard!' And you're right. . . . But to whom can I be responsible, when you refuse to see me?"

Now, after three centuries of black submission and black servitude, "the long habit of deception and evasion," as Ellison once called it, was about to end. The Supreme Court of the United States had pondered the matter and concluded that Negroes were real people after all, and that as such they must become visible to their white compatriots and treated as equals everywhere, beginning in the public schools.

It took Earl Warren, formerly governor of California and now the newly appointed Chief Justice, more than half an hour to read the Court's opinion, but the crux of it lay in just two sentences totaling 24 words: "We conclude that in the field of public education the doctrine of 'separate but equal' has no place. Separate educational facilities are inherently unequal."

The Deep South (its epicenter in Birmingham, which Martin Luther King would call "the most racist city in America") reacted in a state of shock. So equally, though he made no public display of it, did President Eisenhower. In the belief of many, his appointment of Warren to head the highest bench was a straight political payoff: Warren had run for Vice-President on the Republican slate in 1948 and was California's favorite-son candidate at the party convention in 1952; his stance in the close contest between Eisenhower and Senator Robert A. Taft of Ohio was instrumental to Ike's gaining the nomination.

But beyond that, the reward that elevated Warren to the post of Chief Justice had struck the President as a sound piece of Tory business. The main rap on the new man was his lack of judicial experience. But in his dealings with minorities, he had (when attorney general of California) been the prime mover in the concentration-camp internment of Japanese-Americans in the months following the outbreak of World War II. Perhaps he was caught up in the Hearstian/California hysteria of the time, which reasoned that if Pearl Harbor was brought about through sabotage (it wasn't), then Los Angeles could be next (it also wasn't). The only sabotage in Hawaii was the John Dewey brand of liberal education that taught the Japanese-Americans there that even as high school students they had a right to their own opinions. The result was that they volunteered for, and served with matchless distinction in, the armed services of the United States. Meanwhile their Nisei brethren on the mainland were being deprived of not only their liberty but their property, which they were forced to sell off at half, one third, and even less of market value. Told that there was no evidence of Japanese-American hostility toward the U.S., Warren replied, "No evidence? There's your proof right there of how clever and devious they can be."

Yet this was the same Earl Warren who would oversee not only the landmark school desegregation decision but a near-unbroken series of opinions thenceforth that supported the rights of minorities. (Twenty-four years later, comedian George Carlin had a truly funny line in the marvelous Victor Borge tradition that depends on using language correctly. ["Pardon my back," Borge would say to one half of his audience at the outset of his one-man piano recitals. Then, turning to the other half: "Pardon my front."] Carlin had just lost a case in the U.S. Supreme Court—a court by now flavored by the legacy of Nixon appointments—banning future playing on radio of a record of his containing dirty words. Asked what he thought of the Court's ruling, Carlin shrugged. "That's their opinion," he said.)

But the era of the Warren Court was something else, like 1954 itself. That was the year an offer came to me to become public relations chief for the March of Dimes in its war against polio. "Don't," Jack Geiger advised me. "This guy Salk's coming out with his vaccine. There's not going to be any more polio." In a hearing room on Capitol Hill, with television covering the event as never before, the so-called Army-McCarthy hearings went forward, and for the first time Senator McCarthy, who up to then had been astoundingly correct both in his estimation of the decency of his opponents and his underestimation of their guts, came under crackerbarrel questioning from an old-line New England lawyer named Joseph Welch and blew his cover. McCarthy's Richelieu, a counsel named Roy Cohn, looked if anything even worse.

By 1954, I had left the INS and was functioning as a free-lance writer, working out of a tract home in Ardsley, New York (the distinction of a Westchester County address). One of my assignments was to ghostwrite a little book by Willie Mays called *Born to Play Ball*. We still did not know each other well, particularly in view of the demands on his time by others, and even after our sessions on the book, there would be the moment when I called him up and he was not sure who I was. "I wrote the book," I said. "What book?" he said. As the ensuing years would substitute friendship for acquaintance, so also would he and I laugh about his early days in New York, but a small part of that laughter always was reserved for the loss of innocence, which isn't particularly funny. It was like referring to some geological period. But it was joyous enough at the time. Our home in Ardsley, on a 75-by-100-foot lot in something called Huntley Estates, came for $16,000 complete with expansion neighbors and attic. We did all the Things expected of newly established postwar suburbanites. At least once a month we joined the Ballingers next door and the Caseys across the street in an ecumenical dinner for six at some area restaurant, and if any of us missed a trick, another would pick up for him. If Casey was the first to buy a deep freeze from a door-to-door salesman, I was the first to buy the flowering-plant landscape package from *that* door-to-door salesman. And if anything, Ballinger went both of us one better, by enrolling in the local carpentry class and constructing his own built-in bookshelves. "Being a writer, you can tell me something," he said to me when I went over to admire his work. "Where can I get some books?"

Some nettled conversations did take place with the wives. In those days the television set was in the living room. And the Giants were on television.

———•••———

The Boys of Summer, Roger Kahn would call them. They were the Brooklyn Dodgers who won the pennants of 1952–53–55–56, the first two of those years under manager Charley Dressen, the last two under Walter Alston. They were Robinson and Reese and Hodges and Newcombe and Campanella, and Erskine and Furillo and Snider. And beyond question they were one of the greatest baseball teams ever to take the field.

But for one year, 1954, they ran into an even greater team: the Durocher-managed New York Giants. It was a year in which Giant pitching held the enemy to two runs in a game 23 times, to one run 22 times, to no runs 19 times; and of those 64 games, the Giants won 60. Their pinch hitters alone delivered ten home runs; nine of them won games. And there was almost a show-biz touch to the way Durocher, blessed with talent-laden bench and bullpen alike, made his managerial moves. In one game that went extra innings he had already used his first-string catcher Wes Westrum and Bobby Hofman, a pinch hitter who could also catch. Now the catching was being done by second-stringer Ray Katt, and in the bottom half of the 12th inning Durocher sent Dusty Rhodes up to bat for *him*. Rhodes was known as a part-time outfielder, pinch hitter deluxe, and drinker of bourbon, and Durocher had not been at pains to keep any of those facts a secret. Here then came Rhodes to the plate with two out, the tying run at third, and the potential winning run at second in the person of Willie Mays. Specific advice in this situation was not exactly necessary, but Rhodes turned to Durocher for some anyway.

"If we tie the score," Rhodes said, "who's going to catch for us next inning?"

"You," Durocher told him.

Appalled, Rhodes went up and singled home the tying run. Directly behind that runner came Mays with the winning run. The same question that occurred to Rhodes had wandered through Willie's mind as he led off second base. "I never ran so fast in my life," he said.

Bobby Thomson, the hero of '51, had been traded before the '54 season to the Braves in a key exchange for lefthander John Antonelli. Now the search commenced for somebody to take Thomson's place at third base for the Giants. "He left the position so fucked up nobody can play it," Durocher murmured, as he tested a succession of candidates during spring training. But the job was won finally by Hank Thompson, and that solidified an infield with Lockman at first, Davey Williams at second, and Dark at shortstop. "The thing I remember about that club," owner Horace Stoneham told Roger Angell years later, "is all the double plays they got that ended up with a baserunner caught out of position—being put out by a throw behind him, or something like that." The something-like-that included a play second baseman Williams had picked up from his predecessor, Eddie Stanky, which Stanky in turn had perfected to cover his own deficiency as the pivot man in the double play. With runners on first and second and a double-play grounder, Giant infielders had taken to relaying the ball to third base instead of first, after the initial force-out at second. Time and again, the lead runner, assuming the normal double-play attempt was in progress behind him, would round third base only to find himself trapped off the bag by the third baseman with the ball. ("He can't hit, he can't run, and he can't field," Durocher had said of Stanky, in total admiration. In a play during the 1951 World Series, Stanky as a baserunner kicked the ball out of Yankee shortshop Rizzuto's glove at second base, then got up and continued to third. Rizzuto argued long and loud with the umpire, and most folk assumed he was complaining about Stanky's foot tactics, but some ten years later, at breakfast with Stanky in St. Louis, I asked him about the play. "Tell me," I said, "did you ever touch second base?" He smiled in reminiscence. "Rizzuto said it didn't look that way." Stanky had moved to St. Louis to become manager of the Cardinals in 1952, rightfully among the first of Durocher's legions to take up managing.)

In addition to Antonelli, who would lead the club with 21 victories, Giant pitching in 1954 included Ruben Gomez, Sal Maglie, Jim Hearn, Don Liddle, Marv Grissom, and Hoyt Wilhelm; and the staff as a whole would post the league's lowest earned-run average and highest total of shutouts. As for the starting outfield, it comprised Mueller in right, Irvin in left, and You-Know-Who in center.

In Phoenix for spring training, the Giants counted the days till You-Know-Who's discharge from the army. They did more than count them, they actually sang them. To the tune of "Old Black Joe," Giant vice-president Chub Feeney roamed the lobby of the Adams Hotel. "In six more days," he sang, "we're gonna have Willie Mays." As Roger Kahn noted, "Each day Feeney warbled, amending the lyrics cleverly enough, say, changing the word 'six' to the word 'five.' The song, like the sandy wind, became a bane." A bane certainly to Kahn, whose love affair with the Dodgers (not excluding their gifted center fielder Duke Snider) had become so pronounced that his paper, the New York *Herald Tribune,* had detached him purposely to cover another team for a while. Not having covered baseball regularly before 1952, Kahn for that reason too had seen little of Mays in action, and knew him mainly by what he took to be a wildly inflated reputation.

But Mays put an end to Feeney's singing countdown by showing up in camp and getting into action that same day midway through an intra-squad game. "The first unusual thing that Willie did was snatch a sinking liner off the grass," Kahn reported. "The ball came out to center field low and hard and Willie charged it better than anyone else could have and dove and made a graceful somersault and caught the ball." Kahn turned in surprise to Barney Kremenko, a veteran Giants writer. "For Willie that's absolutely nothing," Kremenko said. Kahn turned back to the field to watch Mays some more.

> The next time he came to bat, I resolved to look for specific flaws in his form. I was doing that when he hit a fast ball 420 feet and out of the park. An inning later, and with a man on first, someone hit a tremendous drive over Willie's head. He turned and fled and caught the ball and threw it three hundred feet and doubled the runner. Pandemonium. The camp was alive. The team was alive. And Willie had gone through the delays of a discharge, then sat up all night in a plane. I conceded to Kremenko that, given a little rest, he might show me something.

> Then I sat down and wrote an account that began, "This is not going to be a plausible story, but then no one ever accused Willie Mays of being a plausible ball player. This story is only the implausible truth."

What unfolded now was an implausible season. By the end of July, Mays had hit 36 home runs—whereupon manager Durocher took him aside for a talk and told him to stop hitting them. The order made sense. Neither a dead pull nor a slice hitter, Mays was hitting his homers to the roomiest outfield spaces (symptomatic of this, he also led the league in triples). The result, especially in the Polo Grounds, with the deepest center field in baseball, was that he also had more than his share of outfield flies which rival fielders, with all that running room, could track down and catch. Durocher's feeling was that benefit would come now if Willie concentrated more on hitting for average and less for the fences. Accordingly, Mays would have only five more homers that season (and two of them were inside-the-park jobs, products of speed as well as distance). But his hitting overall picked up, to the point where on the final day of the season he came from third place in history's most vivid three-man race for the league batting championship (Mueller .3426, Snider .3425, Mays .3422), got three hits in four at-bats against Robin Roberts, the best pitcher in the league, and wound up with .345 to Mueller's .342 and Snider's .341.

At that time, the "Ed Sullivan Show" on CBS and the "Colgate Comedy Hour" on NBC shared the same hour-length time slot, from 8 to 9 P.M. Sunday nights from New York. Mays got back from Philadelphia after the season's finale there in time to appear on TV at the beginning of the Sullivan, hustle over to NBC, and appear again at the end of the Colgate. At 7:30 the next morning he was on the "Today" show. At 12:15 that night he was on the "Tonight" show. There was a tickertape parade up lower Broadway, and manager Durocher—making sure that not he but Mays and team captain Alvin Dark rode in the first car—mounted the steps of City Hall and told the massive throng that "Willie Mays is the greatest ballplayer I ever laid eyes on." When a television interviewer asked Mays The Automatic Question—what did it feel like to beat out teammate Mueller for the batting title?—Willie responded politely, "If it couldn't be me I was rooting for him." Mueller's precise thinking on the same subject was not known. For one thing, nobody asked him. No one had put him on the cover of *Time* magazine. He had actually led the league in number of hits, with 212, but few were the reminders even of that. Fans were more apt to compare his defensive play in right field with that of Mays in center. In that connection, Durocher had issued specific instructions that left nothing to doubt: on any ball hit to common ground in right-center, Mays, not Mueller, was to handle the play.

On Tuesday, September 28, the day before the World Series was to begin at the Polo Grounds, the Giants assembled in uniform to have the team picture taken. Sitting before his locker in the clubhouse, Mays was bent over, tying a shoe, when Mueller strolled past.

"Say, tell me," he said to Willie, "is it true you're the best center fielder in the game?"

Mays looked up, but only for the briefest of moments. "Best right fielder too," he said, and went back to his shoelace.

I was accompanying Mays at the time, going over material with him for the book I was ghostwriting, and remember precisely to this day the feeling I had when I walked down the steps of the clubhouse and onto the turf of center field. In later years, when I would travel frequently aboard the Giants' team bus from airport to hotel or hotel to ball park, autograph seekers, wanting to be on the safe side, would scan my face as I alighted and ask, "Are you anybody?" No such circumstances applied that day at the Polo Grounds in 1954. For one thing, there were no autograph seekers on the field; for another, the Giants were all in uniform for the team picture. But in my mind's eye I *was* somebody that day. At the age of twenty-eight, I could think back over nineteen years to the first time, replete in my boyhood fandom, I had vaulted the box seat railing and run out onto that same field at the conclusion of a Giants game. Once again, if only for a moment, I became the center fielder, not his ghostwriter. And if it is true that the magnitude of things tends to decrease as one grows older, then center field at the Polo Grounds was the exception to the rule. Standing there, I realized it was just as immense as always.

The odds on that 1954 World Series would favor the Cleveland Indians over the Giants by anything from 8 to 5 to 2 to 1. The record of the Cleveland club was awesome. It had won a record 111 games, lost only 43, for a percentage of .721. Its pitching staff had an earned-run average of 2.78, the only team ERA under 3.00 in the majors that season. Two of the pitchers, Early Wynn and Bob Lemon, tied for the American League lead in victories with 23 apiece; a third, Mike Garcia, had the best ERA. One of the hitters, Bob Avila, was the A.L. batting champion; another, Larry Doby, led the league in homers and runs batted in.

The only flaw in the Cleveland potential was one the odds-makers completely overlooked. A clue to it lies in Roger Kahn's account, earlier in this chapter, of the Giants' trip to Las Vegas for an exhibition game with the Indians during spring training sixmonthsearlier.*Bob Feller pitched for the Indians. Sal Maglie opposed him. My scorebook is lost, but I believe the Giants won by one run.*

"We *always* beat the Indians in spring training that year," Alvin Dark said afterward. "Sure, you're getting into shape and trying things and looking at new players. That's what spring training's for. But any time we were leveling, any time it was our regulars against their regulars, they just couldn't beat us."

In the World Series, they would be leveling, regulars against regulars. And it was no contest. The Giants swept the Indians in four straight, and each verdict was more pronounced than the last. They had to go ten innings to win the first game, and from that moment the Indians never again in the Series had a lead on the scoreboard, not even for a single inning. Mays put the Giants ahead to stay with a two-out single in the first inning of the third game. By the time the fourth game was halfway through, the Giants were in front in that one, 7 to 0. They even wound up in the bizarre state of taking the pitcher out because he was too good! (That happened in the eighth inning, when Giant knuckleballer Hoyt Wilhelm struck out Avila swinging. The pitch was right there when Avila swung, but by the time it reached catcher Westrum, a foot or so farther back, it was over Westrum's head, and the reprieved Avila scampered safely to first. A few dancing knucklers later, the Indians had two men on base, and Westrum called time and summoned Durocher from the dugout. "What's the matter?" Durocher asked. "You want a new pitcher?" Westrum shook his head. "No," he said. "I want a new catcher. If somebody's going to set a record for passed balls in the World Series, I don't want it to be me." Westrum may have had a point. Durocher turned and waved to the bullpen for his ace, Antonelli, who came on and put the Indians out of their misery.)

The Giants had a total of eleven innings in which they scored, over the four Series games, and Mays figured in eight of them. The one thing he had lacked as a rookie—true confidence at the plate—was lacking no longer. Here is a case where the figures are most descriptive. Counting his two partial years of 1951 and 1952 as one full season, which is what they add up to, then comparing them ᵗo his totals for 1954, one observes a striking contrast between the pre- and post-army Willie. Included here is his slugging average, which is computed like a batting average except that for slugging, a double counts as two hits, a triple as three, a home run as four.

	G	AB	R	H	2B	3B	HR	RBI	B.A.	SL.A.
1951–52:	155	591	76	157	24	9	24	91	.266	.459
1954:	151	565	119	195	33	13	41	110	.345	.667

Hitting honors for the 1954 World Series itself, however, would go to Dusty Rhodes, who had the only two Giant home runs of the Series, one of them a pinch homer that won the first game, and two other pinch hits besides; and Durocher dusted off the hoariest of General Grant jokes—that Al Lopez, the Cleveland manager, had asked him what Rhodes was drinking so he could distribute a case to his own men. But even with Dusty's derring-do, the one moment in the 1954 Series that electrified the fans, the moment that lives forever in scratchy kinescope replay, was a play known simply to this day as The Catch.

It came in the top of the eighth inning of the first game with nobody out, Larry Doby on second for the Indians, Al Rosen at first, and Vic Wertz at bat. Wertz had had a perfect day so far against Giant starter Maglie, with a triple in the first, a single in the fourth, another single in the sixth. Durocher went and got Maglie and replaced him with Don Liddle. Wertz swung at Liddle's first pitch, and there it went, on a rising, soaring line toward deepest center field, just to the right of dead center. To be seated in the press section back of home plate, in the imperceptible flash of time it took to focus from the swing to the horizon beyond, was to encounter a sight: the number 24 on the back of Willie Mays's uniform, already in full flight toward the wall.

But an even more arresting view was recorded not by any writer in the press box but by a writer in the bleachers named Arnold Hano, who subsequently built an entire book around that game and that moment, a book called *A Day in the Bleachers*. Hano too watched Wertz as he swung, but

This ball did not alarm me because it was hit to dead center field —Mays' territory—and not between the fielders, into those dread alleys in left-center and right-center which lead to the bull pens.

And this was not a terribly high drive. It was a long low fly or a high liner, whichever you wish. This ball was hit not nearly so high as the triple Wertz struck earlier in the day, so I may have assumed that it would soon start to break and dip and come down to Mays, not too far from his normal position.

Then I looked at Willie, and alarm raced through me, peril flaring against my heart. To my utter astonishment, the young Giant center fielder—the inimitable Mays, most skilled of outfielders, unique for his ability to scent the length and direction of any drive and then turn and move to the final destination of the ball—Mays was turned full around, head down, running as hard as he could, straight toward the runway between the two bleacher sections.

I knew then that I had underestimated—badly underestimated —the length of Wertz's blow.

I wrenched my eyes from Mays and took another look at the ball, winging its way along, undipping, unbreaking, forty feet higher than Mays' head, rushing along like a locomotive, nearing Mays, and I thought then: it will beat him to the wall.

. . . For the briefest piece of time—I cannot shatter and compute fractions of seconds like some atom gun—Mays started to raise his head and turn it to his left, as though he were about to look behind him.

Then he thought better of it, and continued the swift race with the ball that hovered quite close to him now, thirty feet high and coming down (yes, finally coming down) and again—for the second time—I knew Mays would make the catch.

. . . He simply slowed down to avoid running into the wall, put his hands up in cuplike fashion over his left shoulder, and caught the ball much like a football player catching leading passes in the end zone.

He had turned so quickly, and run so fast and truly, that he made this impossible catch look—to us in the bleachers—quite ordinary. To those reporters in the press box, nearly six hundred feet from the bleacher wall, it must have appeared far more astonishing, watching Mays run and run until he had become the size of a pigmy and then he had to run some more, while the ball diminished to a mote of white dust and finally disappeared in the dark blob that was Mays' mitt.

One might argue whether any other outfielder could combine Mays's instinctive jump on the batted ball and his speed afoot, which is to argue whether any other outfielder could have made that catch. Many people, Hano included, seem to think not. For Mays himself, however, it was not the greatest catch he ever made. The ball had stayed up for him and he still had running room when it came down. ("For Willie," as Barney Kremenko had said, "that's nothing.") But it was a money catch, a World Series catch, the high point indeed of an otherwise dull event, as any Series must most likely be when somebody wins it in four straight games. And quite forgotten by now, here resurrected from Hano's book, is what happened next:

Mays caught the ball, and then whirled and threw, like some olden statue of a Greek javelin hurler, his head twisted away to the left as his right arm swept out and around. But Mays is no classic study for the simple reason that at the peak of his activity, his baseball cap flies off. And as he turned, or as he threw —I could not tell which, the two motions were welded into one —off came the cap, and then Mays himself continued to spin around after the gigantic effort of returning the ball whence it came, and he went down flat on his belly, and out of sight.

But the throw! What an astonishing throw, to make all other throws ever before it, even those four Mays himself had made during fielding practice, appear the flings of teen-age girls. This was the throw of a giant, the throw of a howitzer made human, arriving at second base . . . just as Doby was pulling into third, and as Rosen was scampering back to first.

The containing effect of the throw on the Cleveland runners enabled pitcher Liddle to get out of the inning unscored upon, and two innings later Rhodes hit his game-winning homer, which actually was an unremarkable pop fly along the right-field line which met the grandstand just to the fair side of the foul pole. Along the lines, the park was as short as it was deep to center, and the phrase "That would've been a home run at the Polo Grounds" was heard repeatedly in other parks to deride routine fly balls such as Dusty's.

Many years later, following a tour the Giants had made of Japan, I served as master of ceremonies at a Giants Boosters Club luncheon, and in introducing Mays to the audience, I described a play he was said to have made in a game at Tokyo. It seems that with bases loaded, the batsman put up a fly ball to center field. The ball was caught up in one of the winds that are sacred to the Japanese, and Mays saw it was going to carry out of the park. But he also noticed that the exit gate in center field was open. So he raced through the gate and found himself on a tree-shaded avenue running away from the ball park. Going in the same direction was a fire engine in the process of answering an alarm, so Mays jumped aboard. Three blocks farther, he put up his glove and made the catch. One fireman at the back of the truck turned to another and said, "Home run at the Polo Grounds."

The tale having been told, I presented Mays and sat down while he fielded questions from the audience. Toward the end, one rather unexpected query came up. "About that time you caught the ball while you were riding on the fire engine in

Japan," the questioner said, "did the guy on third score after the catch, or was your throw in time to get him?"

That got a bigger laugh than the story itself. Mays, however, handled it straight-faced. "I didn't make any throw," he said. "Didn't have to. There was two out at the time."

———◆———

Quiz shows were the hottest thing on television in the mid-fifties. One of them, "The $64,000 Question," had a sep-tuagenarian lady named Myrtle Power who was known as "the baseball grandma." She won $32,000 in her category before call-ing it quits. As the questions grew more difficult, contestants would be placed in a glass-enclosed isolation booth to ponder their answers under the spell of *mysterioso* music. If you reached the final $64,000 plateau, you could take an expert into the booth with you, for coaching. (The joke was told about the contestant whose category was lovemaking and who chose a Parisian boule-vardier as his expert coach. The final question asked the respon-dent to list in order the three things a man must do to seduce a woman in the briefest period of time. "First," the man re-sponded, "he touches her on the shoulder." "Right!" cried the master of ceremonies. The contestant bit his lip. "Second," he said, "he kisses her on the cheek." "Right!" the m.c. cried. "Now, for $64,000, what's the third thing he has to do?" Inside the booth, the contestant turned to his expert and hissed, "What's the third thing?" "Do not ask me, monsieur," the Frenchman replied. "I missed ze first two.")

In time, the suspicion would gain currency that not all the quiz shows were on the up and up. I always wondered if I made a small and indirect contribution to that sensation with a phone call I put through to my father, who lived in Beverly Hills, California. The call was from Arizona, where I had moved my family in 1956 and where network programs of the quiz-show type were seen earlier than on the Pacific Coast. One evening, after watching such a show—this one called "Twenty One"— I was on the phone with my father and reviewed the outcome of the show for him. It occasioned that he was having some people over for the evening, including a prominent judge, and they would be watching the identical show an hour or so hence. So they did, and for the thirty-minute run of the program my father sat there, predicting in advance every decision the contestants would reach, every reply they would make. His guests were properly impressed. "How can you be so accurate?" the judge asked him. "Simple," my father answered. "The show is fixed."

Turned out it *was* fixed. Having first denied being given the answers ahead of time, let alone being rehearsed in facial expressions, timing, and general agonizing, Charles Van Doren, scion of a literary family and most renowned among quiz-show winners, responded to a Congressional subpoena and told all, just as other quiz contestants, before and after, had come to do. One view was that Van Doren deserved commendation for telling the truth. A second was that he and others, including the producers of "Twenty One" and other shows, were guilty of massive and unprecedented fraud. If that was the crime, a third view asked, where was the victim? Besides entertaining and educating millions of Americans, what else had the quiz shows done? It was symptomatic of the times not only that the public sided largely with Van Buren in his front-page exposure but that it was front-page at all.

Symptomatic of the times too was something that was front-page only in affected locations. It began in 1953 when the Boston Braves, having told Warren Spahn they did not have enough money to fix his nose, discovered they did not have enough to remain the Boston Braves. In accordance with this they moved to Milwaukee. In 1954 the St. Louis Browns moved to Baltimore. In 1955 the Philadelphia Athletics moved to Kansas City.

And for a baseball map that had gone unchanged for more than half a century, this was just the beginning. Predictably, the trend of exodus at the outset was from two-team cities: the Red Sox would remain in Boston, the Cardinals in St. Louis, the Phillies in Philadelphia. That left only Chicago and New York with more than one major league team, and the latter would be next to go. When it went, it went big. Now the DC-7s and the Super Constellations were flying; the pure jets were only two years away, making escape feasible not just from the dwindling markets of the East, but to the glistening new markets of the Far West. If Giants and Dodgers had baseball's best known rivalry, then San Francisco and Los Angeles offered incomparable municipal rivalry to match it.

The era of stadium-building had not yet dawned, but an era it would be. (San Francisco's Candlestick Park, first of the new stadia, would open for business in 1960; barely a decade later it was the second-oldest park in the National League. Of the eight parks Willie Mays played in throughout the league when he broke in, seven had disappeared by the time he retired.) It remains academic conjecture whether the Dodgers would have stayed in Brooklyn, and the Giants in New York, if they had been given new parks to play in, with locations and parking facilities suited to the shift of population. But the lead time in stadium construction was itself a factor. When the Giants reached San Francisco in 1958, they had to play for two years in a park unequipped for major league baseball before Candlestick was ready; the Dodgers in Los Angeles had to play four years in a park unfitted for any kind of baseball. (This caused no particular commotion. By the tens of thousands, the citizens of Los Angeles showed up for the games carrying transistor radios so Dodger broadcaster Vince Scully could tell them what they were looking at.)

For the fact that they could now call themselves big-league, San Franciscans welcomed the Giants with open arms. The greeting for Willie Mays, superstar, was somewhat more restrained. To chauvinistic residents of the Bay Area, Mays was the hated embodiment of New York. Also he had the temerity to play center field at Seals Stadium, where the native-born DiMaggio had played it in his minor-league days. Also Mays was black. The brick that crashed through his apartment window almost as soon as he moved in had to reflect at least one of those viewpoints, if not all three.

Via television, the local fans had seen Mays make the catch off Wertz in 1954. In 1955, he hit 51 home runs to lead the league. In 1956, he led the league in stolen bases; among other things, he stole third 13 times in 13 attempts, causing the legendary Ty Cobb to observe that Willie had single-handedly restored the art of base running to the game; in 1957, he became the first player in league history ever to record 20 or more doubles, triples, and home runs in the same season. In 1958, his first San Francisco season, he led the league in runs scored and stolen bases and batted a career-high .347. "The jury's still out on him," said Walter Judge, a local baseball writer. Player of the Year, in a poll of Giant fans, was a rookie named Orlando Cepeda. Late in the 1959 season, the Premier of the Union of Soviet Socialist Republics paid a visit to San Francisco. Accompanying him was Frank Conniff, national editor of the Hearst newspapers. "This is the damnedest city I ever saw in my life," Conniff said. "They cheer Khrushchev and boo Willie Mays."

By then I had arrived in San Francisco too. If the linkage of my habitat with that of the Giants lay in some set of tarot cards, I remain unaware of that fact. But in March of 1956 my wife and I, beset by the snows and sicknesses of a long New York winter, flew to Phoenix for a vacation. The first thing we saw was the Giants in training under blue, warm, cloudless skies; it was reunion time with old friends among the club officials and the New York sportswriters covering the team. We bought that. The next thing we saw was a house we liked in a desert-mountain setting twenty minutes' drive from downtown. We bought that too. Three months later we moved in. The Giants were gone by then, of course. The 5 P.M. temperature outside our western windows was 115 degrees.

We watched the political conventions on television. It would be Eisenhower against Stevenson once again, the President having declared for re-election despite the heart attack he had suffered the previous September. But the bulletins describing his recovery at the time were enthusiastic. They were also candid, with one network newscast reporting that "the President had an excellent bowel movement." ("That's nothing compared to the one Leonard Hall had," Jerry Green remarked. Hall was the Republican National Chairman.) Came February and Ike's official announcement that he would run again despite his heart condition. With that, a story began to make the rounds, giving the following futuristic scenario: It is now January 1957. President Eisenhower and Vice-President Nixon, having won re-election, arrive together at the base of the Capitol for the inauguration ceremonies. Nixon turns to Ike and says, "Race you up the steps."

Eisenhower did win re-election, and by inauguration time the economic recession of 1957 was taking hold. As a free-lance writer, I watched the erosion of the magazine field and in due course returned to the newspaper business, this time as a daily general columnist for the San Francisco *Examiner*. It was a heady way to come on in a new town, let alone a place with the magical properties of San Francisco, but understandably one of the first things I noticed, and took up in my column, was the local feel for Mays, Horace Stoneham, Johnny Antonelli, and whoever else carried the New York connection.

Upset by a windblown pop fly that had cost him a game, pitcher Antonelli said something about Seals Stadium, something like "How can you pitch in a bush-league park like this?" All four San Francisco papers jumped on him; one editorial suggested that he go back where he came from.

In Mays's case, the most commonly expressed (if not privately felt) source of resentment on the part of the fans went curiously to the way he caught the ball—his famous "basket" style. While serving in the army, Willie had perfected the basket catch, which consisted of his dipping his hands at the last instant and catching the ball at hip level or even lower, much as a grocer might turn up his apron to catch a box of raisins from the topmost shelf—this in contrast to the standard hands-up, palms-out, head-high method, with the glove in the line of sight.

"Is it a flair?" Leo Durocher was asked, when Mays returned from the army with the new catch in 1954.

"Call it what you want," Durocher replied.

"Are you going to tell him to change back to normal style?"

"Why should I? He catches them, doesn't he?"

If he ever did drop one—which he did, at the old Polo Grounds—it could only make him look ridiculous, which it also did that one time. Mays has had his imitators over the years—Lee Mazzilli of the modern-day Mets became one—but he tries to discourage them. "You just plain look like a fool if you drop it," he told a group of Little Leaguers at a typical baseball clinic. "There I was throwing the ball back after the catch, only I didn't have any ball to throw."

Mays's official rationale for the basket catch (I should know: I wrote it) appeared in *Born to Play Ball,* the book we did together following the '54 season:

> One of the big things with me is getting the ball back to the infield as fast as possible once I make a catch. Most outfielders make their throws from the back-of-the-ear throwing position. Most of my throws, though, are made from lower down and farther out from the body, tending toward the sidearm. It occurred to me I could save a fraction of time by catching the ball lower down, too.

The chief fan gripe about it, when Mays first reached San Francisco, was the element of flair as mentioned in the Durocher interview. Putting it another way, as one letter I received at the *Examiner* put it, "He's nothing but a goddam showboat."

There just may have been a stage touch or two in Willie's

style. The interesting thing, though, is that such a touch, so strongly resented by some fans, was precisely what they would go to the games hoping most to see.

Inevitably, too, some people were easier to convince than others. With the overthrow of the Batista government, the new leader of the Cuban people, Fidel Castro, flew to New York in 1959 to go on the "Ed Sullivan Show."

"Let's get something out of the way right now," Sullivan said, as 25 million viewers watched. "There's been a rumor that you might be a Communist. That's not true, is it?"

"Who, me?" Castro said. "A Communist? Never!"

In the 1959 All-Star game at Pittsburgh, Willie Mays batted in the winning run for the National League with a triple in the eighth inning. "Harvey Kuenn gave it an honest pursuit," wrote Bob Stevens in the next morning's San Francisco *Chronicle*, "but the only center fielder in baseball who could have caught it hit it."

PART THREE

JFK

Does the Wind Always Blow Like This?

Hear THE TRAIN A'CALLIN' HOO-EEE! The lonesome whistle of the steam locomotive. The people in Bloomfield Hills and Highland Park heard it on the afternoon of Sunday, March 27, 1960, and in Royal Oak and Holly, just as they had heard it all the days of their lives, as the Grand Trunk Western's train No. 21 plied its course to Durand from the Brush Street station in Detroit. Just west of Brownville Junction, Maine, the Canadian Pacific's train No. 518 sounded her whistle too that day, signaling the end of her run from Megantic, Quebec, 117 miles away, through densely forested hills that had lived generations with the sound of that high, nervous wail.

Next day, March 28, trains No. 21 and No. 518 ran as always —but, as Don Ball records in his book *Portrait of the Rails*, now with "the muttering drone of internal combustion diesel engines and bleating air horns. What had started one hundred and twenty-nine years earlier, when the steam locomotive, 'Best Friend of Charlestown,' hauled the first steam train in regular service, now had come to an end. During the preceding incredibly short span of ten years, the fires had been dropped, one by one, from the steamers on virtually every class I railroad in America."

The king was dead, long live the king. Six miles from the railroad tracks—straight up—the sky was ribbed with the contrails of the passenger jets.

What a convenient piece of contrast to feed that reliable old parlor pastime: *What would it be like if...?* The publicity department at American Airlines was particularly adroit at the game. What would it be like, they wondered, if they found somebody who was ninety-seven years old and had never been outside a 25-mile radius of his own home, let alone ever flown in an airplane, and put him aboard their first transcontinental 707 jet flight from New York to San Francisco? Leave it to the airline;

they found such a man, in Metuchen, New Jersey. The bonus was that he had three great-great-grandchildren, whom he had never seen, living in South San Francisco.

I observed the ancient gentleman for myself as he boarded the plane at Idlewild Airport in a perfumerie of photographers' flashbulbs. Having flown in from San Francisco on the preview press flight of the new service, I now after two nights in New York was reboarding for the first commercial flight westbound. The flight would include a stop at Chicago—American, unlike United and TWA, was not yet privileged by the Civil Aeronautics Board to fly the New York–San Francisco route nonstop—and, when we touched down at Chicago's O'Hare Airport, the jet flunked. Some mechanical difficulty had arisen—nothing major, but, with replacement parts not yet in general distribution, nothing that could readily be fixed either. So we were offloaded and placed aboard a propeller-driven DC-7, newly arrived from Detroit, for the continuation to the Coast.

The DC-7 was hardly a form of slumming. Up to a week ago, it had been the acknowledged queen of the sky, and today especially it was still agreeable, for the way the airline was pouring whiskey to cover its chagrin. Even the ninety-seven-year-old man from Metuchen, who had appeared moribund when they half carried him aboard at Idlewild, seemed peppier, and over Iowa I undertook to interview him for my column. He was on his fourth Old Overholt when I leaned across the aisle and asked The Automatic Question: What did it feel like, after all these years, suddenly to be traveling in this fashion?

The only thing truly soundproof about the plane being the old gentleman himself, I had to shout the query several times, but finally the meaning got through. "Well, I'll tell you," he answered. "It's like being on a goddam bus, that's what it's like."

(No help for it, the airlines' zeal for promotional triumphs could have quixotic effects from time to time, like the experience, early on in the jet age, when the carriers sought to stimulate the family trade by advertising to transcontinental business travelers that they could take their wives along for half fare. The scheme was an instant success, and American Airlines, ever in the vanguard, undertook courteous follow-up notes addressed to the couples at their homes, thanking them for flying the American way. The businessmen also got divorced the American way, as one wife after another herewith discovered that her husband, on his last business trip, had not flown alone.)

My column dealt occasionally with politics, too, and early in 1960 it offered the observation that what some people feared was not a Catholic President but a good Catholic President. In time came a personal note of thanks from the candidate, one sign of an effective campaign apparatus. And in quest of another column I stood bemused beside the batting cage at Candlestick Park, the afternoon before that stadium's official inauguration with the opening of the 1960 season, as the first practice pitch came in to Willie Mays and—in critical combination of an inside fast ball and a knifelike thrust of wind—literally sawed the bat off in his hands.

Chub Feeney, then the vice-president of the Giants, could recall going to the Candlestick site while construction was still in progress and seeing whole carloads of assorted debris sail past him through the air. "Does the wind always blow like this?" Feeney asked a workman. The latter shrugged. "Just between the hours of one and five," he responded. This was not the best of news, since all but 23 of the 77 home games that first season would be daytime affairs, nor did it come as visible relief that the workman had his facts wrong: the wind at night was even worse, and with it came bone-petrifying cold. That last at least the Giants had anticipated—it was why they had held down the number of night games to begin with—and architect John Bolles, who designed Candlestick Park, had drawn into the plans a unique provision for heating the exposed grandstand seats. One disadvantage in this system—most likely the predominant one—was that it didn't work. In due course, the prominent local barrister Melvin M. Belli sued the Giants for his money back on his season's ticket, claiming that the warranty implicit in the blueprints entitled him to watch the games, not watch his life pass in review before his frozen eyes. Belli got his refund. (His witnesses, had the case gone to trial, included a man from Abercrombie & Fitch who deposed that he had sold heavier clothing to Giant ticket holders than in outfitting an expedition to Little America. Yet even such winterized apparel had its yield point. Enveloped in a parka, St. Louis broadcaster Joe Garagiola found his teeth doing the principal chattering as he described a Cardinal night game at Candlestick. A solicitous aide fetched him a cup of hot coffee. "Never mind the coffee," Garagiola advised. "Get a priest.")

For a time, the same protective instinct that had repudiated Antonelli at Seals Stadium was employed by San Franciscans to discount conditions at Candlestick, with Force 8 on the Beaufort scale translated for out-of-town consumption as a gentle breeze. Sooner or later, however, the truth must out. In the 1961 All-Star game, a nationwide television audience saw pitcher Stu Miller literally blown off the mound in mid-delivery by the wind. (He was charged with a balk.) And when the embryo Mets reached Candlestick the following season, another network audience not only saw the fate of a windblown pop-up in short left field but heard Met manager Casey Stengel describe it later. "I have to think the wind got ahold of it," Stengel reasoned. "Otherwise, my mind tells me my fielders would have been running towards it instead of away from it." And let alone its slight resemblance to the Antonelli gripe, one fly hit by Willie McCovey in 1960 matched the fable of Willie Mays and the Japanese fire engine. The second baseman had his glove up for McCovey's ball, waiting for it to come down, when it encountered the jet stream and began traveling east instead, clearing the distant fence for a grand slam home run.

As fabled a perfectionist as Roberto Clemente, the great Pittsburgh right fielder, would confess years later that he plotted ways to get sick just in advance of the Pirates' visits to Candlestick. "You had to be out of your mind to play the outfield in that park," he said. "How do you catch a ball in that wind? Unless you're Willie Mays?"

Yet Stu Miller's case in the forefront of proof, it was not just batted balls that caused concern. Bob Schmidt, a Giant catcher in 1960, had his own troubles. The wind had a way of taking his *thrown* balls off course. In one bases-loaded situation, Schmidt fired a pick-off throw. The wind took it. On the return throw to the plate, Schmidt was barreled over and the run scored, but he came up throwing again. The sequence repeated itself. He tried it a third time. Hoo boy. The action over at last, Schmidt lay there while anxious teammates dug him out of the dirt. "How many scored?" he asked hoarsely. Three, he was told. Schmidt shook his head. "I counted four. One of them must have been a coach."

One could not blame architect Bolles for such events. "After all," said a line in Herb Caen's column in the *Chronicle*, "it's his first ball park." The designer had his problems nonetheless. One stemmed from a complaint by the local baseball writers that they could not see home plate. The management proclaimed Candlestick's press box to be the most up-to-date in the land, but in truth the heights of its seats, workshelf, and window were such that nobody could see out of it. Bolles sent one of his assistants out to the park to check out the complaint. The assistant arrived in the press box two hours before game time. The Braves were in town that day. The only man in the press box at that early point was the Braves' public relations director, Don Davidson. Seated on a pile of pillows, he was pecking away at his typewriter. Davidson happened to be a dwarf. The architectural emissary took it all in, added 2 and 2 to get his own 4, and went away convinced the only purpose behind the writers' complaint was to stage an elaborate practical joke at his expense. It was three years before a false floor was installed in the press box, enabling journalists finally to see all of the game they were covering. Meanwhile, the eminent architectural expert Allan

Temko wrote a piece for *Harper's* magazine about Candlestick Park. "How Not to Build a Ball Park," the article was entitled. The expansive parking lot struck him as a "tundra." As for first impressions, he went at once to the stadium's "uninviting main entrance," which, he found, bore "some resemblance to a prison gate." (It was Jacques Barzun who observed at one point that "Anyone who would know the heart and mind of America had better learn baseball.")

The reaction of the typical San Francisco fan to the surrealism of Candlestick Park was not unpredictable: fire the manager. Not the manager of the stadium, the manager of the team, who at that point was Bill Rigney. The novelty of big league baseball having by now worn thin, the natives, conspicuous by their impatience, wanted a winner. The club had finished sixth in each of its last two years in New York, and third in each of its first two years in San Francisco. (In Los Angeles, by way of contrast, the Dodgers in their first season came on as pennant favorites and showed the estimable good sense of finishing in seventh place, next to last, leaving them, as their own novelty wore off, with no place to go but up.) For the Giants, their new fans perceived no problem: the move to ensure a championship was simply to hire Lefty O'Doul, a long-time local baseball favorite, to manage the club (and, just incidentally, stamp the San Francisco imprimatur on that New York product for good and all). It took the mob, its blood cry goaded by garish page-one stories that bellowed for Rigney's scalp, till June 18 of that first Candlestick season of 1960 to get him. At that point, the Giants had won 33 games, lost 25, and were lodged respectably in second place, but to a citizenry stimulated even to the point of wanting to change the name "Giants" back to the "Seals" of venerated Pacific Coast League memory, second place in June was no longer good enough.

No readier to hire O'Doul than he was to take the team richest of all in baseball history and call it the Seals, Horace Stoneham did nevertheless relieve Rigney. Into the latter's place went a house functionary, Tom Sheehan, part-time scout and full-time raconteur. Born in 1894 at Grand Ridge, Illinois, Sheehan had been a teammate of Babe Ruth's on the 1921 Yankees. (He told me of one time when Ruth asked him to pick him up at his apartment en route to the ball park. "Come by a little early," the Babe said. "I don't want to miss batting practice." Sheehan, impressed, called for Ruth in a taxicab. The Babe got in and the cab proceeded on its way for a few blocks. Then Ruth told the driver, "Stop here and wait for us." They went upstairs in an apartment building. The Ruth-pushed doorbell was answered by a winsome lady. She and Ruth went into the bedroom while Sheehan waited in the living room. Then out staggered Ruth, and he and Sheehan resumed their journey to the ball park. A few blocks farther on, Ruth told the driver, "Stop here and wait for us." They went upstairs in another apartment building. The Ruth-pushed doorbell was answered by a winsome lady. She and Ruth went into the bedroom while Sheehan waited in the living room. Then out reeled Ruth, and he and Sheehan resumed their journey to the ball park. Listening to this story, I found myself intrigued. Did the Babe ever get to take batting practice? "Not at the ball park," Sheehan said. Well, then, how did he make out in the game itself? "All I remember is one ball he hit," Sheehan said. "It was the longest home run I ever saw in my life.")

A pitcher by trade, Sheehan himself saw little service with the Yankees in 1921. The most work he got was five years earlier, pitching for the Philadelphia Athletics under Connie Mack, when he started 17 games and posted a won-and-lost record of 1-and-16. His roommate, Jack Nabors, saw even more action. He started 29 games and was 1-and-19. Bullet Joe Bush, another starting pitcher on the 1916 A's, lost 22 games. The other starter, Elmer Myers, lost 23. In all, that was a famous team. It won 36 games, lost 117. Its shortstop, Whitey Witt, made 78 errors. The third baseman, Charlie Pick, led the league at that position with 42 errors, but, as he was wont to point out in his later years, "I didn't get to play every day." Wally Schang, the old catcher, was in left field that year, with Billy Myer doing the catching, but Myer was then disabled by appendicitis. In an interview with Jack Orr, Sheehan recalled what happened next:

"After Myer got lucky, everybody caught. Remember Val Picinich? He was 19, just breaking in. He hit .195. On other days total strangers would catch.

"Once we were playing the Yankees and I'm pitching. Picinich warms me up, but as the first hitter gets in, Val goes back to the bench and takes off the tools.

"Another guy comes out, a guy I've never seen. He comes out to the mound and says, 'My name is Carroll. I'm the catcher. What are your signs?' I tell him not to confuse me and get back there and catch. He stuck around for about a week and nobody ever saw him again.

"We pitchers lost a lot of games, but that collection couldn't have won behind Matty or Grove [Hall of Fame pitchers Christy Mathewson and Lefty Grove]. Once we go to Boston for a series. I pitch the opener and give up one hit, by Doc Hoblitzel. But it happens to follow a walk and an error by Witt and I lose, 1–0.

"Now Nabors pitches the second game and he is leading, 1–0, going into the ninth. He gets the first man. Witt boots one and the next guy walks. Hooper is up next, I think, and he singles to left and the man on second tries to score.

"Well, Schang has a good arm and he throws one in that has the runner cold by 15 feet. But we have one of those green catchers. (Never forget his name, Mike Murphy.) The ball bounces out of his glove, the run scores, the other runner takes third and it is 1–1.

"Nabors winds up and throws the next pitch 20 feet over the hitter's head into the grandstand, the man on third scores and we lose another, 2–1.

"Later I asked Nabors why he threw that one away.

" 'Look,' he said, 'I knew those guys wouldn't get me another run and if you think I'm going to throw nine more innings on a hot day like this, you're crazy.' "

(To me, Sheehan's recollection of the 1916 Athletics epitomizes baseball's unique capacity to celebrate failure as well as success. What other sport—what other enterprise in any field—distills such profit and sheer enjoyment from the negative? It does no disservice to the truth to say that when Babe Ruth, Willie Mays, Henry Aaron, Roger Maris, or Sadaharu Oh recorded record-breaking home runs, the newspapers next morning gave about as much space to the individual who threw the ball as to the one who hit it. In reflection of an unsuspected strain in the Japanese sense of humor, Oh's man, though not particularly wild about it, found himself the winner of a vacation trip to Saipan, whose cliffs symbolized his nation's World War II preference for suicide rather than disgrace. And the greatest pictorial preservation of Bobby Thomson's homer is a photograph of Ralph Branca.)

But in his interim tour as Giant manager in 1960, Tom Sheehan, contemporary to both Babe Ruth and Connie Mack, would, however reluctantly, model himself after the latter. Both were creatures of longevity, and both did their managing in street clothes, though Sheehan at least sat in the dugout alongside his players. (Mack, who was still managing the Athletics in 1950, going on eighty-nine, preferred to occupy a spectator box, calling the shots but leaving their execution-in-uniform to two of his coaches who happened also to be his sons, Earle Mack and Connie Mack, Jr. This technique presented American League umpires with something of a dilemma. To be called a bleeping blankety bleep was clear grounds for ejecting the speaker, but to be approached by a middle-aged man who said "My father says to tell you you're a bleeping blankety bleep" presented a situation not wholly covered by the prevailing rules.)

The Sheehan approach to managing was nothing if not informal. On one occasion, he drew up his lineup for the day, then found himself confronted by one of his outfielders, Willie Kirkland, who wanted to know if he was starting that game. Sheehan shook his head in the negative. "Why not?" Kirkland inquired. "To tell you the truth," Sheehan said, "I don't know why not." He took his pencil and wrote in Kirkland's name. Actually, in

Sheehan's philosophy, the alteration didn't make all that much difference. "The closer you get to these guys," he was heard to say of the 1960 Giants, "the worse they look." Some charges of dissension within the ranks had surfaced, but if anything the opposite was true. Noisily sociable card games, far into the night, were the rule on the road. When Sheehan complained, one of the players said privately, "Old Tom's right. From now on, the rule's going to be, 'Shut up and deal.'" Once, manager Sheehan encountered one of his players escorting a female companion through the lobby of the Warwick Hotel in Philadelphia at three o'clock in the morning. "He ought to know better than that," Sheehan said sadly. "He's been in the big league long enough now to know there's a back entrance."

"He may last a week, or three weeks, or the rest of the season," club owner Stoneham intoned in announcing Sheehan's appointment. "It all depends on how the team does." In a week, the team had won 1 game out of 6, in three weeks it had won 7 out of 24, and Sheehan lasted the rest of the season.

Bob Greene did a syndicated newspaper piece in 1978, about wine. "It is all a straight-faced charade," he wrote, "designed to convince the consumer that he is guzzling something with a semblance of character, rather than a pale imitation of a true alcoholic beverage. Wine is to liquor as allergy is to real sickness. Wine is the racquetball of the drinking world." The Greene article had a San Francisco dateline. "This is wine country," it said. "It ought to be declared a federal disaster area." A semblance of the same had hit me twenty years earlier when I took up my *Examiner* column. It was the business of the salad all over again, with a California product being pushed first for local consumption, then foisted upon the nation as a whole—and tomorrow the world. And it seemed that every other press agent I met was pushing wine.

But with salad and wine, California was just beginning to flex its muscle. Another local product then being readied for export would put them both to shame. This one, a banner with a strange device, was revolutionary in the true sense of the word. It was impeccably sponsored, dignifiedly produced. It was still a revolution. They called it BankAmericard.

In my New York boyhood, I would roller-skate after school on the marvelously wide sidewalk surrounding the Central Savings Bank, an isosceles trapezoid that occupied the compressed city block of Broadway to Amsterdam Avenue and 73rd Street to 74th. Inside the bank itself was my money—as much as $1.05 of it, I believe, saved at the basic rate of 5 cents per week through passbooks circulated in the classrooms at P.S. 87, where an officer of the bank who looked like George Washington would appear periodically before the fourth- and fifth-graders to lecture them in the virtues and the machinery of thrift. With that memory, it has always struck me as bizarre that banks and what they stood for would, a quarter century later, have undergone such revolution as to urge upon their customers the ultimate doomsday weapon for going into debt. (The BankAmericard people, soon to be joined as well by another California invention called Master Charge, demurred that what they were doing here was nothing more than traveling a way already paved by Diners Club, American Express, and Carte Blanche, but the comparison was not in all ways apt. For one thing, the three majors were there essentially for the travel and entertainment convenience of the well-heeled, not the everyday shopper. For another, they did not at the time offer their patrons the option of extended payments at interest, something the bank cards made not only possible but well-nigh irresistible. And finally and most simply, the big three were not *banks*. Far from any moral requirement to preach saving over spending, the accepted function in their case was precisely the other way around. Whatever else the

Diners Club might have done, it never sent George Washington to P.S. 87.)

An old story describes the lady cruise traveler who asked the ship's captain if he told the passengers what to do for seasickness. "We don't have to tell them, ma'am," the captain replied. "They just do it." In this vein the bank-card people did discover that when it came to spending, some folk required little if any encouragement. And one such customer proved to be Willie Mays. In 1960, his baseball pay was $75,000, fifteen times the scale minimum he started at in 1951; but far from having anything to show for it, he was actually borrowing from the Giants against his salary. Several ill-advised ventures (not the least of which would prove to be his first marriage in 1956) had worked against his chances of putting something aside. So did his generosity toward his family in Birmingham. So did his generosity toward himself. So, inexorably, did the income taxes against someone with his earnings who lacked the shelters that good investment counseling can produce. One divorce, two business managers, ten years, and a by-then doubled salary later, it could finally be said with some certainty that Mays had turned the corner. But in 1960 he stood—to what would have been the total astonishment of the people at large if they had known about it (and what was pretty much the astonishment of the few who *did* know about it)—on the brink of filing for bankruptcy.

One wonders idly what if anything this might have done to the Mays image if it had become general knowledge. It would not be easy to say it affected his performance on the field: playing in all but one of the team's 154 games in 1960, he had more than 100 runs both scored and batted in and led the National League in hits with 190.

That year too the league set an all-time attendance record, breaking the former mark, established in 1947. The Giants' move to Candlestick, with its additional seats, had to have something to do with that, but there were offsetting factors: the league in 1960 had nothing resembling a tight pennant race, and a sluggish hangover from the Eisenhower recession still obtained. What may have been at work instead was the onset of a factor that would grow increasingly noticeable over the years: baseball's ability to keep its prices down. By 1978, the price for a bleacher seat at a Giant game had gone up only 45 cents in 45 years, and a *TV Guide* poll, also taken in 1978, reported, "When asked if they prefer sports ranging alphabetically from auto racing to wrestling in person or on TV, in every case but one, substantial majorities of viewers vote for television. That one exception is pro baseball, with its pastoral summer panoramas —and comparatively cheap tickets."

As a road attraction—this an index of a team's nationwide appeal, measured by the crowds it draws in the cities away from home—the Giants in 1960 outdrew the Dodgers, even though faring worse in the standings. This was not exceptional: over the fourteen years of 1958 through 1971, San Francisco's team totaled the largest road attendance in baseball, even with only one league championship during that period. In 1972 it was the Mets who led the league in road attendance, though they whetted no public appetite as a contender either. The secret ingredient in all of this could not have been that close-held a secret: from 1958 through 1971, the Giants had Willie Mays; in 1972, the Mets had him.

Mays was without question the biggest gate attraction in baseball history. The only man who would come close would be Babe Ruth. Comparisons here on the basis only of attendance figures would be hugely unfair to Ruth. He did his playing in a league compressed to eight cities within just the northeast quadrant of the United States, so fewer people had access to him; and there were fewer people, period. Ruth had been a major leaguer for five years before the American population reached 100 million; Mays's career still had nine years to go when it passed 200 million.

The case for Willie asserts itself instead in the aspect of crowd appeal. Ruth's was unilateral. His early career work as a pitcher was splendid; his work as a fielder and a base runner did not invite reproach. But where Mays would electrify a crowd simply with the way he caught a ball, or threw it, or ran, or merely took his lead off a base, Ruth in those same elements was uninteresting. With Mays, the capacity to hit home runs was the additional thing; with Ruth it was the only thing—unless you count those fans (and there were more than a few of them) who got their jollies from watching him strike out. The ability to generate hostility, however, was only partly the Babe's personal accomplishment; such resentment as he encountered was not infrequently as much for his New York Yankee uniform as for the man who wore it. Today's emotional custom, under which fans are ready to weep and faint at presentation of the opening lineups, should not be permitted to blur the distinction here. The most implacable hatred on the part of the fans at Dodger Stadium in Los Angeles has been perennially for the visiting Giants, yet repeatedly those fans rewarded Willie with standing ovations. It was the same throughout the league. On the Giants' first trip to Montreal in 1969, when that city was new to the majors, I noticed how early the crowd arrived and mentioned it to one of the local journalists. First he said something succinctly in French; then, observing my uncertainty, he translated it, first by pointing at Giant slugger Willie McCovey, who was taking batting practice. "They expect him to hit a home run," he explained. Then he pointed at Mays. "They *want* him to hit one."

Can a man hit a home run on purpose? The story, though categorically denied by some of the participants, endures that Ruth did so in the 1932 World Series against the Cubs. But if he did it once, Mays did it half a dozen times. To television producer Lee Mendelson, then completing the filming of an NBC documentary on Willie and wondering when he would hit his 400th home run, Mays, on the afternoon of August 27, 1963, said, "I ought to hit it tonight." He did. (The statement may not have been totally egregious—Willie had taken the measure of the weather and the man scheduled to pitch against him.) The dramatic necessity was there even more for Mays to hit a home run in his first game as a Met, against his former Giant teammates. He did, and columnist Pete Hamill recorded the moment:

> It flew high and proud through the New York air, over the infielders, traveling sweetly and purely, obliterating the rain, landing at last in some summer afternoon in 1957. Willie Mays ran the bases, carrying all those summers on the 41-year-old shoulders, jogging in silence, while people in the stands pumped their arms at the skies and hugged each other and even, here and there, cried. It was a glittering moment of repair, in a city that has been starved too long for joy. Don't tell me New York isn't going to make it. Willie Mays is home.

Back in San Francisco, another columnist, Charles McCabe, took a different view of the same event. The Giants, he wrote, must have agreed before the game to let Willie hit one for old time's sake. (If McCabe had written instead that Mays had an educated idea what pitch was coming, he could have been more right than wrong. With the score tied in the bottom of the fifth, Mays leading off with good hitters coming up behind him, the count 3-and-2, and a twenty-two-year-old rookie pitching for the Giants, Willie could have been pardoned for guessing fast ball. Anything else on 3-and-2 increased the chance of ball four and a lead-off baserunner, precisely what the Giants wanted least to see.)

Was an encore required? If so, it would have been on the occasion of the Mets' first visit to San Francisco following their acquisition of Mays. Again it was the fifth inning, again a rookie pitcher, again a fast ball. (Accused of not liking fast pitching, Mays had replied mystically, "Who do?"—but he could still handle the pitch now and again, particularly when his instinct and experience told him to look for it.) Again, just as in New York, he hit the ball out of the park. Again, just as in New York, his home run won the game. If it was McCabe's notion that the Giants let him have that one for old time's sake, too, his column was silent on the point.

"The Ruth is mighty and shall prevail." So wrote Heywood Broun of the Babe in the 1921 World Series. "Intentional" home runs to one side, there is no doubt that Ruth and Mays each had the touch of the showman: they "came up" to big moments and big crowds. Mays, because he could do more things on defense and on the bases, provided the more complete glamour spectrum on the field. Off the field, both men had the need to stay away from crowded places and the hounding of autograph seekers and celebrity buffs. What socializing they did do was marked by Willie's laughter and Ruth's vocabulary. Robert Creamer, in his book *Babe*, said that Ruth at times would be consciously circumspect in his language when in the presence of women; at other times, nothing if not extroverted. Wrote Creamer:

> After Ruth came back from a trip to the Far East in the 1930s, a friend who had just been married came to visit, bringing along his new wife. Babe told [one] story about sitting next to Lefty Gomez' wife at dinner one evening on the trip. "They brought out this great caviar, and they started it around the table from one side of me. Lefty's wife was sitting on the other side. It goes all the way around the table, and there's only a little left when it gets to her, and she takes it all. 'Oh, I love this stuff,' she said. So I asked the waiter to bring some more, and they bring it and it goes around the table again, and damn if she didn't take the last bit again. She was sitting there eating it on bits of toast. My God, she ate so much of that stuff she looked like a seagull eating shit."
>
> The friend was wondering uneasily how his lovely new wife was taking this, and he got Ruth to talking instead about his trophies. Babe gave them a quick guided tour. He pointed to one silver cup and said, "Look at this one. You know what I got it for?"
>
> "No, what?"
>
> "I won first place in a farting contest. Honest. Read the writing on it. Boy, I had to down a lot of beer and limburger to win that one."
>
> The friend left the apartment a bit shaken. In the elevator he looked nervously at his wife. But she seemed exhilarated.
>
> "What a fascinating man," she said.

Elsewhere in his book, Creamer deals with another facet of the Ruth legend:

The story of Johnny Sylvester is one of the most famous in Ruth lore. The simplest version says that Johnny, a young boy, lay dying in a hospital. Ruth came to visit him and promised him he would hit a home run for him that afternoon. And he did, which so filled Johnny with the will to live that he miraculously recovered. The facts are parallel, if not so melodramatic. In 1926 eleven-year-old Johnny Sylvester was badly hurt in a fall from a horse and was hospitalized. To cheer him up, a friend of Johnny's father brought him baseballs autographed by players on the Yankees and the Cardinals just before the World Series that year, as well as a promise from Ruth that he would hit a home run for him. Ruth hit four homers in the Series, and after it was over paid a visit to Johnny in the hospital, which thrilled the boy. The visit was given the tears-and-lump-in-the-throat treatment in the press, and the legend was born. After that, few writers reviewing Ruth's career failed to mention a dying boy and the home run that saved his life.

There were of course other occasions where Ruth's visits to youngsters in hospitals were not so well publicized, if at all. Similarly unpublicized were the hospital calls Willie Mays made in his time . . . and those of many other ballplayers as well. But the Ruth legend did occur to me one time when I accompanied Mays to the hospital bedside of a young boy who had been struck by a car and was having trouble speaking to or even recognizing familiar faces. Mays brought him a cap and an autographed ball, set them on the bedtable, and leaned down to say hello. The boy opened his eyes, looked, and grinned. "Hi, Willie," he said.

They chatted lucidly for a time, as the boy's parents and the family priest looked on. Then it was time to leave, and at the door the father said, "Mr. Mays, I don't know how to thank you for . . ." and then broke down and wept. The mother and the priest were crying too.

To the boy he was Willie. To the parents he was Mr. Mays. They were white and he was black, and yet he was Mr. Mays.

That was a phenomenon of Willie's time, never of Ruth's.

Even in the business of hitting home runs, there would be a pressure on Mays, multiplying far worse in the case of Hank Aaron, that Ruth did not have. The Babe did feel pressure going for his 60th home run in 1927, in order to eclipse his own previous mark of 59 in 1921, but aside from that single season he was so established all by himself as baseball's first mass producer of homers that no one bothered to keep a running count on him as he went along. Difficult though it may be to believe, his 500th home run came and went without notice. He had, after all, nobody to catch. When Aaron ultimately passed Mays and now had only Ruth to beat, the pressure became inexorable. And with it came the sacks of hate mail, outraged that a black man could pretend to the crown.

Ruth could not have known what that felt like. Or maybe he did, in passing, for, as Fred Lieb told Jerry Holtzman:

> What Aaron doesn't know, and I suppose what most people don't know, is that some of Babe's teammates were convinced he had Negro blood. There was quite a bit of talk about that. Many of the players, when they wanted to badger him, called him "nigger." Ruth had Negroid features, Negroid nose, mouth, lips. But when you saw him naked, from the neck down, he was white, a good deal whiter than most men.
>
> Ty Cobb once refused to share a cabin with Ruth. I'm sure of the authenticity of this. They were assigned to the same cabin, but Cobb objected and said, "I've never bedded down with a nigger and I'm not going to start now." . . . Cobb and Ruth never did get along.

Of all the ovations he received in ball parks throughout the land, the one Willie Mays remembers foremost took place at Yankee Stadium in late July of 1961. It was the first appearance of the Giants as a team in New York since their departure for

San Francisco following the 1957 season. They were there for an exhibition game against the Yankees, nothing more than that, and it was raining, and the game—if there was a game—could be seen on television. But 50,000 fans showed up. The game is not included in the record book, but various newspaper accounts survive. Here is part of one:

> The Giants had come home, and in a driving, steaming summer rainstorm, the big town turned out to say hello.
> There was no pre-game practice. It was raining. The pre-game home run contest was called off. It was raining.
> Game time was held up half an hour past the scheduled 7:55 P.M. start.
> "We'll never play tonight," Alvin Dark said.
> "Look outside and you'll change your mind," he was told.
> He went down the runway and up into the visiting dugout along the third-base line and looked.
> There in the rain sat the people. Waiting. . . .
> "Ladies and gentlemen," said the Yankee Stadium announcer, giving the lineup for the San Francisco Giants, "at second base, number fourteen, Joe Amalfitano."
> The cheering started.
> "Number seven, Harvey Kuenn, right field . . ."
> It got louder.
> "Number twenty-four, Wil—"
> You never heard the rest of the Giant batting order announced here tonight.
> An unbroken, throat-swelling peal of adulation sprang from the hearts of Giant-starved New Yorkers. It rolled and volleyed off the great tiering of this triple-decked palace and against the vague outline of the Bronx County court house, looming in the gray-black mist out beyond the huge scoreboard in right-center field.
> They rocked and tottered and shouted and stamped and sang. It was joy and love and welcome, and you never heard a cascade of sound quite like it.

The closest I ever came to hearing a crowd sound like that one was a year earlier, when I was doing my column from Los Angeles during the Democratic convention at the Sports Arena there. The crowd was a smaller one, but like the electronic guitar its noise fed upon itself in the equally smaller confines of the indoor arena, and what moved the ovation—it was for Adlai Stevenson—was curiously similar to the applause for Mays at Yankee Stadium. Stevenson's appearance on the convention floor came at a point where John F. Kennedy already had the nomination locked away, and his managers let Stevenson's fans have their moment. Their emotional response to his brief appearance was conditioned—and strengthened therefore—by the realization that he would be gone again tomorrow, just as Mays would be gone again from New York.

I came away from that convention with bleak thoughts about the winner. One vivid scene stuck in my memory: the sight of the way Kennedy's Boston henchmen manhandled longtime party dignitaries when they sought to pay their respects to him following his victory on the first ballot. His formal speech of acceptance was a disaster. It took place at the outdoor Los Angeles Coliseum. "His face was tired and haggard," Theodore S. White reported. "His voice was high and sad." On top of everything else, the speech, timed for the peak viewing hours in the East and Midwest, forced the candidate to squint directly into the setting California sun.

In contrast, Richard Nixon's speech of acceptance at the Republican convention in Chicago two weeks later was impressive. It should have been: at its most eloquent it borrowed liberally from Stevenson's famous 1952 acceptance speech. (Stevenson: "Let's talk sense to the American people. Let's tell them the truth, that there are no gains without pains. . . ." Nixon: "Our next president must tell the people not what they want to hear but what they need to hear.")

With the impact of the Nixon speech as I saw it on television, combined with the impression of Kennedy that I had so recently taken home from Los Angeles, I was possessed by an overnight decision that I must vote for Nixon. Like the one thing I had in common with President Eisenhower—a twelve-hour body rash that came from eating oyster stew—the state would recede almost as fast as it came on, but for a little bit there I was a Nixon-lover . . . of which, history would come to record, there were never enough, even when he won. "Nixon liked Kennedy," Teddy White wrote, "which was not reciprocally true." And, at another point: "Nixon was above all a friend seeker, almost pathetic in his eagerness to be liked."

The two candidates shared the dais *pro forma* that campaign season at the annual Alfred E. Smith dinner, by custom presided over by the senior prelate of the Catholic Church in New York. In the course of a literate and witty speech to the 1960 Smith dinner, Kennedy said, "I would not want to give the impression that I am taking former President Truman's use of language lightly. I have sent him the following note: 'Dear Mr. President: I have noted with interest your suggestion as to where those who vote for my opponent should go. While I understand and sympathize with your deep motivation, I think it is important that our side try to refrain from raising the religious issue.' " To this, historian White appended: "Such speeches always disturbed Mr. Nixon, whose light touch is never publicly evident and whose private touch is sprinkled with normal profanity." (White's use of the "Mr." in front of Nixon's name is to me a fascinating by-product of Nixon's ability to leave with people exactly the opposite impression he sought so assiduously to create. This was no case of a Mr. Mays in a hospital room. Nor was it a case of gratuitous pejorative. I believe instead it was simply what comes to people who try too hard to be liked.)

If Kennedy was the acknowledged star of that Smith dinner, it didn't change a vote in the audience. Wrote Arthur Schlesinger, "The audience had been strongly pro-Nixon, and Kennedy was ironically entertained by the fact that the wealthy Catholics obviously preferred a conservative Quaker to a liberal of their own faith. 'It all goes to show,' he said to me later, 'that, when the chips are down, money counts more than religion.' " When Kennedy finally won the election, Harry Truman had his own thoughts: "Nixon is a shifty-eyed, goddamn liar, and people know it. I can't figure out how he came so close to getting elected President in 1960. They say young Kennedy deserves a lot of credit for licking him, but I just can't see it. I can't see how the son of a bitch even carried one state."

But Nixon did carry more than one state. He carried five more than Kennedy, including—incredibly—Hawaii, which four years later would go 78.8 percent Democratic. To those who claimed fecklessly that it was the Catholic vote in the big cities that inched Kennedy across, a horde of proper analysts would point out that it was the anti-Catholic vote across the country that carried the greater weight and nearly defeated him. Ironically, if any one factor could be singled out to account for Kennedy's victory, it was an unforeseen twist in that very prejudice. Three weeks before election day, Martin Luther King was arrested and sentenced to four months at hard labor for staging a sit-in in the restaurant of an Atlanta department store. In contrast to Nixon, who had no overt reaction to the news, Kennedy phoned King's wife to express his outrage, the following day his brother Bob called the judge who had leveled the sentence, and straightforth King was released on bail pending appeal. His father, the Rev. Martin Luther King, Sr., had already declared for Nixon, but now he switched. As White records it in his book *The Making of the President 1960:*

"Because this man," said the Reverend Mr. King, Senior, "was willing to wipe the tears from my daughter (-in-law)'s eyes, I've got a suitcase of votes, and I'm going to take them to Mr. Kennedy and dump them in his lap." Across the country scores of Negro leaders, deeply Protestant but even more deeply impressed by Kennedy's action, followed suit. And where command decision had been made, the Kennedy organization could by now follow through. . . . A million pamphlets describing the episode were printed across the country, half a million in Chicago alone, whence they were shipped by Greyhound bus. On the Sunday before election, these pamphlets were distributed outside Negro churches all across the country. One cannot identify in the narrowness of American voting of 1960 any one particular episode or decision as being more important than any other in the final tallies: yet when one reflects that Illinois was carried by only 9,000 votes and that 250,000 Negroes are estimated to have voted for Kennedy; that Michigan was carried by 67,000 votes and that an estimated 250,000 Negroes voted for Kennedy; that South Carolina was carried by 10,000 votes and that an estimated 40,000 Negroes there voted for Kennedy, the candidate's instinctive decision must be ranked among the most crucial of the last few weeks.

(The elder King had earlier told reporters he never thought he could cast his ballot for a Catholic. On hearing this, according to William Manchester's account, "Kennedy murmured, 'Imagine Martin Luther King having a bigot for a father.' Then he added, 'Well, we all have fathers, don't we?' ")

My one remaining piece of political commentary was to vote for Kennedy. Almost as soon as I returned to San Francisco from the Democratic convention, I was caught up in the swirl of new policies, new editors, new resident publishers all trying to keep Hearst's flagship paper, the *Examiner*—"Monarch of the Dailies," so its masthead said—from going belly-up. The compression in the newspaper industry had hit San Francisco, and the *Examiner* was fair game, rich though it was in history. One of its former city editors, a man named Bill Wren, would have fit in splendidly at the old INS. He was a horseplayer and close companion to world figures, including P. G. Wodehouse, the eminent author. At one point, Wodehouse arrived in San Francisco and phoned Wren to ask him out for lunch.

"Can't make it," Wren said. "We've got a meeting of the editors."

"Really?" Wodehouse said. "What's the crisis?"

"No crisis. We meet every day to plan the next day's paper."

"My God," Wodehouse said. "You mean you publish intentionally?"

I was taken off my column and made entertainment editor. That lasted six months. By then a new man was in charge and there was talk of my covering the forthcoming trial in Jerusalem of Adolf Eichmann, the captured Nazi SS general. Then the new editor had second thoughts and called me at home to inquire whether I would rather cover the Giants than Eichmann. I suppose it is the symbol of a generalist that he can go general column–entertainment editor–Eichmann trial–Giants in just over half a year, but barn swallows are generalists, yet they still have a barn. Maybe my barn is a baseball press box. Maybe it was the chance to get away from the turmoil at the paper to covering a ball club at a serene remove. Maybe it was the prospect of revisiting my Phoenix haunts for six weeks of spring training at the nicest time of year. Whatever, I leapt at it, and that was it.

I went to Phoenix to pick up the spring training of 1961 and Chub Feeney said, "It's about time." Willie Mays said, "Einstein? Where you been?" And Alvin Dark, newly installed as Giant manager, said, "We both go back to New York together."

His reference was of course to the fact that I was the only writer covering the team who was in New York while the Giants were there. For Dark the enemy was San Francisco, and he had his reasons. "What's he like?" the city's leading disc jockey, a man named Don Sherwood, asked of a co-worker who attended Dark's first press conference in January of 1961. The other man started to tell him. "Well, he was the star shortstop for the Giants when they won the pennant in 1951 and 1954—"

"In New York?" Sherwood broke in.

The man nodded. "And he doesn't drink, or smoke, or swear. And he's a tithing Baptist—"

"From the South?"

"Yes. Louisiana. And he says he's going to love San Francisco with those cute cable cars and he doesn't think it's important that he never played or managed in the Pacific Coast League, and—"

"Stop right there," Sherwood said. "I've already counted eight insults to our city. There can't be any left."

There was one left, but thanks to a benevolent press agent named Dick Skuse it never surfaced. On learning that Dark was to be the new manager, Skuse wrote him a note welcoming him and offering him the various facilities of his clients. Dark wrote back a note of thanks, saying, "I hope to see you often in Frisco." Skuse sent a prompt reply: "Don't ever call it Frisco." It was a straightforward admonition, and certainly one of the friendlier ones Dark would receive. For virulence, he could match the hate mail Henry Aaron received almost letter for letter. "You ought to see our mail from Catholics," Dark's wife, Adrienne, told me.

Even the manager's southern stress on the off syllable—what a *dis*grace it was to see the *po*lice and the ambu*lance* in front of the *ce*ment *ho*tel in *De*troit—fell gratingly on San Francisco ears. Worse than that, as spring training began he openly avoided the ever-present Lefty O'Doul, assigned by Giant owner Stoneham to help coach the Giant hitters as a sop to San Francisco pride. Bill Rigney had tolerated the O'Doul presence in the past, but Dark snubbed him so obviously that Lefty stayed in camp barely a week. (Watching Harvey Kuenn hit in batting practice, O'Doul said, "He lunges when he swings." Kuenn had come to the Giants from the American League, where in nine seasons he had compiled a batting average of .313. He also had to be one of the all-time artisans when it came to doing what Ted Williams said was the most difficult thing in all sports: making contact with the pitch. In 1954, when he came to the plate some 700 times, Kuenn walked only 29 times and struck out only 13. Overhearing O'Doul's observation, Willie McCovey, who had been the object of Lefty's attentions the year before and had gone on to hit .238, murmured, "What I need is some lungin' lessons.")

The San Francisco writers resented Dark's treatment of O'-Doul, and their dispatches reflected this and so inflamed the populace back home. There was resentment, too, for the presence of touring New York writers who continued nostalgically to home in on the Giants. With Mays as a player, Dark as a manager, and Lockman, Larry Jansen, and Westrum now as coaches, the 1961 San Francisco club had five men who were actually in the lineup that storied 1951 moment when Thomson hit the home run. "Sober up the one guy and get the other out of jail," Bob Stevens said to me, in reference to Dusty Rhodes and Hank Thompson, "and you can have a hell of a reunion."

I had never covered Pacific Coast League baseball, and thus had no reading on that. It appears to have included jolly times: Bob Stevens and Bucky Walter sang one of the writers' songs for me which went on for some length, though the only lines I still recall from it are:

> The hippopotamus, so it seems,
> Seldom if ever has wet dreams.

Which of course did not go to the problem at hand. San Francisco's baseball tradition still was that of the old Pacific Coast League Seals, and indeed the Bay Area had the tradition also of having sent more native sons to the major leagues than any other place of comparable size. The importing of Dark to manage the ball club seemed to the locals only further proof that you could take the Giants out of New York, but you could not take New York out of the Giants.

Things did not improve with the beginning of exhibition play. "Alvin Dark hasn't been quite sure what went wrong with the Giants last year," my story of that opening game began, "so today his players showed him. The result was a 9–1 loss to the Cleveland Indians."

Or, a couple of days later:

> How to be happy though defeated in the last of the ninth is the subject of Alvin Dark's sermon tonight.
> Dark's Giants dropped a 6–5 duke to the Boston Red Sox, but San Francisco was at its sharpest to date.

GIANTS SHARP, said the first bank of the headline on that story in the next morning's *Examiner*. BUT STILL LOSE! said the second.

And it helped neither Dark's born-again Christianity nor San Francisco's deep-seated suspicion of same that upon one Phoenix midnight, three of the players, baited by drag-racing teddy boys as they returned to the team's hotel, responded heatedly and found themselves jailed on drunk-and-disorderly charges. It proved helpful here that I had lived in the area before; I was able to roust a great and dear friend named Robert Begam, later to become the president of the American Trial Lawyers' Association, out of bed, and he was able to secure the trio's immediate release on bail—no mean feat, since local law dictated a mandatory overnight jail stay on all drunk arrests. The premium on instant liberation was to get the three players out of the jailhouse before photographers from the local papers showed up.

As for the papers back home in San Francisco, the story did not make the sports pages. It made the front pages. I reported the manager's account of what happened:

> "It's something that happens all the time," Dark said. "A bunch of hoodlums going by in a car recognize ballplayers and shout abuse at them. This is what happened here."
>
> The arresting officer, Dark said, claimed there was alcohol on at least one of the player's breaths and that his eyes were red.
>
> "They never ran a drunk test on them, though," Dark said. "As for the red eyes, if you'd played a ball game in the desert in 100 degrees of heat, your eyes would be red too."
>
> Dark added: "My eyes were red, and I've never had a drink in my life."

This didn't go over all that hot at home either. Of the three players, two—Schmidt and Jim Davenport—were established Giants, held over from the Tom Sheehan regime of the previous season, while the third was the newly acquired Harvey Kuenn. Thus the *Chronicle* ran a lead editorial wondering whether Jack Daniel would be in Dark's opening-day lineup, with an accompanying cartoon showing Kuenn being welcomed to the club— the boozers' club.

Dark publicly announced he was taking no disciplinary action against the players. In private, he fined them $100 each— as much to protect his scale of fines for lesser offenses as to pass judgment on this one. He was in all ways the thinking man's manager, and firmness of purpose went with it. As the attorney for the accused, Begam was permitted to go upstairs with the turnkey that night at the jail, to confer with his clients in the tank, and when he came back down he took me to one side. "There's a small problem," he said.

"Don't you think you can get them out?"

"I'm not sure they *want* to get out. They heard their manager was downstairs, and I think they'd just as soon stay where they are."

On the field or off, Dark was a caution in the way he managed (overmanaged, to use his own admitted word for it). He was the first to popularize the stunt of bringing in a relief pitcher to issue an intentional base on balls—something the layman might suppose the outgoing pitcher might have done as well, if not better (since a relief pitcher is supposed to come in throwing strikes). What Dark was doing here was making full use of the rule that says a pitcher must face at least one batter. Thus, if the other team resorted to pinch hitters, Dark's new man could himself be replaced by someone else without having to risk pitching to an unexpectedly dangerous batsman.

In truth, little if anything went overlooked. It is traditional, and makes all kinds of geographical common sense, for a team's bullpen to be on the same side of the field as its dugout. But at Candlestick, where the Giants occupied the first-base dugout, Dark used the bullpen in *left field* for his relief corps. That way they would always be in his view, and unlike the bullpen in right field, the one in left field had no handy doorway leading underneath the stands, where one might sneak a puff at a cigarette, gulp a needed beverage, or just plain get in out of the cold. It was noted, too, that Dark shipped one of his pitchers home a day early as the Giants wound up their first road trip of the season. "It's for his stamina," Dark explained to me, "so he won't be a *dis*grace when he opens up the home stand for us. He's married. This way he can get his screwing in a day early."

Thrown out of a game by an umpire, Dark would later tell the press, "I said un-Christianlike things to him." In a following season, he actually called a clubhouse meeting to discuss his extramarital life. As a number of his players and coaches described it to me later, it was one of the strangest clubhouse meetings they ever attended; but they were in the minority. More typically, most of the players were either apathetic to Dark's presentation or simply slept through it. Nor was the response all that great the night the Giants blew a game to the Phillies, when Dark in his post-game fury threw a stool across the clubhouse, oblivious—till he saw the blood—to the fact that the stool had taken a sizable piece of one of his fingers with it. Manager or no manager, that Giant team was something else. When I covered the 1961 World Series—the Giants weren't in it; this one was between the Yankees and the Reds—I wandered into the Cincinnati clubhouse at Yankee Stadium and saw the walls papered and festooned from end to end with floral arrangements and telegrams and messages from well-wishers. The following year I wandered into that same visiting-team dressing room at Yankee Stadium—this time the Giants were in it—and the walls were bare. The only visible message was one chalked on a blackboard by the Yankee management. WALK ON THE MATS, it said.

This of course did not indicate any absence of fan support for the team. It was just that the Giants did not regard themselves as a club that needed to decorate its clubhouse with get-well cards. From the instant I began to cover the team in 1961, when Dark came aboard as manager, they gave off the unmistakable scent of ingrained professionalism. And they had a pretty good professional to work off of: the one in center field.

In 1961, watching Mays day in, day out, was a revelation even for me. "I knew he was the greatest in the business even before I came over from the American League," Harvey Kuenn told me. "But actually *playing* with him, it opened up new things I never would have believed."

Poetically enough, it was in game number 1,234 of his big

league career, on April 30, 1961, that Mays hit four home runs in a single game. It happened at Milwaukee, and there is a strange background to it. On that road trip Dark had decided to room Mays with McCovey, in the hope that Mays's abstemious habits would prove a healthful influence. The health went the other way. McCovey brought some take-out spareribs to the hotel room for a late snack, and they made Mays actively sick to his stomach.

He was, by his own admission, weak as a cat before the game the following day, and more than that, he was disconsolate. His hitting was off. I sat down next to him in front of his locker.

"You writing I'm in a slump?" he asked.

"Not the way you put it, no."

"Everybody else is."

"No, they're not."

"I'll come out of it," Mays said. "I always do."

"You'll come out of it faster," I said, "if you stop thinking you're in it to begin with."

Willie thought that was funny.

"I mean it," I said. "The worst thing about your streaks is you think they've got to happen. You go oh-for-six, you say to yourself, 'I'm in a streak. I won't get a hit the next fifteen times at bat.' There's no law says this has to be this way. You make them worse by talking yourself into them."

"I know, I know," he said, and the way he said it gave me the unnerving impression he suddenly felt he had to cheer *me* up. But then, out of nowhere, he said to me, "What do you do when *you* get in a slump?"

"Well, I'll be a son of a bitch," I said.

"Well?" he said. "What do you do?"

"I never have slumps."

"Bullshit," Mays said, and for the first time he laughed, a high cascade of laughter. "I read you. I know you get your slumps, same's the rest of us."

"Sooner or later I come out of it," I said. "That's the best I can tell you. I don't know how."

"Same with me," he said. "Quit worrying, I'll get me four hits in a game and be right back up there. Don't you worry about nothing."

"Damn it, *I'm* not worrying," I said. "You make me sound like *I* got to go up there and hit Burdette today. *I* know you're going to come out of it. And you'll come out of it faster when you quit eating ribs at midnight, that's all."

He was laughing again as I stalked away. "Don't go 'way mad," he called after me. And went out and hit four home runs in one game, becoming the seventh man in history to do so in a nine-inning game (two others did it in extra innings).

I've kicked myself from that day to this for missing what has to be one of the two or three most delightful pieces of baseball trivia of all time. Of the players who hit four home runs in one game, three were contemporaries of Willie's: Gil Hodges, who hit his four in 1950; Joe Adcock, who got his in 1954; and Rocky Colavito, in 1959. Trivia question: What one player was present on all three occasions? Answer: Billy Loes. He was a right-hander with something of the reputation of an eccentric, being among other things the only pitcher who ever lost a ground ball in the sun, and he was with the Dodgers when Hodges had his four-homer day for them; again with the Dodgers when Adcock had his against them; and with the Orioles when Colavito had his against them.

A nice side touch. But stretching it a bit to tie it in with the Mays occasion in 1961? Not exactly. The winning pitcher for the Giants when Willie hit his four homers against Milwaukee? None other than Billy Loes. He had been present on all four occasions in baseball's modern era when somebody hit four home runs in a nine-inning game, yet the fact went unnoticed at the time. "Why didn't you say something?" I asked him, weeks later. He had the perfect answer: "Nobody asked me."

Loes did attract some attention in the press on another pitching occasion in Milwaukee in 1961 when he suddenly strode off the mound, handed the ball and his glove to the home plate umpire, and told him, "Here, you pitch." ("I came running off the bench to keep the umpire from throwing him out," Dark said. "By the time I got there he'd thrown himself out.") And another silent record-setter the day Mays hit the four homers had to be Giant shortstop José Pagan. (Dark called him *Pa*gan.) In the same game that Mays hit four homers, Pagan, for the one and only time in his career, hit two. Understandably, the feat did not receive the notice it deserved.

After the game, photographers posed Mays holding four baseballs. In one hand.

Later in the season, Willie got three home runs in one game, this time at Philadelphia, and the total of seven homers in two games in a single season is among the trunkful of miscellaneous major league records he established during his career. (In 1963 he would again hit three homers in a game, but that is not close to a record. In a space of 13 seasons, Johnny Mize hit three home runs in a game six different times!)

Philadelphia was a home away from home for the Giants in 1961. They won nine of the eleven games they played there, and with the Mets still a year away from their New York debut and the Phillies going nowhere, the crowds at Shibe Park owed not only their totals but their loyalties to Giant fans who rode the Pennsy down from New York and cheered louder, it often seemed, than the spectators at Candlestick.

"What do you do in this town?" Chuck Hiller, the Giants' rookie second baseman, asked me on the first of our four visits there. "I don't know what anybody else does," I said. "If you're asking me what I do, I go to a place called the Thirtieth Street station and get on anything that moves." And I did make several trips to New York from Philadelphia, feasible for the fact that all except Sunday games in Philadelphia were played at night. That was a plus, but it had its minus side, too: Sundays were getaway days, meaning we would leave directly from the ball park for the airport; all other games being night games, there was never a chance for a decent dinner. One night game was called off because of rain, early enough in the afternoon to make a plan. I picked up the phone in my hotel room and called Russ Hodges, whose room was down the hall. His line was busy, so I decided to walk down the hall to his room. Actually, we met halfway.

"I was trying to get you," he said.

"I was trying to get *you*."

"Old Bookbinder's?"

"Old Bookbinder's."

Remarkable within this dialogue was not just its simultaneity but the sotto voce quality, the conspiracy of two monks breaking the vows of silence in some dank abbey corridor probably not all that dissimilar to the hallways at the Warwick. And dine at Old Bookbinder's we did that night, on clams on the half shell, then steamers, then two-pound lobsters, cackling to each other all the while that San Francisco had no restaurant to match this one. The appraisal may not have been inaccurate. For all its fame as an eating town, San Francisco had its bare spots. It lacked a class-I steakhouse, and its ethnic places were like the climate at Candlestick: unusual, invigorating, and not quite the world-beaters the natives wanted the world to suppose. It was instructive to watch "Mr. San Francisco," a real estate baron named Louis Lurie—father of the future Giants president Robert Lurie—hosting his daily celebrity round table at Jack's on Sacramento Street, where unfailingly he urged the two local specialties, Rex sole and Dungeness crab, upon the visiting notables among his guests. One time, though, he invited my wife and me to his penthouse apartment atop the Mark Hopkins for dinner with actress Rosalind Russell and her husband Frederic Brisson, in celebration of their wedding anniversary. Here Lurie wore his private face. We got Dover sole and Maine lobster.

In fact the best dining in town was the private kind. In later years, an invitation to eat at Willie Mays's home in Atherton, some forty minutes' drive south of San Francisco in posh suburban surroundings, was highly prized. Supervising in the kitchen was his Aunt Ernestine, who had helped raise Willie from his birth, when she was only nine. In that four-room frame house in Westfield, Alabama—three bedrooms and kitchen, coal stove, wood-burning fireplace, privy out back—the first consideration was for food.

A neighbor in Westfield wet-nursed Willie when he was new-born. "We didn't have three cent to buy a can of milk," Ernestine has recalled. "That's what it cost then, three cent, for a small can. So really, we didn't know what to do. So there was a lady living next door to us. But she had a baby the age of Willie, and we would go over next door, me and my other sister and my brother, and take Junior over and tell Mrs. Josephine, that was her name. She would let him nurse her breast, so that he would get some fresh milk, sweet milk."

Willie's father and mother had parted, though both lived nearby, and Mays, Sr.—Kitty Kat—contributed what he could when he could to his son's care. As in many places hit by the Depression (and in white communities no less than black) children in the same family might live apart from each other and from their parents. Where there was food and a bed for one, you settled for that, then made other arrangements elsewhere. The sleeping population in Willie's house when he was born included other children—cousins and the like, and his two aunts, the nine-year-old Ernestine and the twelve-year-old Sarah—and one adult male, a demi-relative named Otis Brooks, known to all as Uncle Otis, who worked with Kitty Kat at the TC&I steel mill. Uncle Otis and Willie shared the same bed for several years until the morning Willie awoke, found himself in the strangely cold grasp of the man's arms, and realized Otis had died in his sleep.

Otis and Kitty Kat worked at the mill—when there was work. If there was, the pay was $2.60 a day. If there wasn't, they would "catch heel"—scrounge elsewhere for any odd jobs they could find. Westfield and Fairfield were company towns, and the steel mill would issue scrip money for use at the company store, then withhold it from wages any time work became available again. It was a prescription both for survival and indenture. The extra money Kitty Kat could pick up in season for playing baseball went to buy clothes for his son. But the food was the province of aunts Ernestine and Sarah. Out front were the flowers—they were proud of their flowers. But on back was their garden: green beans, peas, corn, tomatoes, squash—fresh in summer, home-canned for winter. They would trade off with neighbors for chicken and eggs, and make vegetable soup with a stock of lean beef bones—"old back bones"—as its base. They baked their own bread and rolls. From time to time there might be ham, liver, pork chops. One neighbor had a cow, and Willie was one of a group of boys who got to tend to it; the reward would be a slab of fresh-churned sweet butter. And Aunt Ernestine had her own churn. In it would go a mix of peaches, yeast, malt, raw "ice (white) potatoes" and raisins. She would let it set for a number of days, then strain it, bottle it, and cap it. The fermented result was not moonshine whiskey (known locally as "long tong") but an utterly magnificent peach brandy. It is no mistake that the world's greatest cuisines all stem from poverty. It is no mistake that the greatest native-American eating town in the United States is New Orleans, with its abundance of "poor people's" food. And it is no mistake that the senior master chefs of New Orleans are, almost without exception, all black.

TWO or three times during the 1961 season, Mays joined me in the daytime escape from Philadelphia. The most plausible way was via the Pennsylvania Railroad, but on one occasion we drove it in a rented car, with Bob Stevens of the *Chronicle* along. Mays drove on the way up to New York, I on the way back while Willie slept, slumped in the front passenger seat. It was an eerie experience. Face to face, Mays commanded instant recognition. But little more than his forehead was visible to passing motorists on the New Jersey Turnpike as we motored back to Philadelphia for that night's game. Yet cars to left and right of us were damn near going off the road, their occupants waving and whistling at the sleeping scalp. I have no way of being sure that the alchemy of charisma bears fruitful analysis. General Lee had it and General Grant didn't. Mays and Babe Ruth had it. Henry Aaron and Stan Musial didn't. For a Mays or a Ruth, the unpublicized hospital visit went beyond the ordinary straight-arrow virtue of not seeking to make headlines out of such occasions; it was the only way they would get out of the hospitals in one piece. Not just other patients, but storming doctors and nurses abandoning their posts to waylay Willie or the Babe, could and in fact did trap Mays or Ruth in a frightening hornet swarm. Both men in their careers gained a peculiar distinction: they were known to promise to appear at some event or other, then not show up. Both gained reputations therefore for being glib, forgetful, and uncaring. The truth may have been a shade more complex, for inevitably those who had most cause to complain over such treatment were those with no cause to fear rupture of their own privacy. To me, a lasting wonder in Babe Ruth is not how many appointments he failed to keep, but how many he did keep. Was it a case of being virtuous that Ulysses S. Grant kept his appointments, or was it that he was Ulysses S. Grant?

Findings and observations such as these, when reported for a Mays, a Ruth, or any other baseball luminary, are subject to one exception: the case of pitcher Leroy (Satchel) Paige. Majors, minors, black league, semi-pro, barnstorming, in some posted appearances even *à deux* (himself and catcher; no infielders or outfielders), Paige probably pitched more games than either Ruth or Mays *played*. He too did not always keep appointments, including in his case some at the ball park on days when he was scheduled to pitch, but according to the best information he showed up often enough to record more than 2,000 pitching victories. He too was charismatic: when he reached the majors in 1948, the crowd that turned out to witness his first start totaled 78,382. In the net (excluding the repeaters that make up the overwhelming majority of any baseball audience) he may well have drawn more viewers than Mays. These things may never be known for sure. In one new town, Paige was recognized instantly by a cab driver, with one reservation: "I know you're Satchel Paige," the driver said, "except that by now I also know he's dead."

According to Paige, he was born in 1908; according to his draft card, 1906; according to his mother, 1903; according to a careful biographer, Richard Donovan, perhaps 1900. In 1965, Paige started a game for the Kansas City Athletics, pitched three complete innings, allowed one hit and no runs, struck out one, walked no one. This was seventeen years after his major league debut with the Cleveland Indians, at which time many regarded him as too old. "Many well-wishers of baseball emphatically fail to see eye to eye with the signing of Satchel Paige, superannuated Negro pitcher," wrote publisher J. G. Taylor Spink of baseball's trade journal, *The Sporting News*, on that 1948 occasion. "To bring in a pitching rookie of Paige's age is to demean the standards of baseball in the big circuits." ("I demeaned the big circuits considerable," Paige reflected at season's end. "Win 6, lose 1.") What was demeaned was the reputation of big-circuit batsmen swinging too soon at Paige's famous "hesitation pitch," an offering delivered at unpredictable intervals and consisting of a wind-up and follow-through completely normal in all respects save for the release of the ball, which might come as much as a full second later, like an afterthought.

In 1951, Paige was a guest of the Second International Gerontological Congress, being held in St. Louis. Of this, Richard Donovan wrote:

Paige was almost as interested in the gerontologists as they were in him. The doctors had gathered to report on their studies of the effects of age upon the human body. "They heard there was a man ninety years old playing major-league baseball in the United States," says Paige, "so, naturally, we had to meet."

The doctors interested Paige because he had the impression

that only one of them spoke English. "They was all from Venice (Vienna)," he explains. Everything about Paige interested the doctors—his legs, which resemble golf-club shafts, his great feet, his stringy chest and neck muscles. When they got to his right arm, there was acclaim and astonishment.

"Most of you could be between thirty-five and fifty-five," translated the English-speaking doctor, tensely, "but your arm"—the doctor hesitated—"your arm doesn't seem to be a day over nineteen."

"I just explained to the gentlemen," Paige says, "that the bones running up from my wrist, the fibius, which is the upper bone, and the tiberon, which is the lower bone, was bent out, making more room for my throwing muscles to move around in there. I attributed most of my long life, and so on and so forth, to them two bones. The gentlemen was amazed to hear about that."

In his article about Paige in *Collier's*, Donovan also set down what may be Satchel's most enduring legacy: his six rules for How to Stay Young:

1. Avoid fried meats which angry up the blood.
2. If your stomach disputes you, lie down and pacify it with cool thoughts.
3. Keep the juices flowing by jangling around gently as you move.
4. Go very light on the vices, such as carrying on in society. The social ramble ain't restful.
5. Avoid running at all times.
6. Don't look back. Something might be gaining on you.

In consideration of the Mays/Ruth package, the thought occurs that the Babe went his entire adult lifetime in open violation of Nos. 1 and 4, while Mays ignored No. 5—vividly so at times. The day we drove from Philadelphia to New York and back, in 1961, was the day before his thirtieth birthday. At that night's game at Connie Mack Stadium, Willie scored from first on a single to left. And there was another time that season, this one at Cincinnati, when, with the score 0–0 in the top of the seventh, the Giants had one out, bases loaded, and Ed Bailey at bat. Bailey grounded to Cincinnati first baseman Gordon Coleman, who stepped on first, then threw home. That meant there were now two out, but it also took the force off the play at the plate, so the catcher had to tag the Giant runner coming from third. Of Coleman's decision to touch first base before throwing home, I wrote:

> This was clearly the right play—unless you want to say that catcher Jerry Zimmerman had caught only a dozen games in his major-league lifetime, and that the greatest baserunner in the game was bearing down on him. And here in the seventh inning of a scoreless tie, you were choosing a tag play on Mays instead of the simple force.

Branch Rickey is quoted earlier here as to how Mays could hit a catcher. In Zimmerman's case, the visual memory I retain is that he exploded upon contact. The ball, the glove, the mask, and several pieces of Zimmerman appeared to disassemble in midair, like the cat in a Looney Tunes cartoon. By the time things fell back to earth, Mays had scored, a teammate had scored, and a third Giant was on third base, whence he would score a moment later.

(One of Willie's all-time favorite scoring plays at the plate was a non-play. The pitcher was Don Sutton of the Dodgers, who had hit Willie with a pitch that Mays took to be deliberately aimed. Willie now stole second, then took third daringly on a ground out. Now Sutton unleashed a wild pitch and came in to cover the plate as Mays tore home. But four feet away from his goal, Sutton stopped short. The ball and Mays arrived at home together, and both continued on, Mays into the dugout and the ball into the infield. Sutton had decided he wanted no part of this.)

All told, for Mays aficionados, 1961 had to be a vintage year. There were the home runs and the base running. There were the throws, including one that got Maury Wills trying to score, the ball so placed in catcher Tom Haller's mitt from 300 feet away that it did not even matter how soon it got there, since Wills had no way to get around Haller and touch the plate in any event. And there were the catches you remembered seeing

—not to mention two you never saw. One of these was not a catch at all. With men on second and third and two out, Mays rushed in from his center-field position (as it was, he played the closest center-field since Tris Speaker) and with a graceful somersault nabbed a sinking line drive off the grass and jogged on into the dugout with the ball held aloft as the umpire signaled the third out. "I knew he trapped it instead of catching it," rival manager Jimmy Dykes said afterward. "I said so to the umpire, and he told me, 'If he trapped it, it's still the best play you've seen all year, so forget it.'"

The other catch no one saw went to the matter of Willie's peripheral vision. The Mays career was astonishing for how few were the times he collided with outfield walls or fellow fielders. Sometimes he literally seemed to wrap himself around other bodies without touching them, like the dancing laser-beam ghosts in the Haunted Mansion ride at Disneyland. He did this to Bobby Bonds in a network-telecast game at Candlestick one time, running simultaneously against Bonds and the fence without appearing to touch either, and it has become one of the great action shots of baseball's film archives. But there was no telecast of the game of May 13, 1961, when Charlie Lau came to bat at Candlestick for the Milwaukee Braves. This was with two out and bases empty in the ninth, with the Giants ahead 8–5. Here Lau put up a little pop fly back of second base. Chuck Hiller went charging out for it; Mays came charging in. Hiller had the bead on it, but it seemed the two men must collide. Then in the final instant Mays performed a sudden and entire counter-clockwise turn around Hiller as the latter reached up for the ball. And, knowing the catch had been made, Willie—never having touched Hiller though they came within a feather's breadth of a grinding and perhaps disabling collision—simply continued on his way, exited the arena through the right-field bullpen door, and went to have his post-game shower.

Hiller remained, marveling at the near miss. Then it occurred to him to show the ball to the nearest umpire, Dusty Boggess, so the latter could complete the formality of calling the final out. So Hiller turned to display the ball. Boggess looked. Hiller looked. Nothing. The two of them now began examining the ground. Nothing.

"Where's the game ball?" Boggess said.

"I'm sure I caught it," Hiller said. "It's got to be around here someplace."

As noted, there was no telecast of that game, but photographer Charlie Doherty of the *Examiner* did record stop-action stills of the final play. The last one in the sequence shows Hiller, convinced he had made the catch, staring open-mouthed at his empty glove. The one before that shows Mays completing his turn around Hiller, his glove held at such an angle that one cannot glimpse its contents. The only giveaway is the onset of a lovely smile on Willie's face.

Hitting . . . running . . . fielding . . . yet the play that first made a believer out of Harvey Kuenn came earliest of all, in spring training, and it belonged to none of those categories. With Kuenn on first base and Mays at bat, manager Dark flashed the hit-and-run sign, only to see Mays knocked down by the next pitch. He tumbled flat on his back but somehow, in the act, his bat was still protecting the runner. The ball shot on a searing, low line all the way to the left-field wall. "He hits it while he's lying on his back in the dirt and I score from first base," Kuenn said later. "I didn't know whether to laugh, shit, or go blind."

———◆———

Early in the summer of 1962, Senator Barry Goldwater of Arizona wrote a piece for *Look* magazine predicting a conservative sweep in the Congressional elections in November. One thing about Goldwater's predictions was that you never had to worry whether he spoke from conviction or political necessity: he turned out just as wrong either way.

The year before, there had been 2,525 attacks on New York police. Robert F. Kennedy, U.S. attorney general, said, "What's wrong with the two-dollar bet? That frequently raised question might just as well read: 'What's wrong with a multimillion-dollar narcotics ring, or widespread prostitution, or a corrupt mayor?' The two-dollar bet is the key to all these evils, for it bankrolls the underworld." A picture essay in *Look* had this introduction:

> The most famous baby boy in America, with the possible exception of Caroline Kennedy's little brother, is John Clark Gable of Encino, Calif., the son of the late Clark Gable. Born four months after the death of the movie actor, the baby immediately inherited the admiration that a worldwide public held for his famous father.

On the fashionable south shore of Long Island, two-bedroom oceanfront condominium apartments were selling for $7,900. EVEN IF YOU DON'T GO IN THE WATER . . . THE BEACH CAN BE FUN read the skyline of a Tampax ad. "Seeing the Bahamas through blue-colored glasses," said *Look* in another article,

> girl picks up lush reflection of Paradise Island, a palmy new resort.
> . . . Against summer's brilliant sky and sparkling waters, blue is a natural. This season, there is a rebirth of the blues in clothes for both men and women. The new, refreshing range in the coolest of all colors runs from pale azure to deep navy. As shown here and on the following five pages, there are day blues for sunning, swimming and sailing; night blues for romancing—fashion's reflections of the brilliant blues of tropical sky and sea. Below, arriving at Paradise on the clipper launch from Nassau, girl meets boy. She wears ultrafeminine powder blue: tapered pants of needlepoint cotton; back-buttoned overblouse with lace-trimmed border (Lanz, $29). He mixes stronger tones: striped-cotton sport shirt (Izod, $10) with gendarme-blue walk shorts (Corbin, $17).
>
> LOOK comments: Co-ed blues are risky. A quarrel may have you seeing red by August.

"And now," said a Metrecal advertisement, "the chocolate wafer . . . nine make a 225-calorie meal." "Don't look for a small-size Chrysler—we don't make any jr. editions: a fact that protects your pride and your resale value." "SPECIAL OFFER—get a genuine $3.00 Airguide Outdoor Thermometer for only $1.50! Tear out this ad. Attach to coupon in each package of Duofold underwear you buy. Mail with check to Duofold."

In Washington, D.C., Irv Lichtenstein, the program director of radio station WWDC, sent a letter to Nikita Khrushchev, proposing a cultural exchange of popular hit tunes as a means to thaw the cold war. To Lichtenstein's astonishment, back came a tape from Moscow with the Soviet Union's Top Ten: "Pear Tree," "Evening Bells," "The Broad and Rolling Steppe," "From a Far-off Land," "All Alone I Stood in the Road," "Do Not Blame Me—Do Not Scold Me," "At the Smithy," "Will I, Won't I?" and two others the WWDC translator could not make out. In return, Lichtenstein mailed back America's Top Ten: "King of the Whole Wide World," "I Remember You," "What Kind of Fool Am I?," "You Don't Know Me"—so far so good, but then: "Ramblin' Rose," "Alley Cat," "You Lie to Me," "If I Had a Hammer," "You Beat Me to the Punch," and "Monster Mash." In line with this was a cold-war joke of the time: the Soviets had placed an order with the Du Pont Company for 20 million condoms, each to be 14 inches in length. Nervously, Du Pont took it up with the State Department. Back came the decision: fill the order, but stamp them *U.S. Medium.* Meanwhile a lengthy piece appeared in *The New Yorker* called "Letter from a Region of My Mind." The article was the work of a Negro author named James Baldwin. "The price of the liberation of the white people is the liberation of the blacks," he argued. "The total liberation, in the cities, in the towns, before the law, and in the mind." He ended his piece with the words of an age-old spiritual:

God gave Noah the rainbow sign.
No more water, the fire next time!

Another spiritual was surfacing too. In the minds of most Americans the words kept repeating the phrase "We Shall Overcome," but the real words were those of an old Baptist hymn:

We shall stand together, we shall stand together,
We shall stand together—now.
Oh, deep in my heart I do believe
We shall overcome some day.

"Why don't you settle back and have a full-flavored smoke? . . ." asked the Marlboro ad. "More body in the blend, more flavor in the smoke, more taste through the filter," argued L&M. And: FIRESTONE WINS AGAIN . . . 39TH STRAIGHT VICTORY IN "500" CLASSIC!

———◦●◦———

Willie Mays led the National League in runs scored in 1961. Most of that season, as for most of his career, he batted third in the lineup, as did so many other champion-class hitters, like Ruth and Williams. (No other spot in the batting order so maximizes the combined potential for runners to drive in and hitters to drive you in.) It is fascinating how near-equal will be the great hitters' totals for runs scored and batted in. For Mays over his major league career, he would score 2,062, bat in 1,903. For Stan Musial, who like Mays played 22 seasons, the totals were 1,949 and 1,951! Babe Ruth, also in 22 seasons, drove in just 42 runs more than he scored, Ted Williams 41. With numbers so equal as those, is it fantasizing to point out that among these four all-time batting greats Mays was the only one who scored more runs than he batted in? Possibly not, for in Willie's case there was the extra dimension in run-scoring: he stole 113 more bases than Ruth, Musial, and Williams combined! . . . *Statistics:* I can hear Abe Kemp snarling the word, yet the fact obtains that among the game's top sluggers, Willie's 1:2 ratio of stolen bases: home runs is unique.

Having earned $85,000 in 1961, Mays went to $90,000 in 1962 and in 1963 became the highest-salaried player in history at $105,000. (Shortly after he signed at that figure, Mickey Mantle signed with the Yankees for $100,000, and columnist Jimmy Cannon wrote that Mantle actually had signed first for his $100,-000 and Horace Stoneham gave Mays $105,000 only to top the Yankees and keep Mantle from being known as the game's first $100,000 player. Cannon's timetable was wrong, but that would be moot, because his history was wrong too. Fifteen years earlier, in 1948, Joe DiMaggio had signed for $100,000. And from the standpoint of greatest purchasing power and least taxation, none of the above came close to Babe Ruth's $80,000 in the depths of the Depression. Told this would pay him more than President Hoover was earning, Ruth got off his deathless line: "I had a better year than he did.")

What can be said is that the Mays and Mantle raises in 1963 had to be honestly come by, since both had keyed their clubs into the World Series of 1962. Willie's work was especially vivid: he led his league in home runs with 49 and had career-high totals of 130 runs scored and 141 batted in. In winning, the Giants provided the National League with its fifth different league champion in as many years, and it was to be the Giants' only pennant in the fourteen seasons Mays was with them on the Coast. (The league broke into two divisions in 1969, and the Giants won their division in 1971, but then lost to Pittsburgh in the pennant playoff.) Mantle with the Yankees, on the other hand, was with a team that won 12 pennants during his career. Was a Mantle more important to his team's success than a Mays to his team's success? In his book *A Thinking Man's Guide to Baseball*, Leonard Koppett took up the question:

> Only a handful of players, in all baseball history, have been as important to winning teams, and have been able to contribute as much to eventual victory, rather than statistics, as Mickey Mantle.
>
> Willie, on the other hand, I can sum up very simply: he's the best baseball player I ever saw.

"The Great Debate," Koppett labeled that chapter in his book. Interestingly, it had by then replaced the earlier Great Debate, involving Mantle's predecessor Joe DiMaggio vs. Mays. A part of this shift could be attributed to the passage of the years: 1962 was the Giants' fifth season in San Francisco, and inevitably passions for Lefty O'Doul and the old Seals would begin to spend themselves and recede into history. Another fact was that after five years of seeing what Mays could do, a number of locals began to agree that the center fielder from New York rather did know how to play this game. And another fact joined the testimonials. One such came from Tommy Henrich, who'd played right field alongside DiMaggio with the Yankees and who later became a Giant coach and saw Willie make one of his fabled catches off Roberto Clemente in a game at Pittsburgh. Inevitably, Henrich was asked if DiMaggio could have made the same play. His answer was a study. "I think," he said slowly, "that DiMag *might* have covered that same distance in the same amount of time, and *might* have got a glove on the ball." He took a deep breath. "But he couldn't have caught it." And in 1962, another of DiMaggio's ex-teammates—Joe Gordon, a longtime favorite among Coast fans—spoke at a banquet and found himself being asked The Question: DiMaggio or Mays, who was the greatest he ever saw? "You're not going to like this," Gordon said flat-out, "but the greatest player I ever saw is Willie Mays."

(Not to be overlooked here is that San Francisco's memories of DiMaggio were memories of the great Yankee dynasty of the late thirties, and that was a Yankee team that had other San Franciscans in its lineup as well, like the sterling second base–shortstop combination of Tony Lazzeri and Frankie Crosetti. Another front-line Yankee of those days, pitcher Lefty Gomez was from the town of Rodeo, just across the Bay. Understandably, San Franciscans viewed those Yankees not just as Di-Maggio's team but as their team. On occasion, the view got house support, such as the time Gomez was pitching in a bases-loaded situation and suddenly wheeled and threw the ball to Lazzeri, who was at his customary fielding post in between first and second. Puzzled, Lazzeri brought the ball back to the mound. "Why'd you do that?" he asked. Gomez shrugged. "I read a piece in the paper yesterday about how smart you were, so I wanted to see what *you'd* do."

(Now Gomez pitched out the inning successfully, and when he reached the bench Yankee manager Joe McCarthy asked him the same question Lazzeri had asked. This time Gomez had a different answer. "We've got so many San Francisco Italians on this team I got confused," he said. McCarthy stared at him. "You've got one in center field," he said. "Why didn't you throw it to him?")

If the Giants could not have won the pennant in 1962 without Mays, neither could they have won it without Billy Pierce, a lefthanded pitcher acquired from the White Sox in a midwinter trade, who had a won-and-lost record of 13-and-0 at Candlestick in 1962. The prevailing winds at Candlestick make it a good park for lefthanded pitchers, and Pierce got added help from the Giants' chief groundskeeper, Matty Schwab. Any time they played the Dodgers, Schwab would ostentatiously wet down the dirt area around first base—so much so that on more than one occasion the umpires ordered him to put sand on the man-made swamp—presumably to keep Dodger base stealer Maury Wills from getting a jump on the pitch. It made for headlines and controversy. What made for neither was Schwab's far more private exercise in wetting down the grass on the left side of the

infield hours before game time on days when Pierce was scheduled to pitch. This had the effect of slowing down ground balls
that righthanded batsmen would get off lefthanded pitching,
reducing the number of hits that would go through to the outfield.

All told, Pierce had 16 victories in 1962—Jack Sanford had 24,
Billy O'Dell 19, and Juan Marichal 18. One thanked God for a
Matty Schwab, for five other teams in the league had better
pitching, gauged by earned-run average. Lowest ERA on the
Giants belonged to Marichal, but his 3.36 was grievously above
his career figure. The Giant starting lineup had an infield of
Cepeda, Hiller, Pagan, and Davenport, an outfield of Felipe
Alou, Mays, and Kuenn, and the catching shared by Tom Haller
and Ed Bailey. Chief pinch hitters and part-time outfielders
were McCovey and Matty Alou. The leading relief pitcher was
Stu Miller, known as the killer moth, who threw change-ups
(slow balls) and nothing else. Miller was an interesting man.
Owner of a slew of master points, he was easily the best bridge
player in the in-flight game whose other participants were Dark,
Kuenn, and me, and he had other intellectual feats to his credit.
Once he threw a spitball to strike out Frank Bolling of the
Braves. The rules said anyone detected throwing a spitter would
be ejected from the contest. But Miller's pitch to Bolling was the
last pitch of the game. How do you eject a man from a game
that's already over?

The spectacle of the slight-built Miller pitching to the Dodgers' 6-foot-7, 250-pound behemoth Frank Howard was worth the
price of admission all by itself. Time and again, Howard would
miss connections, flailing at Miller's change-up like a housewife
attacking a hovering bumblebee with a broomstick. On one
memorable occasion, the confrontation took place with neither
man in the game. In a tight Dodger-Giant game, pinch hitter
Howard stood up in the Dodger dugout. Instantly, relief pitcher
Miller stood up in the Giant bullpen. Noting this, Howard sat

down again. Noting that, so did Miller. One time, he mentioned idly to Mays that he had been a catcher in high school. Mays was interested. "What'd you throw to second?" he asked. "The change?"

The 1962 Giants were noteworthy also for their complement of Spanish-speaking players: Marichal, Cepeda, Pagan, the two Alous. They were wont to jabber to one another in the native tongue, and this occasionally upset the enemy. One Cincinnati pitcher stepped off the mound, glared at Cepeda as the latter led off second base, and said, "Don't you know how to talk English?" "Kiss my ass, you cocksucker," Cepeda replied. "Is that English enough for you?"

The actual pennant race that year was theater-of-the-absurd. The Giants trailed the Dodgers by four games with seven left to play, lost two of those seven, and still wound up in a tie for first place. One of the games they lost featured a Willie Mays who wandered off third base, thinking three were out when it was only two, and got tagged. This points to the mythology that grows around any great ballplayer, to the extent that in memories, not just of the fans, but even his own ex-teammates, no one can ever recall his ever making a mistake. One point of interest here is the way the less two players got along, the more one would praise the other on his departure. Men who disliked Babe Ruth the most were the first to say they never saw him make a bad play. Casey Stengel, who managed Joe DiMaggio in the latter's final years, heaped the same praise on DiMag. Yet as Phil Rizzuto recalled for Maury Allen:

I think the real trouble with DiMaggio and Stengel happened when DiMaggio was hurting and playing this game. He was in center field and all of a sudden here comes Cliff Mapes. Stengel had decided to make a change and he didn't wait until DiMaggio was on the bench. He was going to take him right off the field. You can't do that to a great star like DiMaggio. He has too much pride. Mapes got to center field and DiMaggio waved him back to the dugout. "I'll tell Casey when I want to come out." Di-Maggio came to the bench when the inning was over and went right to the clubhouse without a word. I don't think they ever talked again.

One reads today that DiMaggio never had a hitting slump. I saw him in the course of one: he was something like 0-for-August, and finally beat out a hit to the shortstop. As he then took his lead off first, you could see his shoulders sag in relief. He took a deep breath, put his hands on his knees, and relaxed in the knowledge that the hitless streak was over. He was still standing that way when the pitcher threw over to first and picked him off.

Ruth had his times, too. He came to bat with two out in the last of the ninth in the seventh and final game of the 1926 World Series. The Yankees trailed the Cardinals 3–2. Bases were empty. Ruth walked. Now coming to bat in order were the other two .300 hitters in the Yankee lineup that year, Bob Meusel and Lou Gehrig. Meusel, from the batter's box, and Gehrig, from the on-deck circle, looked on transfixed as Ruth got it into his head to steal second base. He was out from here to breakfast and the Series was over.

As in the case of pitchers throwing record-setting home runs to hitters, baseball has an engaging way of making celebrities out of sinners. It goes back to Casey at the Bat, and includes the Merkles who forgot to touch second, the Snodgrasses who dropped the ball, the Peskys who held the ball instead of throwing it; the case of Babe Herman, who is supposed to have doubled into a triple play (in real life he tripled into a double play), and the well-remembered Smead Jolley, who once made three errors on the same play: playing left field at the old League Park in Cleveland, he let a hit go through his legs for an error; turning to play it off the wall, he saw the ball go through his legs again coming back; retrieving it finally, he threw it into the dugout. There was Gee Walker of the Tigers, who got picked off first so often he finally was ordered to take no lead at all, but simply to tap his foot repeatedly on the base as evidence of contact. Promptly the pitcher picked him off. "He got me between taps," Walker explained. One of my favorites involves a Mets outfielder named Don Hahn, who passed teammate Rusty Staub on the bases. Realizing his mistake, he doubled back and passed Staub again, this time going the other way. Momentarily crazed, the nearest umpire called him out twice. And there was the case of Ping Bodie, another San Francisco product whose true name was Francesco Stephano Pezzolo. Like Ruth in the 1926 Series, Bodie sometimes got it into his head to steal against the odds. "He had larceny in his heart," Bugs Baer wrote. "But his feet were honest."

It was not for any mistake he had made, however, that the San Francisco fans booed Willie Mays when he came to bat for the first time on the final day of the 1962 season. To force a playoff for the National League pennant that day, the Giants not only had to win over Houston; the Dodgers had to lose to St. Louis. The parlay was not a particularly bright one for San Franciscans, and they held Mays primarily responsible for it—not for the way he played, but the way he didn't.

(When he became Giant manager in 1961, Alvin Dark was told the San Francisco team had never won a game in which Mays did not play. Since the number of such occasions could be counted on the fingers of one hand, Dark professed not to take it seriously. "We'll be resting him from time to time," he said. "Willie comes on just that much stronger after he's had a day off."

(But as it turned out, Dark rested Mays only one game in all of 1961. "The point wasn't that Mays shouldn't be given a rest," *Examiner* sports editor Curley Grieve wrote after that game. "It just wasn't the right time or place." Actually it was mid-June, and Willie's arm was hurting. Doc Bowman diagnosed it as a cold that had settled in his shoulder. It happened in Milwaukee the night after the Giants had played an exhibition game against their farm team at Tacoma, and manager Dark had another theory: "I don't think there *is* anything wrong with his arm," he told Bob Stevens and me. "I could be wrong. What happened last night in Tacoma was that we had to play the regulars, because it's the one chance those people get to come out and see the big-league stars in the Giant organization. Anyway, Cepeda came out of the game before Willie did, and I think Willie noticed it. *He* had to stay in. He sees other players getting time off, and he isn't getting any."

(I said, "I don't think he'd quit."

("It's not a question of his quitting," Dark said. "He told me he'd play tonight if I wanted him to."

("But," Stevens said, "you said you didn't think there was anything wrong with his arm."

("It can hurt," Dark said, "without there being anything wrong with it."

(Such theorizing to one side, the record was kept intact: Mays didn't play that one game in Milwaukee in 1961, and the Giants didn't win.)

Again, in 1962, Dark renewed his pledge to rest Willie. By September 12, with the Giants at that point trailing the Dodgers by half a game in the standings, Mays had appeared in every game. That night, in the second inning of a game at Cincinnati, he collapsed in the dugout. He regained consciousness almost immediately, but an ambulance rushed him to the hospital. He was kept there for three days, under diagnosis of tension and exhaustion (the doctors found nothing clinically wrong). All three of those days, once again to keep the record intact, the Giants lost. Mays rejoined the team in Pittsburgh, and a wire service photo showed a miserable ballplayer hunched in a jacket. ACHING TO PLAY, the caption said. This was true, though it was a photo of the wrong man, a reserve outfielder named Carl Boles who bore considerable facial resemblance to Mays and who *was* aching to play.

Mays celebrated his return to the lineup the following day with a game-tying three-run homer, and the team was to come out of its spin. But it had lost precious ground to the Dodgers, and once again manager Dark may have had a private reservation or two about the non-playing Mays. Asked when Willie would re-enter the lineup, he said cryptically, "When he says he's ready." And far less private were the rumors printed in the San Francisco papers. One said Mays had had a heart attack, another an epileptic seizure, another that he was an alcoholic, another—cited by the city's leading columnist, Herb Caen of the *Chronicle*—that he had been punched by a teammate.

So the large Candlestick crowd for the season's last day, September 30, 1962—a crowd grown all the larger for the fact that it was Fan Appreciation Day and the Giants were giving away five automobiles and other prizes—vented the baseball portion of its interest by booing Willie when he came to bat in the first inning. In his first at-bat on opening day that year, Mays had hit Warren Spahn's first pitch, as of yore, for a home run. As he had done with his first pitch of the regular season, so today would he do with his last, slamming a long drive into the left-field seats off Turk Farrell in the eighth inning to break a 1–1 tie and bring his team a 2–1 victory.

The boos changed to cheers, mingled with new injections of hope supplied by the bulletins from Los Angeles, where the Dodgers and Cardinals were locked in a scoreless battle. Los Angeles was considered a good liberty town, and we heard that the Cards, on their final road swing with nothing at stake for themselves, were taking complete advantage of its attractions. One story said they were so drunk the catchers were calling audibles.

But at least they were loose, while the Dodgers—no reproduction of the Boys of Summer, that club—found it difficult to remember the last time they'd even scored a run. Pitching was their forte in any event, and their offense was geared to the stolen base and the odd run it might produce. Maury Wills stole 104 bases that year, and the league's runner-up in that category, with 32, was his own teammate, Willie Davis; the rest of the

Dodgers stole more bases than did any of four other entire *teams* in the league. There was some good hitting from Tommy Davis, the league batting champion, but he was the only Dodger over .300, and the demands on the club's pitching staff remained severe. On one occasion, Don Drysdale, having pitched and won the evening before, was enjoying a night off away from the ball park when a phone call reached him with the news that teammate Sandy Koufax had just pitched a no-hitter. "Did he win?" Drysdale asked.

The famine in runs was to cost the Dodgers a 1–0 loss to the Cardinals on the last day of the season and force a best-of-three Giant-Dodger playoff beginning in San Francisco the following day. In this one, with Mays homering twice, Billy Pierce pitched the Giants to an 8–0 triumph. And in the second game next day, held at Los Angeles, the Giants held a 5–0 lead going into the last of the sixth. At that point, the Dodgers, having now gone 35 innings without scoring, broke through for a 7-run inning and held on to win, 8–7. And so, eleven years to the day of the third playoff game between the two teams in New York in 1951, they met again in California to settle a near-identical playoff. Again, as before, the Giants had won the first game, the Dodgers the second. Again as before, the Giants would come up in the ninth inning trailing in the score, and it was almost the same score as before: 4–2 this time, as opposed to the 4–1 in 1951.

One difference was that this time the Giants were the visiting team, but all that meant was a difference in crowd noise—which in this case was no noise at all. The Giants, who had broken through for four runs in the ninth in 1951, would break through for four runs in the ninth again in 1962. But they managed it this time on only two hits, an inning-opening single by Matty Alou and a key single, ripped off the glove of pitcher Ed Roebuck, by Willie Mays.

Alou had been forced at second by Kuenn after his hit, but Willie McCovey walked, and so did Felipe Alou, loading the bases. Now came a moment that did distinguish 1962 from 1951.

The same Willie Mays who as a rookie was sick with fear he might have to come to bat now stood in the batter's box with bases loaded, coolly and characteristically tamping down the dirt with his left foot so he could dig in. So subdued were the Los Angeles fans that the nationwide television audience could hear the encouraging shouts of the Giants as they called Willie's name—a mini-babel in itself, since to his friends he had several names, used interchangeably. They called him Willie, and Will, and 24 (for his uniform number), and Buck (for Buckduck, his boyhood nickname, itself a transfiguration of "Duck-butt" . . . "He always had a high behind," his Aunt Ernestine explained). Now Roebuck threw and Buck-24-Willie-Will rifled a base hit up the middle for one run, leaving the Dodgers ahead 4–3, bases still loaded, still one out.

Los Angeles manager Walter Alston brought Stan Williams in to replace Roebuck and pitch to Orlando Cepeda, who flied to right field, scoring pinch runner Ernie Bowman from third after the catch to tie the score at 4–4. A wild pitch now put runners at second and third and dictated an intentional walk to Ed Bailey. And then, quite unintentionally, Williams walked Jim Davenport, forcing in Felipe Alou with the go-ahead run. Ron Perranoski replaced Williams, and a moment later Dodger second baseman Larry Burright kicked a ground ball and Mays scored to make it 6–4.

Billy Pierce came on to pitch the last of the ninth for the Giants, and got Maury Wills on a grounder and Jim Gilliam on a fly. Then pinch hitter Lee Walls hit a 1-and-1 pitch on a line into right center. The crowd yelped in sudden hope, but the Giant center fielder, moving to his left, struck the pocket of his glove with the fist of his right hand as he ran. With Mays that was a reflex signal meaning only one thing: no problem. "Minute I saw Buck pound that pood, I knew we were home," catcher Bailey said. Mays was waiting for the ball when it got there. He caught it chest high for the final out and then, in an unusual gesture of personal celebration, threw it into the right-field grandstand. (Throughout his career, Mays would eschew the hand slaps, hugs, and dancing that came more and more to characterize the joyous athletic moment. Not for him was it to spike the ball or boogie in somebody's end zone. His reserve was honestly come by, for even as early as 1962, at the age of thirty-one, he represented baseball's older generation. After just five seasons in San Francisco, he was the only Giant left from the team that had come west from New York, and to the rookies on the club, few if any of them old enough to remember *not* seeing his name in a big-league box score or the headlines trumpeting his accomplishments, he was known in simple logic as the old man.)

In the clubhouse following the pennant clincher, someone asked Mays why he had not used his basket catch on Walls's game-ending ball. Willie's high laugh was tinged with amazement at the question. "You crazy?" he responded. "That was $15,000 a man!" Now the Giants dressed and flew home to San Francisco, where a crowd of 75,000 overran the taxiways to make a shambles of airport traffic control. Delayed in landing, the Giants' plane finally got down and was shunted to a remote area where a couple of taxicabs and a bus awaited. Two or three in the traveling party, Mays included, made their getaway by cab, but the crowd caught up with the others and surrounded the bus. "We want Willie!" the people roared. "We want Willie!" Inside the bus, another reserve Giant outfielder, Bob Nieman, looked around uncomfortably. "For God's sake," he husked, "throw 'em Boles and let's get out of here!"

Downtown San Francisco was just as much a mess, wall to wall with celebrants, automobiles, church bells, horns, and firecrackers; and—precisely as had happened eleven years before—the ensuing World Series with the Yankees would prove to be an anticlimax. Again as in 1951, the chief emotional binge, and the most lasting memory, would be provided not by the Series but by the outcome of the playoff. Maybe Bobby Thomson's home run had the theatrical edge over four walks, a couple of singles, an error, and a sacrifice fly *(maybe?)*, but both times the Giants had turned defeat into victory with a four-run ninth in the final inning of the final playoff game, and when the Series began the following day it was difficult to care. The '62 Series was subject too to record prolongation. To two days of travel, add four of rain, and the thing lasted thirteen days. That includes the fact that it went the full seven-game distance and came down to the ninth inning of the final game, when with two out, the tying run on third, and the winning run on second, Willie McCovey smote a savage low liner only to see it picked off by the perfectly positioned Yankee second baseman, Bobby Richardson.

It was the rain that saved Alvin Dark from a second guess that would have been both virulent and rather unfair. The instant in point came in the fifth inning of the fourth game of the Series, at New York. Giant pitcher Juan Marichal was tooling along with a 2–0 lead at the time, having among other things struck out Mickey Mantle swinging twice in a row, and now was at bat with one out, teammates on first and third, and a count of two strikes. At this juncture, Dark signaled for a squeeze bunt—though if Marichal bunted foul, it would go as a strikeout. Marichal did bunt foul. Worse than that, the pitch struck the index finger of his pitching hand. But the Giants went on to win that game, and after that the rains did come, resting the other Giant pitchers so there was no call on the injured Marichal. The second guess never materialized.

Dark was a curio with Marichal and the other Latin players on the team. At one point he called Marichal the best pitcher he ever saw at protecting a lead in the late innings. At another, Marichal was motoring along with a 6–3 lead over the Dodgers. It was the top of the eighth inning. He had struck out pinch hitter Duke Snider on three straight pitches to end the Dodger seventh, and now started off the Dodger eighth by striking out Willie Davis. By this point in the game, he had struck out twelve men. Now Tommy Davis dribbled a ball to the left side and beat it out. Instantly Dark emerged from the dugout, waved to the bullpen for a relief pitcher, and strode to the mound.

Marichal could not believe it. "You taking me out?"

"Yes."

"Why?"

"Just to be safe. You may be tired."

"I strike out Snider and Davis. Is that being tired?"

"I want to make sure I win this one," Dark said. "You get credit for the win even if I take you out. And ain't no way you can be the losing pitcher. So don't complain."

(The Giants lost the game 8–7. Later the same season Dark staged an innovation, again with Marichal pitching. This time there was *no one* occupying the bullpen. "I just got tired of seeing my starting pitchers standing out there and looking for help," Dark explained.)

The baserunner setup for McCovey's Series-ending liner had been established by the previous hitter, who was Mays and who had doubled to right field with Matty Alou on first base. This completed a Mays trilogy that went as follows:

- Last game of regular season, 8th inning, Giants tied, none on, none out: Mays homered.
- Last game of playoff, 9th inning, Giants trailing 4–2, three on, one out: Mays singled.
- Last game of World Series, 9th inning, Giants trailing 1–0, one on, two out: Mays doubled.

(Extra-base hits tend to speak for themselves, but most vivid in my memory is the ninth-inning single off the pitcher's glove in the playoff at Los Angeles. I am not alone in this reminiscence. More than sixteen years afterward, veteran St. Louis sportswriter Bob Broeg, recollecting Willie's career, said that 1962 single was hit "as hard as I ever saw.")

Yet Mays had been booed when he first came to bat for the last game of the regular '62 season. A principal reason for that has already been reviewed here. A secondary reason was that he'd gone hitless the day before, while the Giants were splitting a doubleheader. And all the time, Alvin Dark was keeping a private "book" on his hitters. Mays, he announced after the season was over, was his best clutch hitter. But Cepeda was awful. He could not deliver in the clutch. *Look* magazine did a story on it, and Cepeda sued. The suit was unsuccessful. Yet in the ninth inning of the final playoff game at Los Angeles, Cepeda was the Giant who hit the ball the farthest—the long sacrifice fly that tied the game. I asked Mays privately what he thought of Dark's estimate of Cepeda. "Shit," Willie said, "a man hits .300 and bats in 100 runs, how you gonna say he can't hit?"

Mays himself conformed to no pattern. "I always start good," he explained to one reporter who sought an explanation of one hot early season. "I always start bad," he explained to another who sought an explanation of a cold one. One such cold one was 1963. Willie was swinging late, bailing out, popping up, striking out. I wandered into Dark's clubhouse office one noontime and found the manager in consultation with club vice-president Chub Feeney.

"Listen," Dark said to me. "When Willie had his physical this winter, did they check his eyes?"

"How do I know?" I said.

"It could be his eyesight," Feeney said.

"Why don't you ask him?"

"No," Feeney said. "You know how he is when he's not hitting. You can't get near him."

"We were thinking," Dark said helpfully, "that you and he being as close as you are . . ."

"Oh, fine," I said. "You want me to bell the cat."

"You could just mention it to him," Feeney said. "You know, just in passing."

"Kind of like an idle question," Dark said. "It's like that if it comes from you, it's not official. It's like that he won't know you've been talking to us."

"Sure he won't," I said, and went out through the tunnel to the field where the Giants were taking batting practice. I fell in alongside Mays at the cage. "Say, Buck," I said to him, "you notice how many players are wearing glasses this year?"

"Like who?" he said.

"Well," I said, "Howard—Frank Howard. He's got glasses."

"He ain't hittin' either," Mays said.

In the opinion of historian Arthur Schlesinger, President John F. Kennedy had "a terrible ambivalence about civil rights."

While he did not doubt the depth of the injustice or the need for remedy, he had read the arithmetic of the new Congress and concluded that there was no possible chance of passing a civil rights bill. Moreover, he had a wide range of presidential responsibilities; and a fight for civil rights would alienate southern support he needed for other purposes (including bills, like those for education and the increased minimum wage, of direct benefit to the Negro). And he feared that the inevitable defeat of a civil rights bill after debate and filibuster would heighten Negro resentment, drive the civil rights revolution to more drastic resorts and place a perhaps intolerable strain on the already fragile social fabric. He therefore settled on the strategy of executive action. No doubt wishing to avoid argument and disappointment, he did not even establish an interregnum task force on civil rights. . . .

In the winter of 1962–63 the civil rights leaders, more bent than ever on legislation, watched the success of the President's strategy with understandable frustration. Martin Luther King, Jr., sorrowfully described 1962 as "the year that civil rights was displaced as the dominant issue in domestic politics. . . . The issue no longer commanded the conscience of the nation." . . .

And more and more Negroes perceived these facts at a time when the sit-in demonstrators and the freedom riders and James

Meredith, Roy Wilkins and A. Philip Randolph and Martin Luther King, Jr., had given them a new pride in themselves and a new sense of the power of direct action. The southern penchant for mass jailing had been particularly helpful. "Words cannot express," King wrote, "the exultation felt by the individual as he finds himself, with hundreds of his fellows, behind prison bars for a cause he knows is just." The hoarded anger of generations, so long starved by despair, was now fed by hope.

The whites wondered why, when the Negroes had come so far, they pushed so hard. "For years now I have heard the word 'Wait!'," replied King. "It rings in the ear of every Negro with piercing familiarity. This 'Wait' has always meant 'Never.'" They could wait no longer: each year rotted away more of the Negro future. Boys and girls whose lives had been crippled by ten could not be easily redeemed at twenty. As John Howard Griffin, the white man who had disguised himself as a Negro and rendered an appalled report to his fellow white men in the book *Black Like Me*, asked, why should the Negro "allow his children to go on being dwarfed and deprived . . . so that the whites can indulge themselves in their prejudices for a little longer?" . . .

And now in April 1963 in Birmingham, Alabama, a new crisis was developing. Under the leadership of [King] the Negroes of Birmingham were launching a great campaign to end discrimination in shops, restaurants and employment. But sit-ins and marches were producing sharp retaliation. When King called for a protest march on Good Friday, April 12, Police Commissioner Eugene Connor obtained an injunction, harassed the marchers with police dogs and arrested King and other leaders. A new and more moderate city administration was about to take office, and the Attorney General three times counseled the Birmingham leaders not to force issues while Bull Connor was still in charge. But the movement by now had a momentum of its own. King told Robert Kennedy that the Negroes had waited one hundred years and could wait no longer. The demonstrations increased. So did the arrests. On May 2 about 500 Negroes, many of them high school students and younger, were hauled off to jail, some in school buses. The next day more students paraded. This time white bystanders threw bricks and bottles. The police turned fire hoses on the marchers, and Bull Connor released his growling police dogs. On Saturday, May 4, newspapers across the United States and around the world ran a shocking photograph of a police dog lunging at a Negro woman.

"In the name of the greatest people that have ever trod this earth," said the governor of Alabama, George C. Wallace, "I draw the line in the dust and toss the gauntlet before the feet of tyranny. And I say: Segregation now! Segregation tomorrow! Segregation forever!" Symbolically, he stood in the doorway of the University of Alabama to thwart the enrollment of two black students. A little more than symbolically, President Kennedy federalized the National Guard, and a brigadier general told Wallace to "please stand aside so that the order of the court may be accomplished." Not displeased at having made his point, Wallace stood aside. "For all the horrors of the American Negro's life," wrote James Baldwin in *The New Yorker*, "there has been almost no language. Rope, fire, torture, castration, infanticide, rape; death and humiliation; fear by day and night, fear as deep as the marrow of the bone; doubt that he was worthy of life, since everyone around him denied it; sorrow for his women, for his kinfolk, for his children, who needed his protection, and whom he could not protect; rage, hatred and murder, hatred for white men so deep that it often turned against him and his own, and made all love, all trust, all joy impossible."

Attorney General Robert Kennedy tried to extend his contacts with Negro intellectuals, and met with some of them. As Schlesinger tells it in *A Thousand Days*:

In the Negro group was also Jerome Smith, a young freedom rider who had recently been savagely beaten in the South. Smith opened the meeting by saying, as the Attorney General understood it, that being in the same room with Robert Kennedy made him feel like vomiting. What Smith was apparently trying to say was that he felt like vomiting to have to plead before the Attorney

General for the rights to which he was entitled as an American, but it came through to Kennedy, who had been fighting hard himself for these rights, as a gratuitous expression of personal contempt. The Attorney General showed his resentment; the group rallied around the freedom rider; and from this already low point the conversation went rapidly down hill.

Jerome Smith added that, so long as Negroes were treated this way, he felt no moral obligation to fight for the United States in war. The group applauded this sentiment. Some spoke of sending arms into the South. Baldwin said that the only reason the government had put federal troops in Alabama was because a white man had been stabbed. Burke Marshall, who was present, said that he had consulted with Dr. King about the use of federal troops; the group laughed at him. When Robert Kennedy, recalling his talk with Baldwin the day before, tried to seek their ideas about civil rights policy, they showed no interest. Baldwin was evidently not even aware that the President had given a civil rights message in February. "They didn't know anything," Bobby said to me later. "They don't know what the laws are— they don't know what the facts are—they don't know what we've been doing or what we're trying to do. You couldn't talk to them as you can to Roy Wilkins or Martin Luther King. They didn't want to talk that way. It was all emotion, hysteria. They stood up and orated. They cursed. Some of them wept and walked out of the room." What shocked him most was that, when the meeting broke up after three hours of non-communication, a representative of King's who was present drew the Attorney General aside and said, "I just want to say that Dr. King deeply appreciates the way you handled the Birmingham affair." Kennedy said, "You watched these people attack me over Birmingham for forty minutes, and you didn't say a word. There's no point in your saying this to me now."

By 1963, Jackie Robinson was seven years retired as a baseball player. An activist for civil rights, he was in Birmingham that week, together with heavyweight boxer Floyd Patterson. They had registered at the Gaston Motel, Birmingham's principal Negro hotel, but it had been firebombed before they got there. According to Robinson's account:

The motel was a scene of destruction. State and local police were massed outside, facing Negroes who were prepared to defend victims of fresh violence. Rumors were current that Klansmen were rallying in the city's outskirts.

The bomb had wrecked the dining room. Floyd and I had not eaten since our arrival in Birmingham, so we decided to look for a nearby restaurant. "There's one about two blocks away," we were told. "But you'd better be extremely careful. Don't speak to anyone on the street. The cops are hoping you'll start something, so they can pin a charge on you."

We looked neither to left nor to right as we walked the two blocks, a police car trailing us at the curb, parking before the little restaurant while we ate. Afterward, it trailed us back to the motel.

The following morning Floyd and I paid our respects to the brother of Martin Luther King, the Reverend A. D. King, whose home had twice been bombed. The first bomb had been tossed on the lawn, twenty feet from the house. If it had hit its mark as the second bomb had, the dwelling would have been demolished, its occupants killed.

Among those we found in Rev. King's shattered home was a young man who said that he had been stopped by police while returning from work the previous evening. "Where's your identification?" an officer had demanded. As he fished for his wallet, a second officer snarled, "Take that goddam cigarette outa your mouth, nigger!" Wallet or cigarette? Which order should he obey first? As he hesitated knuckles crashed into his face, bloodying his nose, knocking loose a tooth.

"Fighting back wouldn't have helped," he told us. "I'd be spending the next five years on a road gang. But in Birmingham Negroes are sick and tired of taking abuse. If it continues much longer we're going to fight back with their weapons."

"I saw five cops standing on a poor woman," another young man told me. "They picked her up, tossed her into a truck and took her off to jail. If they treat my sister like that I'll cut a cop's head off and fling it in the gutter!"

I don't know whether the young man's sister was one of the four innocent little girls who were slain by murderous bombers while learning the lesson of God's love in a Sunday-school class. That massacre revealed the depths to which the godless will go.

Those horrors happened in the United States on the day Giant fans were cheering Willie Mays's two home runs.

It could hardly serve Mays for him to point out that he only hit one home run that day, not two. It would indeed be a form of Jesuit argument: accused of killing three men and a dog, he defends himself by proving the dog is still alive. The Birmingham-born Mays had no intention of going out of his way to return there, if for no other reason than that the white establishment would have loved it. There were blacks—including Mays's own father, Kitty Kat—who took a view other than Robinson's. "Hell," Kitty Kat said, "we got along better with the southern white man than we did with the northern white man. See, when I went to New York, I found out the white man in New York was worse than the southern white man. And I found out one thing . . . if you called a southern white man Mister, you could get the shirt off his back. And I used to get anything I wanted out of those southern guys."

"Fighting back wouldn't have helped," Robinson was told, and apparently he believed it. One supposes that nobody told Jackie what happened in the Negro section, away from the television cameras and Bull Connor's fire hoses and publicity downtown. Robinson, we shall assume, did not hear about the black who walked up to a cop car and fired a rifle into it repeatedly at point-blank range . . . about the white cop dragged from his car and repeatedly stabbed . . . about the police dogs who got their throats cut. In strange coalescence, the violent Bull Connor and the nonviolent Martin Luther King benefited equally from the suppression of such news. Without a Jackie Robinson's willingness to go to Birmingham, the cause would have been hurt. Without a Willie Mays's refusal to go there, again the cause would have been hurt. The world and its historians saw the violence of the whites against the blacks. That did the job. The notion that one black man could have helped things along by staying away would be a complicating exercise. The notion that

others could have matched Connor violence for violence was just as complicating. What would have been complicated was the public appraisal. And the appraisal did not deserve complication. There was nothing—*nothing*—complicated about the fact that on September 15, 1963, Cynthia Wesley, 14, Denise McNair, 11, Carol Robertson, 14, and Addie May Collins, 14, died in a bomb blast at Birmingham's 16th Street Baptist Church. "Who killed Birmingham?" a prominent white lawyer, Charles Morgan, Jr., would later write in the pages of *Look*. "We all did. Not only the hate-filled, demented murderers of four Negro Sunday-school girls, but we 'nice people' who did nothing to save our city from race hatred." And as nothing before it, that one moment ostracized Birmingham not just from the rest of the country and the rest of the world, but from the rest of the South. "Nothing short of a total national effort can help Birmingham now," Morgan wrote. "Only the concern of the American people—and those American business leaders whose decisions shape our city's economy—can revive Birmingham. Only 'outsiders'—not those interested merely in the wealth of our soil, but those who care about the moral well-being of our people—can strike the spark of life. Birmingham is dead—but can America afford not to breathe new life into the city?"

Morgan's article appeared in the issue of *Look* of December 3, 1963, though the magazine actually was on the newsstands some time before then. Its cover pictured what was its main story: THE PRESIDENT AND HIS SON. *Now more than 7,400,000 circulation*, the magazine proclaimed. "Your jeweler," said one of the advertisements, "will show you stunning Bulova watches priced from $25 to $2500." No one had yet heard of Zip Code. But: "We thought you might be interested in this advertisement that ran for Campbell's Tomato Soup on July 2, 1921. It shows that the price was 12¢ a can. If you have a grocery store advertisement handy—or if your memory is really good, we think you'll be mildly amazed to find that this is just about the same price you pay today . . . same size can, of course."

And, said the lead-in for the cover story:

He's just three years old this month, and sturdy, brown-eyed John Fitzgerald Kennedy, Jr., obviously finds White House life just marvelous. Not that he's aware of what his father *does* for a living, or why he gets lifts in helicopters so regularly. Like many a two-year-old, he was a late talker. Then, in Hyannis Port this summer, he bloomed—words and ideas bubble out of this small boy, loud and fast. Off and on, John John dashes into the Presidential office with late bulletins from the playground. The President called him John John almost from the day he was born, to avoid well-worn nicknames like Jack or Johnny. Anything that flies intrigues JFK, Jr.—planes, rockets, blimps, and, oh boy, helicopters, which only six months ago he pronounced "he-precops." Daddy, who always seems to be flying someplace, is good about bringing home surprises: like a life-sized toy parrot, with a mysterious tape recorder inside. Press a button, and a fatherly voice says with a Boston twang, "My name is Poll Parrot. Would you like to fly with me in my helicopter?" "Hi, Poll Parrot," answers John John with aplomb. "Would you like a stick of gum?"

The day after that issue of the magazine actually was published, the UPI night trunk wire, for the next morning's papers, was carrying a story about a murder trial from Minneapolis. It was a half hour or so past one o'clock in the afternoon, New York time, as the teletypes chattered:

DETECTIVES WERE THERE AND THEY "ASKED HIM TO LOOK IN THERE [THE BRIEFCASE] FOR SOMETHING."

THE CASE WAS OPENED AND AN ENVELOPE WAS FOUND CONTAINING 44 $100 BILLS, THE WITNESS SAID. THE STATE HAD SAID IT WOULD PRODUCE THAT PIECE OF EVIDENCE BUT IT HAD NOT LISTED IT AS ONE "OF THE SEVEN LINKS." THE DEFENSE HAS IMPLIED IT WILL TAKE THE LINE THAT CAROL'S DEATH AFTER A SAVAGE BLUDGEONING AND STABBING IN HER HOME WAS THE RESULT OF AN ATTEMPTED   MOREDA1234PCS

It was not customary for a bureau to cut off a story it was sending in mid-sentence, but this was not the doing of the sending bureau. MOREDA 1234PCS meant there was more to come, and the time was 12:34 P.M. Central Standard. The DA stood for the initials of the bureau breaking into the transmission. For the UPI, DA meant the call letters of the bureau in Dallas.

PART FOUR

L B J

——————◆◆◆——————

The Fire Next Time

ACOUPLE OF WEEKS AFTER THE ASSASSINATION of the President, Willie Mays appeared as one of the guest stars at a charity benefit in San Francisco, and I remember that afterward a group of us went to Trader Vic's for a late bite to eat. In the conversation somebody spoke of Lee Harvey Oswald, and how accurate his aim had been. "If that's who he was shooting at," Mays said. Two or three people looked up and blinked when he said that, for he had spoken what rapidly was becoming the unspeakable. I could remember the prominent San Francisco attorney Jake ("Never Plead Guilty") Ehrlich voicing the same thought to me a week or so earlier, and in the most positive manner: "He was shooting at Connally. Oswald had no beef against Kennedy, but we all know he did have one with Connally, from the time he was in the Marines and Connally was Secretary of the Navy. And don't forget, the car was moving—moving away from Oswald. He aims at Connally, but in that space of time the car moves forward so he hits the guy behind Connally instead. Isolate the most logical thing we know about motive and the most logical thing we know about trajectory and they both spell Connally, not Kennedy." And I could remember, too, the first interview with Gov. John Connally, at his hospital bedside, following the shooting. "Martin," Connally said to television newsman Martin Agronsky, "I *know* he wasn't shooting at *me.*" It was almost as though task number one was to lay that possibility to permanent rest.

And laid to permanent rest it was. Nowhere in the Warren Report, nowhere in the latter-day investigation of the House Assassination Committee fourteen years later, nowhere in the endless stream of theories and postulates, of FBI this and CIA that and international-conspiracy the other that surfaced in the years between, will anyone touch in even the remotest way upon the one notion that truly would have proved intolerable:

that the President of the United States was killed by mistake.

A Willie Mays would be one of the handful of people you ever heard allude to it. That was interesting, because ordinarily you might suppose Mays to be politically indifferent, and in the ordinary sense he was. He grew up in a time when Roosevelt was a favorite first name for a Negro father to bestow upon his newborn son, and when the right-wingers of the South established their consistency of common cause with the Republicans of the North and West. The black man perceived the Republican as the oppressor, and he had his reasons. IN YOUR HEART, YOU KNOW HE'S RIGHT was Barry Goldwater's campaign slogan in 1964. No black man needed to decode that.

Yet politically indifferent Mays was. Nothing was there to drive him out to vote on election day, but in that he did not differ that much from anyone else. I offer some citations to this subject, for after covering the Giants for the *Examiner* I left the paper to take up free-lancing once again; I kept my baseball hand in by doing a thrice-weekly column on the sport for the morning *Chronicle* in San Francisco, but my time remained my own and I took up some spates of political speechwriting, advertising, and campaign management, particularly in Arizona. Honed to the historical imperative, Jews and Irish Catholics tended to vote in heavy numbers, and in Arizona the WASP inhabitants of retirement communities like Sun City and Youngtown also voted like there was no tomorrow, which in their case was frequently true enough. A resident senior citizen would spend the morning composing a letter to the Arizona *Republic* in opposition to cradle-to-the-grave government; in the afternoon another letter, this one to Senator Goldwater complaining that the Social Security and Medicare checks were running late. In between times one could go to a funeral, or play shuffleboard, or, come Election Day, vote. It was something to do. As for other voter groups in Arizona, the Republicans liked to single out blacks, Mexicans, and whites of little education and urge them anonymously to "make sure you vote Democratic on

Election Day—and just so there won't be any legal trouble for you at the polls, bring your pink registration slip with you." There was no such thing as a pink registration slip.

The intimidation and "dirty tricks" that so characterized Watergate were everyday facts of political life in Arizona, and the *Republic* and its sister afternoon counterpart, the Phoenix *Gazette*, both under the same right-wing management, joined in at will. One Sunday during the 1966 campaign, a large ad ran in the *Star* in Tucson and the *Republic* in Phoenix—the only two Sunday papers in the state—on behalf of Sam Goddard, the incumbent Democratic governor up for re-election. The ad contained a quote that derogated the opposition. It ran as submitted in the *Star,* but at the *Republic* the quotation marks were chiseled out, to make it look as though Goddard was talking about himself. Such were the climate of the times and the fear of the monopolistic Phoenix press that the Goddard camp—I know: I was a part of it—decided not to complain about it. Television was a more hospitable venue, possibly because it lacked the *Republic's* technical competence, which was enormous; but even there one encountered single-minded forces. Shortly after the death of JFK, Channel 5 in Phoenix presented a symposium on gun control and featured the argument that a broken Coca-Cola bottle was just as deadly a weapon as a bullet. The notion that Oswald could have killed Kennedy by throwing a Coke bottle at him from a sixth-floor window was enlightening.

I first worked for Goddard when he ran for governor in 1964. He was going to win that year and he did: the only major statewide candidate on the Democratic side to do so, but by a comfortable 53–47 margin over his Republican opponent, Goldwater sidekick Richard Kleindienst. Later Kleindienst would be known as Attorney General of the United States and one of the indicted players of Watergate, but to us in Arizona in '64 he was "Dreamy Draw Dick," a nickname he had inherited for a land deal that swapped cemetery space for highway access. There had been an internecine primary in which not even the religion of Kleindienst's opponent (a Mormon who stood politically even to the right of Kleindienst) was safe from attack, and there was no way the wounds from that September conflict would heal by the first week in November; so that all of us in the Goddard campaign, establishing maximum claim to credit for his victory, knew privately there was nothing we could have done to lose it. Our only skitterish moment—and it wasn't a bad one—arose when the Kleindienst forces began circulating the charge that Goddard was an atheist. In truth he was a Unitarian, which few of us viewed as a major defense. "Get some of the boys on this," Goddard said to me. I went to Ben Foote, the campaign manager, and said, "Tell me one thing: who are the boys?"

Certain though we were of victory for our own candidate, we had every reason to want to see the margin as large as possible, and so we joined the rest of the ticket in the push to persuade President Lyndon B. Johnson to make a campaign stop in Arizona. Johnson's people were cool to the idea, but eventually the moment came when Foote received a visit from two men: one from the Secret Service, the other an advance man from the Johnson campaign team.

"You're going to get the President," the advance man said, "but he has to have a guarantee of at least ten thousand people at the airport when he comes in."

Foote, who had helped arrange a turnout of 12,000 for Vice-Presidential candidate Hubert Humphrey at Tucson the week before, saw no real problem in promising this kind of a crowd.

"On a Sunday?" the advance man said.

"I don't see why not," Foote said.

"At seven o'clock in the morning?"

"*Seven o'clock in the morning?*" Foote said. "You don't understand something here."

"No," the Secret Service man broke in, "*you* don't understand something here. See, we have a list of three cities where the President's not supposed to show up at all: Dallas, Amarillo, and this town, Phoenix. So we're not taking him in to Dallas or

Amarillo, because if we do, they'll shoot him. We are going to bring him in to Phoenix, and he'll motorcade downtown, go to church, and motorcade back to the airport and get the hell out. But he's going to do it at seven o'clock on a Sunday morning or not at all, because we don't want anybody in the downtown buildings."

"This is Goldwater's home state," the advance man appended. "And we don't *need* your goddam five electoral votes. Okay?"

Foote did not indicate it was not okay. LBJ did come in, just after seven in the morning, and the crowd did exceed 10,000. At church downtown he sat next to Goddard, who told me afterward about the potted palm in the aisle beside their pew. Inside the pot, he said, were a black telephone and a red telephone. We turned that into a radio commercial, with Goddard simply describing the two telephones, with its whose-finger-do-you-want-on-the-button implication. In some ways it was a nutty campaign. Despite the elaborate security precautions, somebody at the airport hit the President over the head with a Goldwater sign, but that in no way diminished Johnson's enthusiasm. At the next stop, San Diego, a pickpocket, working the crowd pressed against the fence, reached out for the dip and found himself shaking hands with the President of the United States. Meanwhile, Goldwater's running mate for Vice-President, a man named Miller, found himself greeted by such crowds that his salutation on more than one occasion was "Dear Sir." The height of Miller rhetoric was his oratory on why Hubert Humphrey never served in the armed forces during World War II. "Why wasn't he in service?" Miller trumpeted. "I'll tell you why: because he had a hernia and he was color-blind, that's why!" (Some years later, Miller would be turned away as a visitor at the White House gate for being unrecognized; trading on this, he did one of those "Do You Know Me?" TV commercials for American Express.)

Just before his nomination, Goldwater was reported by Daniel Schorr of CBS News to be planning a post-convention vacation trip to Berchtesgaden, Hitler's erstwhile Bavarian retreat. Opponents of the Arizona senator circulated the report, and Goldwater canceled the trip with an angry denunciation of CBS. As Schorr would later write, Goldwater seemed "insensitive to the symbolism and the probable reaction" connected with the Berchtesgaden trip. It wasn't only Berchtesgaden. From his Election Night headquarters in November, the day after he had been buried by Lyndon Johnson, Goldwater began his speech of concession and congratulation—which contained neither concession nor congratulation—by saying, "I want to thank Jack Stewart for the use of the premises." Stewart was the boss of the Camelback Inn, the Goldwater headquarters site just outside of Phoenix, and was known nationally for running the most blatantly anti-Semitic resort in the country. (It was a reputation that went public with the decision to cancel the Camelback Inn as the site of an annual convention of the attorneys general of the forty-eight states. It is also a reputation that belongs to the past. With the takeover of the place by a successor management, the bigotry ceased to apply.)

"I would like to suggest," Goldwater said on January 6, 1964, "that Social Security be made voluntary, that if a person can provide better for himself, let him do it." In his official campaign literature, he said, "I favor a sound Social Security system and I want to see it strengthened. I want to see every participant receive all the benefits this system provides." Whatever else you might think of Goldwater, his partisans insisted, at least he said what he thought. The fact that he could and did think in irreconcilably opposite ways on the same subject never seemed to bother either him or his supporters. "When over and over again during the campaign he would promise, 'I will give you back your freedom,'" wrote Teddy White, "his sincerity would evoke the wildest response. His misfortune was that he could not make clear just how, and by what degrees, he would free the American people from paternalism and central government without exposing them at the same time to some personal loss."

No doubt of it, Goldwater was Sun City Sid: denounce big government, but make sure the check's on time.

In *The Making of the President 1964*, White wrote that Goldwater "had, out of conviction, voted against the Civil Rights Bill in June—against all the warnings, it must be noted, of his political advisers. Thus he had pinpointed himself as the outright anti-Negro candidate of the campaign, clearly on record in an area where the decisive morality of America was against him." Indeed, the entire spectrum of social legislation found Goldwater voting no. Be it housing, voting rights, education, health care, whatever, time and again he pointed out that you could not legislate what was in men's hearts. Presented with the ring of eternal truth, this in fact was miasmous shibboleth. "It may be true that a law can't make a man love me," Martin Luther King said. "But it can restrain him from lynching me, and that's pretty important." Even more to the point, you *could* legislate what was in men's hearts. The same bankers who in the thirties decried the federal insurance of deposits as Bolshevism incarnate turned from haters to lovers when the law went into effect and produced a new generation of customer confidence. And in baseball, the law was administered by president Ford Frick of the National League when in 1947, Jackie Robinson's first year in the majors, the St. Louis Cardinals decided they would not take the field against a team that included a black player. "If you refuse to play," Frick told the Cardinals, "you will never play another game of major league baseball." The Cardinals played. Fade out, fade in, and now again it is 1964, with Barry Goldwater saying you cannot legislate what's in men's hearts and, at the height of Goldwater's campaign for the Presidency, white and black Cardinal players hugging and kissing one another in celebration of their World Series victory over the Yankees. The final out is made, and that is a white catcher exploding from behind the plate like a cork blown from a bottle to throw his arms around the black pitcher who made the dream come true. Nor is it only in victory. In San Francisco, a white player on the

Giants has had marital problems and faces a difficult divorce. For advice he turns to Willie Mays. "I need your help, Buck," he says.

The progress was by no means total, nor by any means rapid enough for some who tasted its fruits. "It should have surprised no one," Arthur Schlesinger wrote, "that, as the Negroes began to gain some of their rights, their determination to claim *all* their rights hardened. Revolutions accelerate not from despair but from hope." And one thing Barry Goldwater perceived correctly was that the law could generate hope, and here and there hope become reality. Four years after his defeat by Lyndon Johnson, Goldwater reran for—and rewon—a seat in the U.S. Senate, and the longevity of his tenure in that body, added to the prominence he had won as probably the most outright Tory to be nominated for the Presidency by either major party in this century, gained him unquestioned title to the label "Mr. Conservative." He began to mellow, too, and in 1976, when the Republicans in Arizona again conducted a primary that featured religious slurs (these delivered by fanciers of a Senatorial candidate who was the son of baseball umpire Jocko Conlan), Goldwater publicly deplored the tactic. He even sided briefly with President Gerald Ford against Ronald Reagan on the Panama Canal issue, which brought him the new sensation of receiving hate mail from right-wingers. When he proclaimed that he knew of no organized crime activity in the state of Arizona, Johnny Carson, on the "Tonight" show, could be heard to murmur that "the Barry Goldwater memory course at the University of Arizona has been canceled." The laugh from the studio audience was loud and long, but not malicious. Goldwater, himself labeled in the 1963 exposé *The Green Felt Jungle* as friendly to Las Vegas mobsters, could be and was viewed as a man of rectitude and principle. One of the things that fed this view was that he had become essentially harmless. His votes in the Senate had the effect of opposing progressive bills, not defeating them. And as the pendulum swung back toward conservatism in the late seventies, Goldwater could even be looked upon as the continuum. After all, he went almost as many years back in national prominence as Willie Mays.

In the final week of Richard Nixon's presidency in 1974, Goldwater even played a leading role in getting Nixon to resign —the theory being that if Barry told it to him, even Nixon would accept that he no longer had any viable political support. In their book *The Final Days*, Bob Woodward and Carl Bernstein wrote:

> Barry Goldwater had driven to his office early. After having spent a brooding evening, he was angry. He blamed himself in part for the current nightmare. He should have pushed Nixon harder to be open and frank. His concern had been the office and the party, not Nixon, but he had been overly protective nonetheless. It had taken him too long to apply his stern, no-nonsense judgment. Christ, Goldwater was thinking, he had never really had a conversation with Nixon, he had never gotten through to him. He would come in to discuss one thing, and damned if the President didn't act as if he hadn't heard it. Now Goldwater realized that he didn't even like the man. Nixon had an obsession with the outward signs of power—trumpets, dressing up the White House guards, ceremonies. To Goldwater, this was, in one of his favorite expressions, "a bucket of shit."
>
> Goldwater thought Nixon was not a man's man, someone with whom he could drink or joke or have a frank heart-to-heart discussion. He was thinking of the contrast with John F. Kennedy. At a particularly tense moment during the Bay of Pigs invasion period, President Kennedy had said to him, "So you want this fucking job."
>
> Goldwater now concluded that Nixon was off his head and had been for quite a while, and that he had probably known about the Watergate break-in in advance. . . .
>
> That evening Goldwater discussed the situation with his wife. Wednesday he would call for resignation, and that would be a political disaster in Arizona, where he was running for reelection. He wondered if he should withdraw from the race. "No," his wife said.

Again here, as in so many other contemporary histories, a certain rough-hewn nobility attaches to Goldwater. There is no evidence that he resented this. In their foreword to *The Final*

Days, co-authors Woodward and Bernstein noted that "Nothing in this book has been reconstructed without accounts from at least two people." One wonders whether in Goldwater's case the two people were Goldwater and Mrs. Goldwater. Some other source—say, the editor of any high school weekly in Arizona—might have tempered the prospect of political disaster for the senator if he called for Nixon's resignation. Goldwater faced no problem in being re-elected. He was going to win in a walk and he did.

Indeed, the only electoral disaster he ever courted was one whose result was never in doubt to begin with: his landslide loss to Lyndon Johnson in the presidential race of 1964. Kennedy had been assassinated less than a year before the '64 election, and there was no way the country was about to change Presidents again within so short a time, let alone hand the office over to a man with no concern for healing. "Extremism in the defense of liberty is no vice!" Goldwater trumpeted from the convention podium in his acceptance speech. "Moderation in the pursuit of justice is no virtue!"

Years later, when Spiro Agnew was riding high as Vice-President, a priest in Milwaukee asserted that by the very virtue of his office he had given respectability to hate. Yet all other things being equal, a winning candidate for Vice-President achieves less prestige than a losing candidate for President. What respectability then did Goldwater give to hate in 1964? If there is a place for statistics in recording the history of baseball, maybe they have an occasional place in politics too. The record shows that Goldwater in 1964 carried 6 states, LBJ the other 44 and the District of Columbia, with Johnson nationwide recording 61 percent of the popular vote to Goldwater's 38.5 percent. Of the states Goldwater won, his narrowest margin was the gift of his native Arizona, where he eked out 50.4 percent. But across the five drop-leaf states of the deep South—Louisiana, Mississippi, Alabama, Georgia, and South Carolina—Goldwater did significantly better. This was before the Voting Rights Act of 1965, and, as Theodore White wrote, "The denial of Negro suffrage had long been an accepted southern scandal. In at least 193 counties fewer than 15 per cent of eligible Negroes were permitted to register; in Mississippi this was true in seventy-four out of eighty-two counties." Nevertheless Mississippi was historically and uninterruptedly Democratic (Roosevelt 157,318, Landon 2,760 was the Mississippi result in 1936), and even when states' rightists were on the ballot, head-and-head the Democrat always outpolled the Republican. And for the first time since Reconstruction, Mississippians could vote in 1964 for a southern President. The result? Johnson polled exactly 12.9 percent of the Mississippi vote. All the rest—87.1 percent—went to Barry Goldwater, his vote total in that one election exceeding the aggregate in that state for all other Republican Presidential candidates since before 1900. As for Willie Mays's next-door state of Alabama, the vote for Goldwater there in 1964 exceeded the *total* vote in Mississippi. His actual percentage vs. Lyndon Johnson's is not known, for in Alabama the President of the United States was not even listed on the ballot!

An added fascination would emerge four years later, in 1968, when that great concert segregationist, George Wallace of Alabama, ran for President on a third-party ticket. The total vote he received in the six states Goldwater had carried in '64 did not differ by even 1 percent from the Goldwater total before him in those same six states. History may wish to endorse the Goldwater position that he himself was not infected with prejudice. If not so diseased himself, he had to be one of the greatest carriers since Typhoid Mary.

Among the Goldwater fans of 1964 was manager Alvin Dark of the San Francisco Giants. He went public with this announcement on a weekly Bay Area television show he had that year in the course of defending one of his pitchers, Bob

Shaw, who also was espousing pro-Goldwater views. The only thing noteworthy here was not what Dark said but that the need existed to say it at all. The manager in truth had other and more pressing problems, one of which was his team. The same Giant club that finished 41 games over .500 in 1962 was to finish only 14 over in 1963 to end up in third place, 11 games back of the pennant-winning Dodgers, and on Labor Day of that year, Willie Mays—who had appeared in all but one game up to that late point—experienced a near duplication of his collapse the previous season, sinking to his knees with dizziness as he approached home plate. He was out for three days, then went back to work. (In 1978, Willie McCovey would be quoted in *Sport* magazine to the effect that Mays's collapses were staged in order to get time off. Afterward, McCovey denied having said that, and stated instead that the cause was probably the intensity with which Mays played the game. What is known is that the '62 and '63 episodes were the only ones of their kind in the Mays career, and in none of the four seasons in which he managed the Giants did Dark fulfill his pledge to rest his center fielder at periodic intervals.

(Mays was the only Giant to play in every inning of three marathon events that dotted the Dark administration. In 1961, the Giants and Phillies played a weird 15-inning tie game, then came back the next night with a doubleheader, the first game of which went 10 innings. In that first game, Mays had three home runs and a single; in the second game a walk, a double, a triple, and a superb double-play throw to the plate. In 1963 the Giants would go 16 innings in a classic game with the Braves—Marichal vs. Spahn, with the Giants winning 1–0 when Mays hit a home run in the bottom of the 16th. And in 1964 they won both ends of a doubleheader with the Mets, the second game of which went 23 innings and in point of time was the longest [7 hours, 23 minutes] game on major league record. The event was staged in New York before a record Shea Stadium crowd of 57,037, not to mention airline pilots whose shuttle flights to and from nearby LaGuardia Field caused some of them to get a glimpse of the action, coming and going, eight times. On their last flight they could have been treated to the sight of Willie Mays playing shortstop, which he did for the final three innings of the second game.)

There had been one flare-up between Dark and Mays in 1963, the result of Willie's failure to go all out in chasing a ball hit to the wall in center field at Chicago. The Cubs had gone on to win the game in extra innings, and Mays was guilty as charged, but with an explanation, which was that it was the eighth inning and the Giants at the time held a six-run lead. "You laid down on me," Dark snapped at Willie after the game. "I didn't cost you no seven runs," Mays snapped back.

Dark's moods were mercurial, but predictable enough: in victory, magnanimity; in defeat, black rage. In this he was not unique. The night he ripped away his finger throwing a stool in the clubhouse, Ed Bailey, who recently had come to the Giants from the Cincinnati club managed by Fred Hutchinson, seemed singularly unaffected by the episode. "Dark throws stools." He shrugged. "Hutch throws rooms." Dark did in truth seem committed to fail-safe. One story told of a time during his playing days when following an especially painful defeat Dark sat before his locker, methodically shredding a discarded uniform to tatters. "Some day," said Herman Franks, "Alvin'll get so mad he'll tear up his own uniform." And there was the time in 1963 when Dark took José Pagan to one side after a game, handed him a $50 bill, and said, "Take the boys to supper," meaning the Latin players on the Giant team. A few days later, following a loss to St. Louis, Dark called Pagan aside once more. "José," he said, "I'm fining you for not hustling." "How much?" Pagan asked. "Fifty dollars," Dark told him.

From the time in his first season as manager when he removed Marichal from the game in which he had a three-run lead and had already struck out twelve Dodgers, Dark had impressed his players as overreactive. His problem here was compounded by his rules for player conduct and his clubhouse lectures, both of them sprinkled with biblical admonitions which, including as they did his own continuing breach of the Third Commandment, did little to improve his authority. By the beginning of the 1964 season, Dark's level of communication with the players was at perigee. And it was in this setting that he named Willie Mays to be captain of the Giants, as he himself had been captain of the Giants under Durocher in New York.

Both from the standpoint of its timing and its conception, this move made solid good sense. As the veteran team leader, Mays now would be entitled, in the official sense of that word, to serve both as lightning rod and funnel in a communication process that the manager unaided had found was a growing shambles. It was easy to admire Willie, but the other players also trusted him, and Dark knew that was not so easily come upon. As for the timing of the announcement, it was unique. The oldest daily starter on the team, Mays had overcome his slow start the year before to hit .314 and lead the Giants in innings played, runs scored, and runs batted in. Yet it would not have been San Francisco to accept these figures at face value. One local sports editor, Roger Williams of the *News-Call Bulletin*, did a column just before the 1964 season saying that Mays was no better than the third most valuable Giant, that his eyes and legs had gone bad, and that '64 would mark his downfall. And in the wake of this, Mays got off to the best start in his major league lifetime. He hit seven home runs in April, eleven in May. At one point in May he was hitting nearly .500 for the season that far. "Boy, do the fans love you," I said to him. "You hit .486, they'll love *you*," he responded. And it was at that point that Dark named him team captain.

What did not go overlooked was that this was the first Negro team captain in major league history. What did not go overlooked also was that shortly before Dark's announcement, Jackie Robinson's book *Baseball Has Done It* was published, and it contained an interview with Dark—or, more accurately, a simple quotation of his views:

> Since I was born in the South I know that everyone thinks that Southerners dislike Negroes or even being with them. This isn't true at all. The majority of the people in the South, especially the Christian people that I have associated with, have really and truly liked the colored people. As for socializing with them on different levels there is a line drawn in the South, and I think it's going to be a number of years before this is corrected, or it may never be corrected.
>
> The way I feel, the colored boys who are baseball players are the ones I know best, and there isn't any of them that I don't like. When I first played with them on the Giant ball club—Willie Mays and Monte Irvin and a boy from Cuba by the name of Ray Noble, Hank Thompson, Ruben Gomez, the Puerto Rican—all these boys were, as far as I was concerned, wonderful boys and I never had any kind of trouble any way with them. In fact, I felt that because I was from the South—and we from the South actually take care of the colored people, I think, better than they're taken care of in the North—I felt when I was playing with them it was a responsibility for me. I liked the idea that I was pushed to take care of them and make them feel at home and to help them out any way possible that I could in playing baseball the way that you can win pennants.
>
> This is the feeling I have always had; I have respected many colored fellows in the National League as far as playing baseball goes. The greatest competitor I have ever seen in my life is Jackie Robinson. He has to be one of the greatest competitors the game has ever seen. Things that happened on the baseball field showed me that he had to be one of the greatest competitors.
>
> As far as my thoughts on integration are concerned, I'd rather stay away from it as much as possible. I think it's being handled a little wrong in that the people in the South, and I think I know them because I've lived with them, although I live in California now, I feel that too many people are trying to solve the Southerners' problems in the North.
>
> . . . The way I run a ball club is just like the way I played. As long as a man does his job, I don't care who he is. I don't pick

on anyone in particular. If a fellow loafs, if a fellow misses a sign, if a fellow doesn't produce, it makes no difference to me what color he is. I want to win and that's why I want my players to put out. There has never been any trouble between colored boys and other players on this club during my connection with it. Colored boys have never given me any trouble as manager. I wouldn't care if I had nine colored players on the field at one time as long as they can win.

... I don't think that a ball club with colored players would change the people in Birmingham or anywhere in the South. The majority of people in the South like colored people. They consider them as human beings, but right now it's being rushed too fast. ...

There might have been some small degree of cosmeticizing here, yet having known Dark well and heard him talk off-the-record on repeated occasions, I thought that overall his views as published in the Robinson book were both candid and unremarkable. He and I had flown back to San Francisco together from the winter baseball meetings at Miami Beach in December of 1961, and I asked him in the course of conversation whether he would ever start a team of nine nonwhites. "I'd never do it," he said, "and neither would you." In the Robinson interview he was now saying he would do it, and if my memory is correct a point was reached later in his managerial career when he did do it. Yet to me this represented neither a contradiction nor a gradual evolution in his thinking. It was a case rather that philosophizing in social midwinter conversation, he viewed things differently than when managing in public midsummer combat. When it came to wanting to win, Dark was truly color blind; and this fact, if not abnormally to his credit, surely was not to his discredit. His taped interview for the Robinson book was in fact an almost prototypical reproduction of the white Southerner's outlook in the early 1960s. It went to the point of being mindless of the buzz word "colored." As Dark and other Southerners used it, it included not just the Negro players but anyone with dark skin, which outraged the hell out of many of the

Latins. The Negroes would use it among themselves to describe themselves, but let a white man use it publicly and they were outraged too.

("Negro" was then the fashionable word; "black" would not surface as its substitute until the 1968 Olympics at Mexico City, viewed by hundreds of millions on television the world around. The key moment in that transfer in language came almost in a single flashpoint in history and was the doing of two black Americans, Tommie Smith and John Carlos, as they mounted the victory pedestal to receive their medals—Smith the gold, Carlos the bronze—for the 200-meter dash. The band struck up "The Star-Spangled Banner," the American flag was raised, and suddenly each of the athletes raised a clenched fist encased in a black glove. "We're black and proud to be black," Smith said afterward. "White America will say 'an American won,' not 'a black American won.' If it'd been something bad, they would have said 'a Negro.' ")

Whether Charles McCabe, sports columnist for the San Francisco *Chronicle*, was a student of such language terms, cannot readily be known. In the wake of Mays being named captain of the Giants in May of 1964, McCabe wrote a column in which he described the Giants as "a largely Negro" ball club. Of the eight pitchers and fourteen non-pitchers used most by Dark that year, only three were Negroes. Most of the Giants did not even know McCabe. He came around seldom, and where the team captaincy was concerned there is no evidence he realized that the job with this team—or any team—was anything more than ceremonial. Where Mays was concerned, McCabe was the columnist who had already written that Willie couldn't hit in the clutch, and would be the one who wrote in a future time that the Giants conspired to let him hit a home run against them in his first game as a Met. Those things to one side, the McCabe column of May 25, 1964, was triggered by Dark's statements in the Robinson book:

I had not intended to make any comment on Mr. Alvin Dark's comments on the Negro in baseball, believing that every man is entitled to one really huge goof a year in his public life.

Mr. Dark's views are those of an educated, committed, Christian Southerner. They are terrible.

The only reason I bring them up is that the manager of the San Francisco Giants, a largely Negro ballclub, recently named Willie Mays to be "captain" of the club. And "managerial material."

Willie Mays has as much reason to be captain of the Giants, even if in name only, as I have to be placed in charge of our space program.

His naming to the fictitious job was, apparently, a public relations gimmick to becalm the Negroes of this area, many of whom are rightly enraged by Mr. Dark's odd views on the race question, most of which could have been pronounced from a podium by Governor Wallace, of Alabama, to wild, wild applause.

Had Mr. Dark's views been made public in New York when the Giants were living there, and had the press there reacted as they predictably would, Mr. Dark would now be seeking employment in a field outside baseball. That he is not doing so is a tribute to the fact that the racial question is not met with such raw emotion in these parts.

If you didn't read the story in the Sporting Green of some time back, I shall refresh you. Not with any real pleasure, mark you, because I'm sorry for an America where the educated class of the South thinks as Mr. Dark thinks. . . . This kind of chit-chat is garbage, and dangerous garbage, whether it comes from a politician or a baseball manager. The appalling thing about it is its obvious sincerity. Mr. Dark clearly believes, to the last comma and syllable, what he is saying.

His comments on the Negro problem are about as meaningful, and as called for, as somebody idly remarking that some of his best friends are Jews.

His remarks quite rightly outraged large segments of the Negro and white community here. Ergo, Willie Mays is named captain.

The function and importance of the job of Giant captain can best be judged by the fact that the team has done without one for the past eight years. The last captain was Alvin Dark.

What Mr. Dark said about the Negro was bad enough, but not surprising. His views are shared by thousands of his fellows in the South, and they constitute the largest single social problem before us.

What the Giants' organization did to turn the heat off itself—naming an innocent as captain and "managerial material"—is another rougher, more sickening thing.

It requires no heavy sociological analysis to discern that in his reflection on Mays's capacity for leadership and intelligence, McCabe was saying far worse things about a black man than anything that he accosted Dark for saying. McCabe did give lip service to the fact that Dark's views were not surprising . . . in the act of himself seeming not only surprised but stunned. To Mays, Willie McCovey, and Giant third baseman Jim Ray Hart, all three of them witnesses from birth to White-Man's-Burden talk, McCabe was simply using Dark as a convenient handle to take another of his shots at Mays. The Latins on the club, who outnumbered the Negroes 5 to 3, and the predominantly white remainder of the players and coaches, saw little if anything in the McCabe invective that affected them in any way. There was universal pleasure that Mays was now team captain, and it began and ended with that.

"I told you something like that might happen," Mays said to Dark.

"Just so long as you don't believe it," Dark replied. "If McCabe walked up to you tomorrow, would you know who he is?"

"I don't think so," Mays said.

"Me neither," Dark said.

In the Giants front office, however, team owner Horace Stoneham was forming a different view. Information, which within a relatively short space of time would prove to be correct, had reached him that McCabe's *Chronicle* was going to become the only morning paper in San Francisco, and Stoneham had already tangled with the *Chronicle*, and to his sorrow. The circumstances were bizarre. Giant custom had been not to fly the American flag at night, in fealty to established practice that the flag flew after sundown only under battle conditions. For this, editor Scott Newhall of the *Chronicle* in 1961 attacked Stoneham for his want of patriotism and, to underline his point, assembled and paid a rag-tail assortment of crippled war veterans to hobble to Candlestick Park and present Stoneham with an American flag. It was a circulation stunt, and Newhall and Stoneham both knew it, but not unpredictably Stoneham caved in, as his fellow club owners throughout both major leagues and other owners in all sports were likewise doing. (The longest holdout was Phil Wrigley, owner of the Chicago Cubs, but the 110-percent patriots got to him, too, and in 1963 the Cubs started playing the national anthem before every game. Today a routine game against the Montreal Expos is preceded by not one national anthem but two: this despite the known facts that no one on the Montreal roster is from Canada and that almost no one in the ball park actually cares one way or the other.)

But it was not only cynical outside pressures that Stoneham had to consider. The Giant owner had his own view of Dark and his ways, during games and after. It could be said of the 1962 club, which won 103 games and the pennant, that the manager might have been doing something right. Yet that was the team that was 4 games behind with 7 to play, and Stoneham's chief comment was, "They backed in." And if '62 failed to entrance him, '63 had to be a doozer. The Giants on August 15 of that year trailed the Dodgers by only 3 games in the standings. Less than a week later they had dropped to a point 8½ games behind, and by season's end Stoneham had fairly well determined that 1964 would be Dark's last year as Giant manager, win or lose.

It came decently close to a win, or at least so is the appearance of the record. The 1964 Giants finished fourth, but they won 9 of their last 14 games and actually were not eliminated mathematically until the next-to-last day of a season in which only

5 games separated the top five teams in the final National League standings. But the Giants could have won it all, and Dark still would have been through as manager. In a late-July home stand, with his team only percentage points out of the lead, Dark was interviewed by Stan Isaacs, a reporter for the large-circulation *Newsday* on New York's Long Island. The Giants had encountered a five-game losing streak, with the loss of first place, and the distraction of it may have contributed to the bluntness of what Dark had to say. Those of us who were accustomed to the way Dark punctuated his agitation with negatives might have been less apt to publish his words, but when Isaacs did publish them they came as no surprise. Here are some extracts of the Dark interview as they appeared in *Newsday:*

• We have trouble [atrocious mistakes] because we have so many Spanish-speaking and Negro players on the team. They are just not able to perform up to the white ball player when it comes to mental alertness.

• You can't make most Negro and Spanish players have the pride in their team that you can get from white players. And they just aren't as sharp mentally. They aren't able to adjust to situations because they don't have that mental alertness.

• One of the biggest things is that you can't make them subordinate themselves to the best interest of the team. You don't find pride in them that you get in the white player.

• You don't know how hard we've tried to make a team player, a hustling ballplayer, out of Orlando [Cepeda]. But nothing has worked for so long . . . he doesn't sacrifice himself . . . I'd have to say he's giving out only 40 percent.

• Stoneham won't trade Cepeda or Willie McCovey. They know it and they know they'll get paid well if their averages are good.

"With the Giants," Cepeda was to write in his book *My Ups and Downs in Baseball,* "if you were Willie Mays, you played with a broken hand. If you were Juan Marichal, you pitched with a broken foot. To complain meant you didn't have 'pride.' " At one point, Cepeda was on third base with Tom Haller at bat for the Giants, when Dark put on the sign for a squeeze play. Considering the runner and the hitter involved, it was an extraordinary move, and the two chief reactors were Cepeda and Haller. At third base, Cepeda clapped his hands to his head in an involuntary gesture of dismay, and at the plate Haller said to the umpire, "Time out. I have to get another bat." He walked back to the dugout and said to Dark, "You want the *squeeze?* I'm not that good a bunter." "That's why they won't expect it," Dark said. "Won't expect it?" Haller said. "The whole world knows why I'm back in here talking to you." Dark shook his head. "You're wrong. Go back up there and bunt." By now Gene Mauch, the rival manager, was actually laughing. With their overview of the Cepeda and Haller reactions, so even were casual fans in the stands. Haller went back up to bat, bunted at the ball, missed. *"¡Pelota! ¡Pelota!"* Cepeda cried hopelessly as he ran into the catcher's tag-out at home plate. In his disbelief he had gone from a run to a pronounced limp. He had been born in Puerto Rico with a malformed leg—a *paralitico*. The limp was his normal gait—except, not so curiously according to medical lore, when he was running all out. To Dark, anything less than all out meant lack of pride.

But the situation was more complicated than that. In Cepeda and McCovey, Dark had two sluggers who both played first base. In 1961, the solution was to play Cepeda in the outfield, where by his own admission he was a butcher. "I've got to change that and put McCovey in the outfield," Dark said to me. I said, "Then *he'll* be a butcher." "What's he going to do?" Dark said savagely. "Ketch?" There is no question that both Cepeda and McCovey were affected by the dilemma, that neither enjoyed it, and that their lack of enjoyment was visible. Dark was also correct about Stoneham's determination to keep both men regardless of this. (Ironically, with Dark's departure following the 1964 season, the situation resolved itself. Cepeda underwent major knee surgery in the off-season and played in only a handful of games in 1965, so McCovey had first base to himself. The following year, at the urging of Dark's successor, Herman Franks, and club vice-president Chub Feeney, Stoneham overrode the wishes of himself and Tom Sheehan and okayed the trading of Cepeda to the St. Louis Cardinals, where in 1967 Cepeda became the National League's most valuable player. McCovey meanwhile would go on to become an elder statesman of the game, and in a comeback with the Giants hit the 500th home run of his career in 1978 at the age of forty. From the date of Cepeda's departure from the club in 1966, both men would complete their careers playing nothing but their beloved first base.)

But the *Newsday* interview with Dark in 1964 obviously went deeper than the question of Who's on First. There was no question of his dedication to fielding the best nine men he had: though the Giant roster was mainly white, six of the eight regulars in '64 were nonwhite; on days when Marichal pitched it was seven out of nine. But the *Newsday* quotes pronounced that Dark had compartmentalized his thinking, whites in one group, nonwhites in another. He had drunks, womanizers, goof-offs among his white players, and he knew it and dealt with it. But no sign of that emerged in *Newsday*. What emerged was the very opposite. Pride, he was saying, was a strictly white commodity.

Predictably, his first reaction to questions about what he had said was to deny that he had said it. That got him nowhere. Isaacs was a good reporter, and too many people knew Dark too well. As he had exempted Jackie Robinson from his comments in Robinson's book, so Dark would obviously exempt Willie Mays in *Newsday*, but that was blatant tokenism, like singling out Louis Armstrong as America's greatest ambassador of goodwill, and Mays as team captain now found a revolt on his hands. The club was off on another road trip when the *Newsday* interview hit. In Pittsburgh, Mays called a meeting of the nonwhite players in his hotel room in the Carlton House. (The city could not have been more appropriate: where the mutineers were

209

concerned, the most prideful was Orlando Cepeda, a Puerto Rican; and Pittsburgh was the home city of the Pirates and the most prideful player in the major leagues, Roberto Clemente, also a Puerto Rican.)

"Shut up!" Mays told the congregants in his room. *"Just shut up!"*

"You don't tell me to shut up," Cepeda said. "I'm not going to play another game for that son of a bitch."

"Oh, yes, you are," Mays told him. "And let me tell you why." Then he told why. It came down to three separate points:

• Horace Stoneham was livid. He was set to fly to Cincinnati, where the Giants would be playing one week hence, and fire the manager. Three men—vice-president Feeney, coach Herman Franks, and captain Mays—were working on Stoneham to keep this from happening. Its sole effect would be to martyr Dark. "I tell you for a fact," Mays said to his listeners, "he is *not* going to be back next year. Don't let the rednecks make a hero out of him."

• The Giants had a chance to win the pennant. "I don't say it'll happen, but it's money if we do, and we ought to take our best shot. We changed managers in the middle of 1960 and look where it left us."

• Regardless of his philosophy, Dark did not discriminate against anyone when it came down to fielding the best possible lineup.

There was tension in the room. Mays and Dark went back as teammates on the Giants of the fifties in New York, and Dark had not only named Willie captain but had specifically excepted him from his blast on the lack of pride among nonwhites. "If I go back with Alvin Dark," Mays said now, "it means one thing: I know him better than any of the rest of you. I know when he helped me and I know why. The why is that he's the same as me and everybody else in this room: he likes money. That preacher's talk that goes with it he can shove up his ass. I'm telling you he helped me. And he's helped everybody here. I'm not playing Tom to him when I say that. He helps us because he wants to win, and he wants the money that goes with winning. Ain't nothing wrong with that." Mays reached for an inhaler and held it to his nose. He had a bad cold and it was getting worse. His whole body ached. Now one of the other players challenged him on why it would be bad if the team changed managers. (There had been cases before, and would be cases again—cases as recently as 1978, when Bob Lemon took over from Billy Martin as manager of the New York Yankees and turned the team around—when a change in field manager was precisely what the players needed the most. The St. Louis Browns of 1952 had chipped in to buy owner Bill Veeck a trophy in gratitude for his midseason firing of manager Rogers Hornsby.) "No," Mays said. "That shit won't go in this case. Ain't one of us gonna have a moment's peace if it does happen. Every place you go, some son of a bitch with a microphone or a camera or a pad and pencil'll be asking you why you quit on your manager. Same way they've used me this year, asking me why I thought he made me captain, now they'll use you. What do you need that for?"

Seated on one of the twin beds in the room, Orlando Cepeda said, "It's more than just money."

"Correct," Mays said to him. "Suppose him or a lady friend of his went to a picture show together in Birmingham, where I come from, and one of them passes out. And somebody shouts 'Is there a doctor in the house?' and it turns out the only doctor there is colored. You think Dark's gonna turn him away?"

Standing beside the window, Willie McCovey bestirred himself. "Be a while for him to get there, that doctor," he observed mildly, "seeing as he'd have to make his way down from the balcony." That broke the tension. The room dissolved into laughter; Mays had carried his point.

But operating on his own track, Horace Stoneham still could

get rid of Dark here and now, and he continued so minded. The next port of call was New York, where Dark had to face newsmen. No one had ever accused him of being more intelligent than San Francisco *Chronicle* columnist McCabe, so now Dark carried out McCabe's unwitting prophecy. He would use Willie Mays as proof of his kindliness toward his black brother. "I thought I proved my feelings when I named Willie Mays captain," Alvin Dark said. "If I thought Negroes were inferior, would I have done that?"

Willie's cold had worsened. The following day he suited up, but the sickness was in his throat and his voice was all but gone, which may have been a good thing. Silently Dark handed him the lineup card for Willie to take out to the umpires. Logically, Mays ought not to play that day. The virus had robbed him of his usual vitality. Logically, also, if he did not start, in the light of what Dark had said the day before, the baseball world would have taken it as a Mays refusal to play for a man who had bailed out on him, and Dark's managerial career would end then and there. Silently, Mays took the lineup card. He looked. His name was not on it.

"I actually felt sorry for the man," he told me later. "So I did the only thing I could do." What he did was to take a pencil, write his name back into the lineup, and go out and hit two home runs to beat the Mets. With this action, Horace Stoneham called off his plan to confront Dark and fire him when the club now flew to Cincinnati. He would let him go the remainder of the season, permit the inflammation to subside, and guarantee a future for him, if not with the Giants then elsewhere in baseball, a future from which Dark was to enjoy, and certainly as a dedicated baseball man deserve, full measure.

There are two follow-ups to this story. One occurred immediately upon the return from the road trip, when I talked with Dark in his clubhouse office at Candlestick. Once before—in 1961, in Milwaukee—I had seen him in a similar state of agitation. He and I had been out for a post-midnight walk after a night game, and across the echoing downtown street, on a corner away from us, three young couples stood beneath a lamppost, nuzzling and laughing. One of the couples was a black boy and a white girl. "Son of a buck, that's a *dis*grace," Dark said. "Somebody's got to break that up!" He started to cross the street, and I reached out vaingloriously to stop him: the man had played fullback ahead of Steve Van Buren at Louisiana State. I said, "Jesus Harrison Christ, Alvin!" At that he stopped and thought better of it. Possibly he wished to give additional contemplation to the Saviour's middle name.

Now at Candlestick, Dark looked at me from behind his desk and said, "There's something I learned." He stood up and began an almost stately dance around the room, like the gryphon in the Lobster Quadrille, punctuating his gyrations with rhythmic wording: "You cannot say colored. Instead, you must say Ne-*gro*, Ne-*gro*, Ne-*gro*. " I thought, but admittedly did not say, that it might be time for his Ovaltine. Dark was intensely bitter at Stoneham's refusal to support him, even more so over what he took to be Feeney's betrayal. I think he was genuinely unaware that Stoneham had been on the verge of firing him, and unaware equally of Feeney's role in helping make the owner change his mind.

The grace period would and did end on the final day of the season, when Stoneham announced the name of Herman Franks as the new manager. And the second follow-up took more than five years to eventuate, when late in 1969 Feeney was up for the post of commissioner of baseball and considered the odds-on favorite to get it. He had the votes of the National League club owners and sufficient American League votes as well, or so everyone thought. But what seemed the safest American League vote, held by Feeney's good friend Gabe Paul, president of the Cleveland Indians, went stunningly against him. Paul never stated his reason, as far as I know, but surely he knew the trouble commissioners could make for managers, as Landis had for Hornsby and Happy Chandler for Durocher. And Paul's manager at Cleveland was Alvin Dark, who had perceived Feeney as someone out to get him. (Instead of becoming commissioner, which he expected, Feeney would be named president of the National League, which he did not expect. It was a Cinderella story with a twist: the slipper fit the sister.) In all, few were those connected with the 1964 Giants who escaped Dark's wrath. "I hear Alvin's telling people it was all a plot on my part," Herman Franks told me.

The turning of events was sad, because of the falling out. The Feeney of 1961 had been an ardent Dark supporter. Even more so had been the Mays. "I never thought I'd say this," Willie told me at the beginning of the '61 season, "but I think more of Cap as a manager than I did of Leo."

But if in 1964 columnist McCabe proved accidentally correct about the recourse an embattled Dark would take to his reason for appointing Mays captain of the Giants, so was he equally oblivious to the role the "innocent/unqualified" Mays would make of the captaincy. It was not for any lack of leadership on Willie's part that he helped save Dark's future; nor by absence of calculation. Nor by the presence of any residual worship. The day a sickness-ridden Mays took the lineup card from Dark and wrote his own name on it was a day two full months before the end of the season. In all that time, Mays never spoke to his manager again.

———◆◆◆———

Willie Mays would be named Player of the Decade by *The Sporting News* for the 1960s and thereby prove to be the second most durable product of the most turbulent and volatile decade in American history. The only thing more continuingly consistent was Polish jokes. Q. Why is it illegal to swat a fly in Poland? A. It's the national bird. . . . Q. How can you tell who's the groom at a Polish wedding? A. He's the one in the clean bowling shirt. . . . Q. What do the following have in common: 1492, 1776, 1812, 1941? A. They're adjoining rooms at the Warsaw Hilton. . . . Q. Why do Poles have holes in their cheeks? A. From learning to use a fork. . . . Q. Why don't restaurants and bars serve ice in Poland? A. They lost the recipe. . . . Q. Why is the Polish suicide rate so low? A. How can you commit suicide jumping out of a basement window? . . . Q. Why is there no zoo in Warsaw? A. The clam died. . . . Q. What wears a robe and rides on a pig? A. Lawrence of Poland. . . . Q. What is a Polish Lesbian? A. A woman who likes men. . . . Did you hear about the Polish terrorists who were assigned to hijack a jet? They came back with Joe Namath. . . . Did you hear about the Polish rapist who has to stand in a police lineup for identification by the victim? The minute she comes into the room, he points at her and says, "That's the one." . . . Q. How many pit stops did the Polish driver make in the Indianapolis 500? A. Three, once for gas and twice to ask for directions. . . . Q. Why do helicopters keep crashing in Poland? A. The pilots get cold and shut off the fan.

This onslaught reached its zenith when a deadpan, little-recognized comic appeared on a Steve Allen television show, representing himself as a spokesman for the Polish Anti-Defamation League who wished to protest this slanderous form of ethnic slur. Naturally, he had to give examples, and so delivered one Polish joke after another while Allen and the studio audience rolled on the floor in helpless merriment. What nobody knew was that there was a *real* Polish Anti-Defamation League, which promptly brought suit against Allen and the network. It was like the Chinese boxes, one fitting inside the next. No judge would touch the case. It went on appeal all the way up to the Supreme Court of the United States. Like all the lower courts, the Supremes refused to hear it. This was understandable. Oral argument in the case would perforce have made the nine robed justices of the highest court in the land sit there and stuff handkerchiefs in their mouths to keep from giggling at the evidence.

A variation on a theme could be seen in a Japanese pitcher named Masanori Murakami, a lefthander with fine control who lasted but a short while with the San Francisco Giants before he got homesick and went back to Japan. Totally dependent on his teammates for schooling in the English language, he nevertheless wished to preserve the baseball custom of his homeland, under which the starting pitcher would greet the plate umpire with a courteous salutation. Came now in 1965 Murakami's one and only starting assignment, and his fellow Giants had primed him in advance. Striding out from the dugout to take the mound, Murakami paused and bowed to the plate umpire. "Herro, you haily plick," he said. "How you like to piss up a lope?" The umpire, Chris Pelekoudas, found himself bowing back. "I couldn't think of what else to do," he explained.

"Do you envy people who fly an airplane?" ran a magazine ad of 1965:

Do you wonder what compels a housewife to fly around the world alone? At the airport, have you seen someone walk to a trim airplane, go around it once with a critical eye, climb into the cabin and shut the door on the outside world? Have you wished it were you . . . taxi-ing out for takeoff?

Wish no longer—here's your opportunity to enjoy the thrill of flying an airplane. For $5 and the coupon at the bottom of this ad, any Cessna dealer in your area will take you up in the easy-to-fly Cessna 150, *and let you be the pilot.*

You'll sit at dual controls beside a government-licensed instructor. Then, when you're up in the sky, it's all yours. Roll into some turns. Try some glides and climbs. Enjoy the view. The feeling is wonderful!

There were captions for pictures in *Life* magazine:

• This foaming machine, demonstrated on a pair of volunteer targets on a West Chester, Pa., street, is the latest thing in mob control. Its powerful fan blows out 40,000 gallons of detergent suds a minute—enough to immobilize a crowd in oceans of slippery white goo that blocks both sight and hearing.

• When Jordan's King Hussein heard of a recent Jordan-Israel clash of border guards, he leaped into his powerful sports car and started out to take a look. En route he ran off the road, hit a wall and injured his back. Then the desert king was off to the French Riviera—where he recuperated on a pair of water skis, whizzing over the Mediterranean.

• The Sculls *(left)* admire a stove created by pop artist Claes Oldenburg, which they display in their hall before a Jasper Johns painting of the American flag. The stove is real, but the food is painted plaster. "Ethel thought I was crazy when the stove arrived," Scull says, "but now she calls it 'my emerald' and she won't let anyone else touch it." The Sculls commissioned popist Andy Warhol to do Mrs. Scull's portrait. He took her to a 25¢ photomaton, got dozens of photos, made silk screens of them and produced the multiple portrait that Mrs. Scull and Warhol are shown with above. At right, Scull sits in dining room in front of a 16-foot-long painting, *Silent Skies* by James Rosenquist. "When I bought it three years ago and paid $1,400 for it," Scull recalls, "Rosenquist just stood there and looked at me. Finally he said, 'I didn't think there'd be anyone crazy enough to buy it.'"

Also, in the pages of *Life* in 1965, Shana Alexander had something to say:

Give me my choice today between a glamorous secret agent with hair like a black comma, and a spindle-shanked, dope-shooting misanthrope, and I will unhesitatingly choose the dope-shooter. It is not that I have become so bored with James Bond. I am well aware that I speak for a fast-dwindling minority of the earth's population. Bond, Secret Agent 007, or, to use his fine Italian handle, "Mr. Kiss-kiss, bang-bang," is the international superhero of modern times. The dozen or so Bond books by the late Ian Fleming have sold some 50 million copies in 11 languages; the three Bond movies are breaking all box-office records; TV is swarming with copycat Bond characters; and the world-wide avalanche of 007 merchandise includes everything from Bond-licensed bedsheets to a complete line of what is known, revoltingly, as "men's toiletries." In short, the Bond image is now so potent it even has the selling power to deodorize armpits.

In my opposition to it all, I stand almost alone, but not quite. The party organ of the East German government is with me; and so, oddly enough, are the Vatican newspaper, the intellectual British journal, *New Statesman*, and Malcolm Muggeridge, the ex-editor of *Punch*. Even for a Bond caper, we are a strange band of bedfellows indeed! My allies found Bond a unique blend of sex, snobbery and sadism so nasty as to be "far more dangerous than straight pornography." I disagree. There is something wrong with Bond all right, but that is not it. He has simply become too dull.

What was not dull was the San Francisco baseball club. Under their new manager, Herman Franks, the Giants finished two games behind the Dodgers in 1965, a game and a half behind them in 1966. (In the four years of the Franks reign, 1965 through 1968, San Francisco won more games than any other team in the majors—and finished second four straight times.) The 1965 and 1966 races against the Dodgers helped generate an unprecedented fan frenzy, not just for the standing rivalry between the two teams but nationwide. Six teams were still in contention in the National League going into September of 1965; four at the same point in 1966. Both Giants and Dodgers set all-time league records for road attendance in 1965, figures good enough to be still the records more than a dozen years later, as this book was being written, except that in 1966 both teams topped their records of the previous year. For their road dates in 1966, the Giants' league-leading attendance of 2,207,530 averaged 79 percent of the seating capacities of the nine parks they visited.

As managers go, Herman Franks would, I think, be the best I ever saw. Like Rigney and Dark before him, he had been a Durocher disciple, but with less of the hypertension and impulsion, though the absence of these dulled neither his enthusiasm nor skill. I remember a time when he had been kicked out of a game in Los Angeles, and I went from the press box down to the clubhouse to talk to him. But he was not in the clubhouse. I found him instead crouched in the tunnel leading from clubhouse to dugout, a lineup card clutched in his hand, just out of the umpires' sight but hissing instructions nonetheless. There are theories that catchers make good managers and stars do not. The catcher is the one defender with a batter's-eye view of the game; the great player tends to inflict his excellence, either directly or by implicit reputation, as a burden on others unequal to his exploits. Within those parameters, to reach for the Ehrlichman locution, Franks had to have the best of both worlds: he had been a catcher for four different big league teams in six different seasons, three before War II and three after, but never a regular. His total number of times at bat was under 200. So was his batting average.

But he was in good company: Sparky Anderson, manager of the dynastic Reds of the seventies, had one season as a player in the majors; Walter Alston, of the dynastic Dodgers of the fifties and sixties, had one at-bat in the majors; Joe McCarthy, of the dynastic Yankees of the thirties and forties, never played in the majors.

Herman Franks meanwhile had played and coached for Durocher, and managed the team Willie Mays played for in Puerto Rican winter ball the season of 1951–52, and of all the Giant managers dating back to Mel Ott in the mid-forties (possibly excepting the seriocomic Tom Sheehan interregnum in 1960), Franks was far and away the one who stood closest on a personal basis to club owner Horace Stoneham. And he had one other advantage, which might have been abused but wasn't: he didn't need baseball for a living. A successful real estate developer in his native Utah, Franks wanted to manage a baseball team because he wanted to manage a baseball team. Critics would and did say this must dull his desire to win; as recently as 1978, a piece in the Chicago *Tribune* portrayed him as a landed squire with no particular care for the fate of the Cubs he was managing. Since there was no other manager who could have got that particular mileage out of those particular Cubs, the criticism had to miss.

In truth Franks never had to manage like a man with an overdue mortgage payment, and so he had the better of a Durocher or a Dark. Paper it over though they would, Durocher and Dark never left any doubt but that they were the smartest men on the team. The more relaxed Franks would give full rein to his coaches and team captain. The blame would be his, but the credit—victory has a hundred fathers, defeat is an orphan— he would happily assign to others. His tactics were sound enough to begin with; his imagination could be inspired. In one game in 1965, he made sure his pitcher walked the Dodger pitcher with bases empty, two out, and nobody on base in the late innings of a close game at Los Angeles. Too late, Dodger manager Alston realized that Franks had finessed him out of his jockstrap. Now Maury Wills, the premier Dodger base stealer, was at bat with a slow-running pitcher on base ahead of him. The greatest Wills potential—to reach base and then steal into scoring position—had been nullified. And if Wills was now at bat with two out this inning, there was hardly a way he could become the lead-off hitter next inning. One could almost see the light bulb click belatedly to the on position over Alston's head. Next series between the two clubs, Franks tried the same stunt again, but he was laughing when he did it. This time Alston had his pitcher intentionally strike out by waving at three bad pitches.

The beauty of Franks's move with Wills was of course its essential simplicity. Unlike Alvin Dark, his successor exhibited little zest for trick plays; at one point Franks actually fined one of his coaches for camouflaging signals so effectively no one, unfortunately including the Giant players, could possibly tell which sign was the real one. Unlike Dark, too, Franks drank, smoked, chewed tobacco, and never said "Son of a buck" in his life. His language not only was graphic, but he had no hesitation in using it on the writers who covered the team. On one occasion he reamed them out for not phoning down to the dugout from the press box to tell him Jim Ray Hart's batting average had exceeded .300. This was on the last day of the 1965 season, a game meaningless to the final standings, and if Franks had known Hart had crested the magic .300 he would have taken him out of the game then and there. As it was, Hart stayed in, made an out the next time at bat, and finished the season at .299. Some of the San Francisco writers never warmed to Franks. They remembered him coaching third base for the Giants in 1958 as another one of Stoneham's New York expatriates, and he had never gone out of his way to court them, nor would he now.

Franks's first season of 1965 was less than halfway along when club owner Stoneham announced he was rehiring him as manager for 1966. "We gave Herman a raise and made it retroactive to the current season," Stoneham said. He then made pointed reference to the way the players were putting out for Franks, and said, "I think we're in a very fine position to overtake the leaders, and this in spite of a succession of injuries that has made the job most difficult for Franks. The way he has handled the case of Willie Mays, who now needs rest, has impressed me very much."

Franks would indeed rest Mays, as Dark before him had not. Mays would appear in 157 games in 1965, only five short of the team total of 162, but that would include six pinch-hitting appearances and other games where he was relieved in the late innings. The same pattern repeated itself in 1966, when the record showed Mays appearing in 152 games. But 1966 was sufficient to establish his major league record for 13 seasons—13 *consecutive* seasons, dating back to his first full season as a Giant in 1954—of appearing in more than 150 games.

Franks's handling of Mays went far beyond that. What Alvin Dark had seen as gainful—but could not put to fruition—in naming Mays team captain the year before, Herman Franks could and did execute in extraordinary measure in 1965. New York *Post* columnist Milton Gross indeed saw in the new Willie something even more than a captain:

Undoubtedly it does Herman Franks a great injustice to ask who will be the next Giant manager. Could it be Willie Mays? Don't snicker. He's been the assistant manager all year.

"Man," Willie screamed in protest, "don't call me that. Herman's a good man. He's been doing a good job. He don't misuse a man. He don't abuse him."

True, true, but Mays is such a great one, he's not only been the team leader this season, he's been a coach, a whip-cracker, a shoulder for the young and an example for the old.

"I don't want to think of things like managing," said Willie. "I got enough to think about playing, but I'll tell you this. In my mind there ain't any job I can't do on a baseball field." . . .

The point is Willie does not completely reject the possibility of becoming the first Negro manager. He'd rather not discuss it seriously, but he's serious when he says he knows in his own heart he could do it.

Item: Second-baseman Hal Lanier is considered the "captain" of the Giants' infield. It is his duty to talk to the pitcher, give him a breather, a moment to think. It was Willie who appointed Lanier to this task, and it is Willie to whom Lanier looks for instructions in the field during the course of the game.

"Nobody in the whole organization taught me more about this game than Mays," Lanier confessed. "I watch him out in the outfield, and when he waves me to go in and talk to the pitcher, I go. The pitcher knows I'm coming in to him on Willie's order, and that's good enough for him."

This is so great a departure from what Mays used to be that it is almost startling to listen to Willie say it. In the past he would never offer advice to another player unless the player came and asked. It is more than a measure of maturity for the 34-year-old. Why the change?

"This year," says Mays, "they talked to me. This year they told me to do it. This year I'm encouraged to say what's on my mind."

"They" are president Stoneham, vice-president Chub Feeney and even Herman Franks.

The Hal Lanier of the Milton Gross account was the son of former St. Louis Cardinals pitcher Max Lanier, and so became known as "Maxie." He idolized Mays, not only as man and ballplayer but as philosopher. His first time at bat in the big league, Lanier was sent spinning by a fast ball aimed at his head. "I'm not that great a hitter," he complained to Mays afterward. "Why would they do that to *me?*"

"It's because you're new, Maxie," Mays explained. "That's their way of saying hello."

The qualities of leadership suggested here of course did not arise overnight, nor did the opportunity to display them. Dark's insecure state the previous season had permitted Mays only one practical moment of any authority, but that was a pretty good one: the meeting he called in Pittsburgh to put down the mutiny against Dark. In 1974, a Grosset and Dunlap book, *The Sports Encyclopedia: Baseball,* would reveal statistically, in Roger Angell's phrase, "a clustering of black and Latin stars at the top levels of baseball accomplishment." In 1975, with the Giants up for sale, Herman Franks tried to put together an offer to buy the club. The effort was unsuccessful; if it had succeeded, his intent was to liberate Willie Mays from the Mets, for whom Mays now was a coach, and install him as Giant manager. Alvin Dark in the meantime had not once but twice undergone the public humiliation of managing for, and being fired by, Charles O. Finley of the A's, and the criticism that went with it. ("You couldn't manage a meat market," Dark's third baseman, Sal Bando, said to him cheerfully at one point while Dark was under Finley's thumb.) Dick Williams and Bobby Winkles were two managers who retained some dignity by quitting the A's job. Wrote Stephanie Salter in the San Francisco *Examiner:*

Dignity to Finley is an unaffordable luxury for anyone who wants to manage a major league club. If ever a person believed each man has his price, it is Finley. He has seen them come and go, usually lesser men when they exit, yet they continue. After every cashiering, he has seen the eyes of the unemployed light up. Along with Dick Williams, Bobby Winkles has become the second man in history to tell Charlie Finley to stick it. Like e.e. cummings' Olaf, he decided, "There is some s——— I will not eat." Although his departure will do nothing more than inconvenience Finley, and perhaps perplex him for a moment or two, it will distinguish Winkles from the rest of the gang. Maybe the desire to be credited with something—besides the ability to repress anger, lie with a smile on his face and make jokes about his own manhood—was behind Winkles' decision to leave.

(Willie Mays with his license plates had nothing on Alvin Dark. Roger Angell did a 1975 spring training piece during the time Dark was with the A's, and reported spotting Dark's car parked outside Rendezvous Park, the club's spring headquarters in Mesa, Arizona—"a big, mocha-colored Imperial LeBaron, with Florida plates and two rear bumper stickers. 'A's, World Champions' was on the left side and 'Jesus Is Coming Soon! Every Knee Shall Bow' on the right.")

It was during Herman Franks's tenure as the Giant manager that he and his Salt Lake City accountant-associate Ernie Psarras convinced Mays to join them in a company that would specialize in apartment-house ownership and give the best application to Mays's financial condition. This went a giant step toward getting Willie permanently well, where management of his money and taxes was involved, and it postulated a unique manager/captain-player association. Not everyone, particularly in the Giant front office, was swatted in the tail with this arrangement. If Mays ever wanted to turn prima donna, his own manager would support him at every point. Though at his own expense, Mays maintained a private room at hotels when the team was on the road, and used cabs rather than the team bus as often as not. On one occasion, the Giant team voted unanimously for a rotation seating basis on airplanes so everyone would get his shot at first-class space. On the second road trip following the vote, Mays found himself in the coach section. Noting this, Franks went storming to the team's traveling secretary, Frank Bergonzi. "What's he doing back there?" he demanded. Taken aback, Bergonzi said, "He voted for it with all the rest. He's as equal as anybody else." "God damn," Franks said, "he's *more* equal than anybody else. From now on put him in first class!" It was one of those purifying cases where both sides were right. A prima donna acts like a prima donna because she is a prima donna. It is as simple as that. There comes to mind Oscar Levant's recollection of the time he and George Gershwin were traveling cross-country in a Pullman compartment, and the question arose of who would occupy what sleeping space. Gershwin settled it. Pointing to Levant, he said, "Talent in the upper berth." Pointing to himself, he said, "Genius in the lower." Or, as Captain Queeg would remark, rank has its privileges.

There is no evidence that Mays's teammates seriously begrudged him his perks. They appreciated his seniority and admired his work, but over and beyond that they perceived that he was paving the way for their own commensurate advancements: the top-paid man on the team enhanced the salary environment for everybody else, particularly when his presence guaranteed a better shot at a pennant, therefore more fans in the stands, therefore more income for the club. The Mays who went to spring training under Franks in 1965 was the same Mays who had gone to spring training under Dark in 1964 and had caused columnist Roger Williams to write that he was through, his eyes and legs gone, no longer any more than the third most valuable Giant. Though it never occurred to Williams, this public assessment, however inaccurate, could serve just as neatly as a favorable appraisal, if not even more so, to implement the salary demands of players earning less. In the late sixties, Juan Marichal actually based a fairly successful holdout on what Willie Mays was making, a technique by no means uncommon.

And the 1965 Giants were a resounding success—by every yardstick save their failure to win the pennant. During his career, Willie Mays played for four pennant-winning teams: the 1951 and 1954 New York Giants, the 1962 San Francisco Giants, the 1973 New York Mets. Ted Williams played for one pennant-winning team. Ernie Banks played for none. Yogi Berra played on fourteen pennant-winners in his nineteen-year career. A catcher named Charlie Silvera, who in his ten-year career came to bat fewer times than Willie Mays averaged for a single season, played on eight pennant-winning teams. It is possible to argue therefore that Charlie Silvera was at least eight times better than Ted Williams, if the connection between individual greatness and team success is taken seriously. Robin Roberts and Rod Carew might argue differently. Roberts as a Phillies pitcher and Carew as a Twins hitter dominated their leagues season in and season out with infrequent semblance of working for even a contending team, let alone a champion.

Within that no-pennant context, the 1965 Giants nevertheless were indeed a resounding success. They won 95 games, which was 2 more than the pennant-winning Cardinals of the year before, and they reversed their previous year's decline in home attendance, while setting the highest road-attendance figure in the club's history. Having won 14 straight games, the Giants were in first place by 4½ games on September 16. The Dodgers then won 13 in a row to capture the pennant, but at least they won it: the Giants did not lose it. Nor was it the worst season Willie Mays ever had. Having led the league in home runs with 47 in 1964, he now hit 52 in 1965 to lead the league again, making him, a decade after his 51 homers of 1955, the only National Leaguer other than Ralph Kiner to hit 50 or more homers more than once. Kiner, who had become a Mets broadcaster, was at the microphone in Shea Stadium the day—it was August 29, 1965—Mays set a record by hitting his 17th home run of the month. It was Kiner who had held the previous mark of 16, and it fell his lot to interview Willie after the game.

Actually, Willie interviewed him. "Are you sore?" he asked. "Of course I'm sore," Kiner replied. "Wouldn't you be?"

In Houston two weeks later, Mays hit the 500th home run of his career, a game-tying shot into the center-field bleachers off Don Nottebart. Waiting for him as he reached the dugout was Warren Spahn, now in the last September of his own storied career, as a spot starter for the Giants.

"I threw you the first one and now I've seen the five hundredth," he said to Mays. His voice broke. "Was it anything like the same feeling?"

"It *was* the same feeling," Mays said. He looked out on the field and at the roaring standing ovation from the Houston fans. Then he turned back to Spahn. "Same pitch, too."

In the ninth inning the following night, again Mays tied the score with a home run, and this 501st homer of his career is the one he remembers most fondly of all. The setting was ideal: two out, a man on base, the Giants trailing by two runs, Mays their last chance to keep them alive. What made matters extra-special, though, was the reaction of Claude Raymond, the Houston pitcher. With the count 2-and-2, he went with his fast ball to see if he could smoke strike three past Willie. "It was like challenging God," Herman Franks said afterward. Raymond wound and threw, and Mays fouled off the pitch. Raymond threw another fast ball. Mays fouled it off. Again a fast ball. Another foul. Again a fast ball. The fourth foul. The Houston team was en route to a ninth-place finish in a ten-team league, but the buildup of tension here was as though the pennant were at stake. The fans were on their feet as Raymond studied his catcher's sign. They weren't rooting for the Giants. They weren't rooting for the home-team Astros either. They were rooting for Willie Mays.

Half a continent away, half the city of San Francisco had the radio tuned to KSFO, listening to Russ Hodges as he broadcast the action. The acoustics from the Astrodome were excellent. Each time Mays fouled a pitch, the contact of bat with ball came over the radio loud and clear, and with that near-indescribable but utterly reliable "foul" sound to it. Aristotelian dramaturgy provided, without a question in anyone's heart or mind, that the next pitch from Raymond would, like the previous four, be in the strike zone. And it would be a fast ball.

Mr. Raymond was to oblige on both counts. He stretched, wound, delivered. And—the acoustics so perfect—*Crack!* said the radio. Nobody in San Francisco even had to wait for Hodges to pronounce his "Bye-Bye Baby!" The sound of it even told the listeners *where* the home run went—it could be nothing other than Willie's power alley to left, far up into the seats.

Charley Callahan, the sports publicist for Notre Dame, was in San Francisco that night and happened to be passing through the lobby of the Jack Tar Hotel at the moment Mays hit the homer. He heard the crashing of a waiter's tray in the adjoining restaurant, saw a registration clerk go straight up in the air and a staid old lady suddenly start hopping like a jackrabbit over the deep-pile carpeting. Given the site, it was Callahan's flash reaction that another earthquake had hit.

Needless to recount, the Giants would go on to win the game in extra innings. Their joyous reaction in the dugout, as Mays circled the bases, took at least one strange form as Juan Marichal, talking softly to himself in Spanish, started searching the seat cushions vacated by his celebrating teammates. Manager Franks picked this up out of the corner of his eye.

"What's he doing?" he asked coach Larry Jansen.

"I think he's looking for his glove," Jansen said.

"Why?"

"He wants to go in and pitch when they come up."

"He pitched nine innings yesterday. Is he out of his fucking mind?"

(Nearly six years later, the night of May 6, 1971, an audience of 700 gathered in the Grand Ballroom of the Fairmont Hotel atop San Francisco's Nob Hill. The occasion was a fortieth birthday party for Willie Mays, who was off to one of his fast starts that season—including home runs in each of the Giants' first four games of the year—and the ceremonial phase of the evening began as the lights in the ballroom dimmed, finally to total darkness, and upon the room came the voice of Russ Hodges, who had died the previous month. It was Hodges's description of Willie's 501st. Partially of course it was a moving and effective tribute to the late beloved sportscaster, but when that *Crack!* sounded, the audience came roaring to its feet in the darkness, as if the home run had just that moment happened.

(Even then, the greening of that 501st homer was to continue onward. In 1979, when Mays was elected to the Hall of Fame, Harry Jupiter, a San Francisco newsman who had covered that 501st in 1965, recalled the event complete to the assertion that Mays had fouled off *eleven* Raymond fast balls before hitting the home run! Nor would it end even there. In separate interviews with Roger Angell in the spring of 1991, more than a quarter century after the night in question, none other than the principals themselves—batsman Mays and pitcher Raymond—would each insist that Willie had fouled off *thirteen* consecutive fast balls before connecting! Is it true that sooner or later the gods of mythology become their own best customers? Bob Stevens' morning-after story of the game in the *San Francisco Chronicle* of Sept. 15, 1965, said the at-bat went two balls, then two swinging strikes, then four fouls, then the homer.)

As he had in 1954, Mays would win the National League's most valuable player award in 1965. For the same man to win that award two different times was not precedential. But for the two awards to occur *eleven years apart* was unheard of. At least one member of the Hall of Fame—Jackie Robinson, no less—is in there with an entire major league career that didn't last eleven years.

(The charge is heard from time to time that the Baseball Writers' Association of America, from whose ranks certain panels vote for Most Valuable and Hall of Fame selections, tilts in favor of media-heavy New York. But the anti–New York strain is there too. There is little question that the influence of that group was what denied election to the Hall of Fame of Joe DiMaggio in his first year of eligibility, and there is little question that the same prejudice cost Mays his shot at becoming Most Valuable Player in 1962, the year he led the Giants to their National League championship. On the voting scale that year, Willie lost out to Maury Wills by 7 points, 202 to Wills's 209. But in 1962 he was still viewed as a New Yorker, and his bid was shot down. In 1978, as his own point of eligibility for the Hall of Fame grew closer—having completed the mandatory five-season waiting period since the end of his playing career, Mays would go before the electorate for winter balloting, the results to be announced in January of 1979 and his induction into the Hall to come at Cooperstown the ensuing midsummer—he wanted little truck with any glowing predictions. "Joe D. didn't even make it the first year he was up," Mays said warily. "And look what happened to me in 'sixty-two."

(He had no such problems in 1954 and 1965. In '54, he was not only Most Valuable Player in the National League but the Associated Press selection as Athlete of the Year. *Time* celebrated him with a cover story. In '65, again it was no contest for Most Valuable, and this time *Life* took up the account. "To his team he gives the best—and he gives baseball its finest hours," ran the late-September *Life* headline over a story that included the following:

> Earlier this month the National League had appeared to be headed into the first six-team dead-heat finish in history. Suddenly—but not inexplicably, for Mays is the reason—five of the six teams were outpaced, outclassed and outplayed by the most brilliant virtuoso performance ever seen in baseball. Whatever the outcome of the pennant race—the Los Angeles Dodgers and the Cincinnati Reds were battling all the way—the incomparable and dazzling Willie had given baseball its finest hour in years.)

Eleven years. One way of expressing that spread in time could be in terms of the U.S. space program. From the first beeping satellite—only a fraction the size of Russia's Sputnik, which Barry Goldwater had dismissed as "a basketball in outer space"—to putting a man on the moon would take America eleven years. Yet for Mays, the eleven years between most-valuable awards were almost a form of time in colloidal suspension. He stole one more base in 1965 than he had in 1954. In the field, he had 13 assists and 7 errors in 1954; 13 assists and 6 errors in 1965. (The figures for assists are shown here for comparison only, that category being a meaningless and potentially misleading index of an outfielder's throwing ability. Teams with good pitching have fewer baserunners to contend with, and often the ultimate test of an outfielder's arm lies in the runner's decision *not* to test it. A better reading comes from the outfielder's total of double plays. Here Mays set a record by leading the league in four separate seasons. Including 1954 and 1965!) That eleven-year spread, of course, actually represents twelve complete seasons. All twelve of those seasons, Mays scored more than 100 runs. He was twenty-two years of age going into the '54 season, when he scored 119 runs. With the passage of time, his legs must weary. He was thirty-four when the '65 season ended. That year he scored 118 runs. In two consecutive seasons beginning with 1954, he hit 92 home runs in 1,145 at-bats. In two consecutive seasons ending with 1965, he hit 99 home runs in 1,136 at-bats. Those latter totals for the years 1964–65 came on the heels of the Roger Williams column proclaiming that Mays was washed up, a column that proved unsettling to TV producer Lee Mendelson, whose special on Mays had aired the previous fall and who started pressing NBC to schedule the rerun before it was too late. The network soothed him with an unusual display of prescience. "We consider the Mays show one of our two perennials," Ed Friendly of NBC told Mendelson. "What's the other one?" Mendelson asked. "Peter Pan," Friendly said.

If Friendly reduced it to two words, the supporting statistics offer their own show of brevity, as Herbert Wind had suggested. With the occasional exception of something like outfield assists, baseball statistics have an authenticity all their own. One reason for this is that the game has changed so little over the years, but another reason, I have always believed, is that the umpires do not have to come equipped with whistles. The plays that never get into the record book in football and basketball, nullified by this penalty or that personal foul, would cram a book all their own. Indeed, infractions have become so much a part of the two-dimensional sports that in basketball, as Red Smith disgustedly pointed out, the strategy of intentionally fouling an opponent has advanced to the level of a graduate science. So long as they go undetected, such infractions are a vital part of winning football too, to the point that even when the whistle blows it is possible to be philosophical about it. The great Hugh McElhenny once had a brilliant 95-yard run called back because of a clipping penalty. Asked if he was disappointed at seeing the yardage and the touchdown wiped from the record, McElhenny merely shrugged. "If he doesn't clip him, I don't go 95 to begin with," he explained.

Baseball certainly has its rules, and the rules have their violators. The more civilized, the less simplistic. . . . So mote it be, as the Masons say. A batter is not entitled to run to first base on a dropped third strike if the base is occupied with less than two out. But suppose he forgets and runs anyway? Now suppose the catcher also forgets, throws to first to get him, and overthrows into right field instead? Answer: All hell breaks loose. On the action calls . . . safe or out, ball or strike, fair or foul . . . the judgment of the umpires is final; but a game may be continued under protest if a team feels a rule has been misapplied. If the protest is upheld after consideration by the president of the league, the game is replayed from the point just before the protested action occurred. The majority of protests never even get to the point of final judgment by the league president: some teams are not alert enough to protest at once, which the rules mandate; others go on to win the game, leaving nothing to protest about. (An exception occurred in 1978, when a minor league manager, having won the game, let his protest stand that a ball hit by an enemy batsman had turned egg-shaped in mid-flight. The president of the league apparently protested in turn to the president of Haiti, where the balls were manufactured.) The wonder of it is that so many protests do reach the point of decision, establishing as they do the infinite subtleties and byways of the great American game. Harry Simmons's marvelous series *So You Think You Know Baseball*, based for the most part on registered protests, ran weekly for years in the *Saturday Evening Post* and later became one of several "knotty problem" books that enjoyed handsome circulation. To this day, Hal Lebovitz features baseball in his "Ask the Referee" column in *The Sporting News*. A master at citing the rules, Lebovitz also can cite what the book does not. "Reminds me," he wrote in reply to one reader's question, "of the time the Indians and Giants were playing a spring exhibition game in Denver. The outfield was ringed with snow. Ray Boone hit one deep to center, far behind the snow bank, but quick-witted Willie Mays reached back, came up with a gloveful of snow, held it high and the ump called Boone out."

The variety and intellectual challenge inherent in baseball—it is almost impossible to watch a baseball game at any level without seeing something, whatever it may be, that is new to the experience—comes close to being certified by the following wire-service story from the mid-sixties:

CINCINNATI – (AP) – National League President Warren C. Giles yesterday disallowed a protest filed by Philadelphia manager Gene Mauch, who claimed that Pittsburgh pitcher Elroy Face "was inside the Forbes Field scoreboard for six innings during the May 28 Phillies-Pirates game."

The Pirates said Face "went into the scoreboard after the fifth inning, and before the Philadelphia club came to bat in the top of the sixth inning," to use the restroom facilities.

Giles said, "It has been common practice to use the ground-level lavatory facilities in the Pittsburgh scoreboard." He added:

"To allow a protest and order

a game replayed, there must be conclusive evidence that the action which is the subject of the protest directly affected the final outcome of the game. I find no such evidence in this case."

Pittsburgh won the game, 6–5, in the ninth inning.

———❦———

The year 1965 was marked by the death of Sir Winston Churchill, and the U.S. delegation in attendance at his London funeral was headed by Dwight Eisenhower. (A story was that LBJ was going to send the newly elected Vice-President, Hubert Humphrey, but he was afraid Hubert would laugh.) Stateside, motion picture distributors were laughing and crying simultaneously. Television and the flight to the suburbs had shuttered one movie theater after another, but there was a counterbalancing boom in drive-in theaters whose very life, in many cases, would be their death: one drive-in site after another would be taken over to house the suburban population whose growth had put the drive-in there to begin with. As Yale law professor Charles Reich would later write, the technology that went with the new America was "surprisingly vulnerable to breakdown." His book *The Greening of America* would expand on this:

> What good is a $250,000 cooperative apartment if, due to the decay in schooling and job training, a robber waits in the hallway or elevator? A luxurious suburban home, if one is a prisoner in it, surrounded by locked gates, private watchmen, and beware-of-the-dog signs to ward off the discontented populace? Shopping in the city if one is likely to get caught in a breakdown of the subway, commuter rail services, or in a giant traffic jam?

The hottest ad agency around was an outfit called Doyle Dane Bernbach, which had pioneered the successful invasion of the small foreign car with its brilliant selling campaign for Volkswagen. The agency insisted on artistic freedom even when it agreed to do the television commercials for Lyndon Johnson's 1964 campaign. The result of that was a TV spot showing a little girl picking petals from a flower, then vanishing in a nuclear explosion. The spot ran only once before the agency pulled it. Once did the job. Almost as short-lived were two Doyle Dane Bernbach billboards for Volkswagen. One showed a front view of a Volkswagen beetle and van parked side by side, with the beetle saying to the van, "FUNNY, YOU DON'T LOOK IT." The other showed a van surrounded by its many occupants, all male except one. Ran the underline: "I'LL TAKE ON THE WHOLE GANG."

As reported by William Manchester, a dying Douglas MacArthur had some advice for President Johnson at the Walter Reed Hospital in Washington: no American soldier should be made to fight on Asian soil. Even more ominously, the old general forecast that the time might be dangerously near when many Americans might not have the will to fight for their country. The dissatisfaction with the war in Vietnam was growing in curious tandem with dissatisfaction over civil rights. But Martin Luther King would tie the two together. "No one," he would say, "can pretend that the existence of the war is not profoundly affecting the destiny of civil rights progress." In the abstract, King thought that Vietnam had turned the United States into "the greatest purveyor of violence in the world today." In the ratiocinative, he saw money that should have been spent in the ghettos going to pay for the war instead. In the concrete, he saw Negroes fighting and dying in Vietnam in numbers strikingly disproportionate to the U.S. population at large.

In his book *The Vantage Point*, LBJ isolates July 27, 1965, as the date on which "two great streams in our national life converged —the dream of a Great Society at home and the inescapable demands of our obligations halfway around the world." It was a cabinet meeting that day that set this tone, and LBJ's solution for it was set before the Congress in his State-of-the-Union address the following January:

"I believe," I said to the assembled legislators, "that we can continue the Great Society while we fight in Vietnam." In that sentence, to which the Congress responded with heartening applause, the turmoil of months was resolved, and the Great Society moved through midpassage into its final years of creative activity and accomplishment.

If contrary to the Johnson belief one sentence did not resolve the turmoil, the LBJ guns-and-butter commitment was real. So (see again the deep-South vote against him in the 1964 election) was his commitment to the Negro. The commitment, in Johnson's remembrance, was evolutionary:

> When I was in the Senate, we had an extra car to take back to Texas at the close of each congressional session. Usually my Negro employees—Zephyr Wright, our cook; Helen Williams, our maid; and Helen's husband, Gene—drove the car to the Ranch for us. At that time, nearly twenty years ago, it was an ordeal to get an automobile from Washington to Texas—three full days of hard driving.
>
> On one of those trips I asked Gene if he would take my beagle dog with them in the car. I didn't think they would mind. Little Beagle was a friendly, gentle dog. . . .
>
> But Gene still hesitated. I didn't understand. I looked directly at him. "Tell me what's the matter. Why don't you want to take Beagle? What aren't you telling me?"
>
> Gene began slowly. Here is the gist of what he had to say: "Well, Senator, it's tough enough to get all the way from Washington to Texas. We drive for hours and hours. We get hungry. But there's no place on the road we can stop and go in and eat. We drive some more. It gets pretty hot. We want to wash up. But the only bathroom we're allowed in is usually miles off the main highway. We keep going 'til night comes—'til we get so tired we can't stay awake any more. We're ready to pull in. But it takes us another hour or so to find a place to sleep. You see, what I'm saying is that a colored man's got enough trouble getting across the South on his own, without having a dog along."
>
> Of course, I knew that such discrimination existed throughout the South. We all knew it. But somehow we had deluded ourselves into believing that the black people around us were happy

236

and satisfied; into thinking that the bad and ugly things were going on somewhere else, happening to other people.

There were no "darkies" or plantations in the arid hill country where I grew up. I never sat on my parents' or grandparents' knees listening to nostalgic tales of the antebellum South. In Stonewall and Johnson City I never was a part of the Old Confederacy. But I was part of Texas. My roots were in its soil. I felt a special identification with its history and its people. And Texas is a part of the South—in the sense that Texas shares a common heritage and outlook that differs from the Northeast or Middle West or Far West.

That Southern heritage meant a great deal to me. It gave me a feeling of belonging and a sense of continuity. But it also created—sadly, but perhaps inevitably—certain parochial feelings that flared up defensively whenever Northerners described the South as "a blot on our national conscience" or "a stain on our country's democracy."

These were emotions I took with me to the Congress when I voted against six civil rights bills that came up on the House and Senate floor. At that time I simply did not believe that the legislation, as written, was the right way to handle the problem. Much of it seemed designed more to humiliate the South than to help the black man.

Beyond this, I did not think there was much I could do as a lone Congressman from Texas. I represented a conservative constituency. One heroic stand and I'd be back home, defeated, unable to do any good for anyone, much less the blacks and the underprivileged. As a Representative and a Senator, before I became Majority Leader, I did not have the power. That is a plain and simple fact.

If that was the fabric, it began to become unstuck. On the day in 1945 when Branch Rickey signed Jackie Robinson, for the purpose of integrating organized baseball, a fourteen-year-old Willie Mays was welcome to buy his clothes in any downtown Birmingham store—but if he wanted to try them on for size and fit, he had to pay for them, then take them home and do it there. He would enter a bus or streetcar by the front door, but only to pay his fare. He then must leave the bus and walk outside to the back door and re-enter that way. The notion that integrating baseball would be the wax impression for the key to the fitting-room door at that department store, to the front door of that bus, may appear grandiloquent, but in point of historical fact it was the first move in that direction. At the point in 1947 when Robinson reached the majors and Ford Frick ordered the Cardinals to take the field against him, Harry Truman had not yet integrated the armed forces. Yet by that time, over two successive spring-training periods, a black man had been using the same shower and toilet facilities alongside whites in ball park after ball park across the old South.

The seed of change was not lost upon Lyndon Johnson. Neither was the degree of power hitherto denied him. Within a few months of the Supreme Court's epic school-desegregation decision in 1954, LBJ would become the majority leader of the Senate, where in 1957 he would lead passage of the first civil rights legislation in eighty-two years. As President, he would sign the Civil Rights Act of 1964, the most sweeping such measure enacted in the twentieth century.

> My thoughts went back to the afternoon a decade before when there was absolutely nothing I could say to Gene Williams, or to any black man, or to myself. That had been the day I first realized the sad truth: that to the extent Negroes were imprisoned, so was I. On this day, July 2, 1964, I knew the positive side of that same truth: that to the extent Negroes were free, really free, so was I. And so was my country.

On March 7, 1965, several hundred Negroes staged a protest march in Selma, Alabama, a community with 15,000 blacks of voting age. Of these, only 325 were registered to vote. The march reached the Edmund Pettus bridge, where Governor George Wallace's state troopers waited with tear gas, clubs, and bullwhips. Television cameras also waited, and the world saw the armed whites wading into the unarmed blacks, saw half a hundred victims fall under the swinging club and lashing whip.

A week later, President Johnson went before a joint session of the Congress with his Voting Rights Act:

> There is no constitutional issue here. The command of the Constitution is plain. There is no moral issue. It is wrong—deadly wrong—to deny any of your fellow Americans the right to vote in this country. There is no issue of states' rights or national rights. There is only the struggle for human rights. . . . This time, on this issue, there must be no delay, no hesitation, and no compromise with our purpose.
>
> But even if we pass this bill, the battle will not be over. What happened in Selma is part of a far larger movement which reaches into every section and state of America. It is the effort of American Negroes to secure for themselves the full blessings of American life.

Music? There was none, but you could almost hear it anyway, and the voices of a Baptist choir singing the old spiritual, as, standing in the well of the House of Representatives, this southern white President finished what he had to say:

> Their cause must be our cause too. Because it is not just Negroes, but really it is all of us who must overcome the crippling legacy of bigotry and injustice.
>
> And . . . we . . . shall . . . overcome.

For those in the chamber at the time, for the millions watching on television and the added millions who would see it on replay, Johnson's memory of what happened next would be wholly accurate:

> For a few seconds, the entire Chamber was quiet. Then the applause started and kept coming. One by one the Representatives and Senators stood up. They were joined by the Cabinet, the Justices, and the Ambassadors. Soon most of the Chamber was on its feet with a shouting ovation that I shall never forget as long as I live.

And well he should so remember it, for it was the high-water mark of his Presidency.

On April 11, 1965, LBJ signed into law the great Elementary and Secondary Education Act.

On July 9, 1965, the Medicare Bill passed the Senate.

I had a special reason for wanting to sign Medicare into law before the end of July. It would mean an extra $30 million in benefits to the aged. I had a particular place in mind for the signing. On July 27 I called President Truman and told him that I wanted to come out and have a special visit with him. On July 30 I traveled to Independence, Missouri, to sign the bill in Mr. Truman's presence in the library that bears his name. He had started it all, so many years before. I wanted him to know that America remembered. It was a proud day for all of us, and President Truman said that no single honor ever paid him had touched him more deeply.

In the LBJ summary:

Altogether, we passed sixty education bills. All of them contributed to advances across the whole spectrum of our society. When I left office, millions of young boys and girls were receiving better grade school educations than they once could have acquired. A million and a half students were in college who otherwise could not have afforded it. Thousands of adult men and women were enrolled in classes of their choice, available to them for the first time. I remember seeing, in the folder of reading material I took to my bedroom one night, the account of a sixty-two-year-old man who learned how to write his name after years of making an *X* for a signature. He was so excited that he sat for a whole hour just writing his name over and over again. Reading about this man, whose life had been singularly enriched, I was almost as excited as the man himself. In his story our striving for increased opportunity in education took shape and became real and valid.

I had the same sentiments about Medicare, whose overriding importance, to me, was that it foreshadowed a revolutionary change in our thinking about health care. We had begun, at long last, to recognize that good medical care is a right, not just a privilege. During my administration, forty national health measures were presented to the Congress and passed by the Congress —more than in all the preceding 175 years of the Republic's history. . . . This is not just a tribute to my administration's concern for the people's health but a tribute to the people themselves—a salute to what they demand of their government and to the system that makes it possible to meet the demand.

One week after his trip to Independence, LBJ returned to the Capitol on August 6, 1965, to sign the Voting Rights Act into law.

Less than a week later, on Wednesday, August 11, in the early evening of a fourth successive day of a heat wave, a California highway patrolman named Lee Minikus stopped a young Negro driver named Marquette Frye for interrogation. Suspicion of drunken driving was the cause, but Frye's mother was one of the spectators to the arrest, and she began to scream at the officer. Other assembled spectators, many of them outdoors, because with nightfall that was the coolest place, began to encourage her. The place was a heavily traveled intersection: the corner of the Imperial Highway and Avalon Boulevard in Los Angeles. It was, Bill Manchester would record,

a busy L.A. intersection through which passed a constant stream of white drivers, often behind the wheels of expensive cars. Most inauspicious of all was the neighborhood. It was 98 percent black, with a population density of 27.3 people per acre (the figure was 7.4 for Los Angeles County as a whole). Negro immigrants had been arriving here in massive numbers since the early 1940s, when an average of 2,000 each month came to work in war industries. Now 420,000 of the 2,731,000 inhabitants of the city were black. Yet in this ghetto there were just five blacks on the 205-man police force. And every month in 1965 another 1,000 Negroes poured into these swarming warrens, often looking for jobs that no longer existed. The temptations of drugs and alcohol awaited their children, and when the children went wrong The Man came after them. These snares, not the inhabitants, were the real transgressors in this district, a region known locally as Watts.

The Watts rioting lasted six days, caused losses put at $45 million, produced 34 dead, 898 injured, more than 4,000 arrested. Its most methodical by-product was looting, which was by no means a Negro invention, but so here it would come to seem. It is no sociological sophistry to pinpoint what encouraged the looters: it was television. There is simply no question of that. Charles Reich would call TV "the riot box for the poor, inflaming their desires without offering them any satisfaction at all." And since one of the products most heavily advertised on television sets is television sets, it requires minimum acumen to detect what product the looters looted the most. Indeed the imperative was to steal two television sets, not one: one to keep, the other to sell.

Watts would set the pitch for other riots across the country, not all of them ghetto-sited. An influence could be felt at other points, one of them Candlestick Park in San Francisco. Said *Time* magazine:

> Most so-called U.S. sports rivalries are frauds, preserved only by tradition. The feud between the Giants and Dodgers is real. It was bad enough when it involved Manhattan and Brooklyn, two boroughs of the same city. Now the principals are San Francisco and Los Angeles, two cities 325 miles apart whose partisans hate each other's guts. In ordinary times, Giants-Dodgers games are still games. Aug. 22, 1965 was no ordinary time.
>
> Dodger catcher Johnny Roseboro was deeply concerned about race riots in the Watts section of Los Angeles near his home. Giants pitcher Juan Marichal had been brooding over the bloody civil war in the Dominican Republic. For tinder, there was the tension of the tightest National League race in history; for fire, a provocative trading of beanballs, curses and threats. In the third inning, with the Dodgers leading 2–1, Marichal came to bat. The second pitch was low inside; Roseboro dropped the ball, then picked it up and deliberately fired it as hard as he could back to the mound—right past Juan's right ear.
>
> Marichal later claimed that the ball had ticked his ear. He spun around, bat in hand. "Why did you do that? Why did you do that?" he screamed. Roseboro did not answer. He charged at

Marichal, and in front of 42,807 witnesses at Candlestick Park, Juan clubbed him three times on the head with the bat, sending blood streaming down the catcher's face from a deep wound in his scalp.

In the bench-clearing brawl that followed, one image stood out above all others. It was the sight of Willie Mays, the shirt of his white home uniform red with blood. The blood was Roseboro's. Mays had come from the Giant dugout, isolated the Dodger catcher from the battle, and walked him away, cradling the bleeding head. Television viewers in Los Angeles could see in close-up the tears coursing down the cheeks of the Giant captain. On the newscasts that night and the following morning, the entire nation would see it.

The action of Mays in going for Roseboro was a blend of the personal and practical. On the personal side, they were friends; on the practical, Mays reasoned that Roseboro, being the one with his head laid open, might be motivated to take up the fight again. The tender way he ministered and talked to the other man was real—and just as real was the comfort of his arms around Roseboro, though it served the incidental purpose of holding him back.

As for Willie's distraught state, it was shared by others. The Giants had not even waited for the umpires to order Marichal off the field: they hustled him out of there themselves. And when play resumed, Dodger pitcher Sandy Koufax found himself walking two Giant hitters and seeing Willie Mays at bat with two out and two on. Mays had homered in each of the three previous games of this series. Now protecting a one-run lead, Koufax did not want to walk him, for that would load the bases and bring up the dangerous Jim Ray Hart. Nor did he want to go to his curve, which broke inside to a righthanded hitter, and if Sandy had thrown close to Mays in these circumstances he ran the risk of being lynched. In short, the greatest clutch pitcher in baseball was facing the greatest clutch hitter with no way to pitch to him.

Koufax did the only thing he could do: throw a fast ball down the middle and hope it stayed in the ball park. It did not stay in the ball park. His tears dried by now, Mays hit it over the fence in center field and over the fence behind the fence for the three-run homer that put the Giants ahead 4–2 and won the game.

It is no exaggeration to say that what Mays did that day, first with Roseboro and then to Koufax, brought him finally, late in his eighth San Francisco season, the true adoration of Bay Area baseball fans, and this would endure without break for the remainder of his career. Likely it is no exaggeration either to label Koufax, as above, the greatest clutch pitcher in baseball, though at that point one man might have challenged him for that title. That one man was Juan Marichal, who had already won 19 games for the Giants that season.

Now it was up to National League president Warren Giles to decide what to do. Fining Marichal was easy, and Giles did so, to the tune of $1,750—not in those days, or even these days, a minor amount. But by itself a fine would not suffice. Giles knew he had to suspend Marichal. But for how long? The league president may have played the part of Solomon in determining what Elroy Face was doing in the bathroom inside the scoreboard that time, but in determining how long he should deprive a contending team of its ace pitcher at the height of a pennant race, Giles faced a truly torturous challenge.

In truth, no one was told how torturous it actually was. Giles put a public face on it: to penalize Marichal, he must penalize the Giants. But the Giants had done nothing wrong. "Shall I penalize Willie Mays?" Giles said in a television interview. "If so, how does such fine and decent conduct deserve a penalty? This man was an example of the best in any of us."

Giles decided to suspend Marichal for eight days, with accompanying implication that under different circumstances the suspension would have been for the entire remainder of the season. But again, that was the public face. The private face was that the Giants would be going into Los Angeles for a two-game series with the Dodgers there on September 6 and 7, and from Los Angeles, Sacramento, and Washington had come the word: Marichal must not pitch against the Dodgers in their home park. In fact, he must not even show up. If there had been nothing primarily racial in the Roseboro episode, nevertheless Watts had happened. It was bad enough that the Giants were coming to town: you could not jam 56,000 people within the confines of four acres and expect them to tolerate Marichal too.

Thus it was that Giles's determination of eight days as the duration of Marichal's suspension was governed more by the schedule than anything else. It would permit Marichal to pitch in Philadelphia, then again in Chicago, the latter stop one day ahead of the Giants' appearance in Los Angeles. Thus he would not be in the normal rotation against L.A. anyway and could be kept away without exciting undue comment.

That was fine unless it rained. It did rain. Marichal's start in Philadelphia was held up one day, but he got it in. Then Herman Franks, knowing the true state of affairs, pitched him on short rest in Chicago, and he never did make the trip to Los Angeles.

He was booed in Philadelphia and Chicago, and in Los Angeles the Giants were booed en masse—until Willie Mays stepped to bat in the first inning. In that moment the Giant-hating crowd came to its feet in an astounding, roaring ovation. It had happened at all the other stops on the road trip that commenced the day after the Marichal-Roseboro game . . . similar ovations for Mays at Pittsburgh, New York, Philadelphia, and Chicago. But Willie was well beloved in those places, and it had not been their man who'd had his head laid open by a baseball bat. Neither were their teams battling head and head with the Giants for first place. Neither had they experienced a Watts riot so shortly before.

The point was inescapable that Mays had become a socio-political figure. He had heard before, and would hear again, the voices of fellow blacks excoriating him for not getting involved.

Yet to a man the black spectators at Dodger Stadium were cheering him just as lustily as the whites. As for not getting involved, that was blood on his shirt that day at Candlestick. And it spoke for decency, a commodity in short supply. And the public knew it.

Opening day of the following season, 1966, Marichal pitched and Mays homered, and Bill Thompson, the interview man in the Giants' radio team, decided to put the two winning heroes on the air together after the game. "Fuck it," Mays said to him. "Use Marichal."

"You don't want to go on?" Thompson said.

"Not with him," Mays said.

The opening-day game was with the Cubs, now managed by Leo Durocher. As always, he worshiped Willie. As always, he was out to win, and ordered his pitcher, Bill Faul—known as "Looney Tunes" to his teammates—to throw at Willie's head. Faul did, and Mays went down, then got up and started out toward the mound to get at Faul, until his reason reminded him this was Leo's doing, not the pitcher's. By unspoken agreement, it was Marichal's job now to retaliate by throwing at the Cubs' leading hitter, Ernie Banks. (Technically, a pitcher was supposed to protect his hitter by throwing at the enemy pitcher who had put him down, but too frequently the other team's pitcher came to bat at the wrong time, if at all.) In this instance, what Marichal threw at Banks was a courtesy pitch: a lazy looper over his head. The reminder was there, but Banks did not even have to duck, and Mays was infuriated. In time, he cooled off and apologized to Marichal, for it had come to him that Juan was in an impossible situation: with the Roseboro incident still so fresh from late the previous season, he could hardly start off this season with a beanball.

(Mays was the last hitter in the National League to take to wearing a batting helmet. He disliked the weight of it, and depended on quick reflex to get out of the way of the pitch. The reflex in his case had to be pretty good. Actually, the practice of "head-hunting," as duster pitches were called, had been reduced since the coming of the Negro to the majors. Too often, it could have smacked of racism, and word went down from the front offices to lay off; in the old days, when it was whites vs. whites, nobody cared. But in the case of Willie Mays, pitcher after pitcher threw at him, not because they disliked him but because they knew what he could do when he was dug in at the plate. It was nearly automatic that Don Drysdale of the Dodgers would put Willie down at least once per game, and others did it almost as regularly. The basic protection for Mays lay in the Giant pitchers, like Jack Sanford, Gaylord Perry, and the pre-Roseboro Marichal, who would retaliate by throwing at the other team even harder and more viciously than the rival pitcher had thrown at the Giant captain. In one surrealistic exhibition game one year the pitchers throwing at each other were brothers, Gaylord Perry of the Giants and Jim Perry of the Indians.)

It was in the Giants' 13th game of the 1966 season, at Houston on April 24, that Mays hit his sixth home run of that young campaign. It was homer number 511 of his career, tying him with the legendary Giant Mel Ott for the most home runs ever hit by a National Leaguer. The following day the Giants would be opening a ten-day home stand at Candlestick Park, and Eddie Logan, the Giants' clubhouse man and equipment supervisor, decided he would bake a cake to celebrate the record-breaking 512th homer. Not just local stations but network television crews descended on Candlestick Park. Mays's 512th would prove to be the most heavily covered home run until Henry Aaron passed Babe Ruth eight years later.

Atlanta came in to play the Giants at Candlestick April 25 and 26. Mays did not hit a home run. Cincinnati came in for the 27th and 28th. Mays did not hit a home run. St. Louis came in the 29th. Mays did not hit a home run. Nor did he on the 30th, but the Giants had an easy win that day and Herman Franks took Willie out of the game early. Gazing at what now had become the latest addition to miles of unused film footage on the floor of the photography booth, an out-of-town cameraman said to his director, "I guess we can go home now." "Keep rolling," the director advised. "They may send him back into the game."

Sunday, June 1, Mays did not hit a home run. Monday was a day off. Tuesday the 3rd, the Dodgers came in. Mays did not hit a home run. Wednesday the 4th, he did hit it, to right field off Claude Osteen in the fifth inning. To say he had planned it this way would be to say too much—or would it? He had hit it at home, and against the Dodgers, and with one game left in the home stand in case something went wrong. "I took a shot at every pitch you saw the past ten days," a TV cameraman said to him. "So did I," Mays said. But the theater of it was perfect, as it had been so many times before, and as it would be yet again.

For the first time before a San Francisco crowd, Willie Mays was brought by the thundering stands to come out of the dugout after the home run and doff his cap. The moment was unique. Not anticipating the extra bow in this town, the umpire at home plate had bade the game go forward. As a result, the photograph of Mays as he emerged to accept the plaudits of the fans shows him in the full forefront, cap in hand, while in the background the fans packed in the stands are all looking the other way. As Mays came out of the dugout, Tito Fuentes, the next Giant batter, had just hit the first triple of his major league career.

As for the ball itself—the one Mays hit for the home run—it turned out he had hit it into a cartel. Anticipating this might be the night, a man had brought his two sons to the game. All three of them had fielder's gloves. One of them prowled behind the right-field fence, another in left, while the father was the spokesman when he offered the ball to Horace Stoneham in the Giant clubhouse after the game. Stoneham offered him tickets to future games and $100. The man said that was not enough and turned to Mays to ask him what he thought.

"Keep it," Willie told him.

"You can send this ball to Cooperstown if the price is right," the man said. "Mr. Stoneham would like that."

"Keep it," Mays told him.

"I'll keep it," the man said, still dealing, "but only if you autograph it."

"Give me your pen," Mays said, and autographed the ball.

The clubhouse meanwhile was a shambles of cameras and microphones. Not all of the interviewers could get close to Mays, and so they fell to interviewing whoever was closest at hand. "And standing by my side here is Eddie Logan," one reporter intoned into his microphone. "He's the clubhouse manager who goes back with the Giants since before Willie joined them. Isn't that right, Eddie?" Eddie said that was right, and indeed it was. He not only went back to the old Polo Grounds but actually lived there with his family, in a windowless apartment underneath the left-field stands. "It was a long wait for this homer, wasn't it, Eddie?" the interviewer said. "Almost the whole home stand." Eddie agreed it had been a long wait. "But now he's hit it," the interviewer said, "and now what's the good word?" It was the old southern railroad joke. "Don't eat that cake," Logan said.

With his 512th homer, Mays now stood behind Jimmy Foxx, an American Leaguer who had hit 534 home runs in his big league career, to make him the top righthanded home run hitter of all time. On August 16, 1966, again at home, Mays tied Foxx. The following day he homered off Ray Washburn of the Cardinals for his record-breaking 535th. The first man to shake Willie's hand at home plate was the umpire, Chris Pelekoudas, who had been the object of Murakami's salutation the year before. Things kept happening to Pelekoudas when he umpired Giant games. This time, he realized that his handshake for Willie might be misconstrued: he turned with a shit-eating grin to the Cardinal dugout, where manager Red Schoendienst stared impassively back. That night, Pelekoudas turned himself in to league president Giles, saying that the handshake had been involuntary and was not intended to favor one pennant contender over another. (Giles responded that he would overlook it this one time, provided Pelekoudas did not do it again. "When was *again* going to be?" Pelekoudas wondered.)

Once again in 1966 it would come down to a pennant fight between the Giants and Dodgers. The night of September 7 was the last meeting between the two teams that season, at Los Angeles. If the Giants won, they would leave Los Angeles trailing the Dodgers by half a game in the standings. They came to the top of the 12th inning, tied 2–2, Willie Mays at bat, two out. He was hurting . . . so hobbled by a pulled thigh muscle that manager Franks had transferred him to left field instead of center, so he wouldn't have to run as much. The pitch rode in . . . low, for a ball. Dodger catcher Roseboro boxed it, and the ball bounced on home plate. One-handed, Mays stuck out his bat, caught the ball with the very tip of the bat, balanced it there serenely, then flipped it back to the Dodger catcher. It was showmanship incarnate—almost a circus act—and the crowd roared at the beauty of it.

Now came ball four, and Mays limped to first base, and Franks sent up a raw rookie named Frank Johnson, newly from Phoenix, as a pinch hitter. In his first major league game, Johnson was now coming to bat before a tense sea of 56,000 faces. He had never seen a crowd like that in his life. He swung at the first pitch and made contact, looping the ball into right field for a single. The right fielder picked it up and whipped the ball back to Jim LeFebvre, the Dodger second baseman.

It was the classic mistake. You did not throw the ball behind Willie Mays when he was on the bases. Anybody else, fine. Not Mays.

Was he limping as he tooled standing up into third base? Nobody remembers. What is remembered is that he was not limping as he suddenly cut out for home plate. A startled LeFebvre threw the ball home, where John Roseboro awaited, blocking the plate. He had the ball before Mays got there, but he did not have it solidly, and as Willie hit him the ball popped loose, and there in a swirl of dirt Willie Mays arose from his slide, one hand keeping the sprawled Roseboro quiescent while the other pointed at the ball. "Out!" roared the umpire, then: "No, goddamn, safe!" as he followed Willie's pointing finger. The Giants were ahead, 3–2. Not for the first time, the rabid Los Angeles crowd could have been mistaken for a rabid San Francisco crowd. Peals of applause followed Mays as he limped to the dugout, greeted him again as he limped out to left field to take up his position for the last of the 12th. There was no problem. The Giants won the game, and in the clubhouse afterward I noticed two things I expected, one thing I didn't. What was expected was the horde of newsmen who would ask manager Franks if he had signaled Mays to continue on home from third base. "Sure," Herman said heavily. "I turned around in the dugout and got a towel and waved it at him." One Los Angeles writer said, "I notice he looks behind him when he runs. Do you advise that?" No, said Franks. "Did you ever speak to Willie about it?" No, said Franks. "What about Charley Fox, your third base coach? Have you talked to him about it?" No, said Franks. "Is it up to Fox to tell Mays what to do?" No, said Franks. Then the horde gathered before Willie. "What made you think you could score from first on a little single like that?" I've scored on singles before, said Mays. "But in a game as important as this one?" They're all important, said Mays. "But not like this one." No, Mays said, not like this one. "Then why'd you do it? You couldn't even run on that bad leg." We had a plane to catch, Mays said. It was time to get it over with.

Then the horde turned to Frank Johnson, the rookie who had hit the ball, and this was what I had failed to expect. Johnson was married and a father. But when Willie Mays first joined the Giants, he was an eight-year-old in El Paso, Texas. Tonight in his first big league game he had got the old man home from first base with a single. He sat in front of his locker and his entire body shook with emotion and excitement. He said the banal, everyday thing: "I was just trying to make contact with the ball." For he had been just as much a spectator as anyone else in the park when Mays, instead of pulling into third, suddenly turned it on and broke for the plate. It comes, once in a joyous moment in a lifetime it comes—and not just in baseball, surely not just in baseball, but baseball has the record book that is ready for it—when the apprentice gets the run batted in for the run scored by the master. I thought of Mays and Franks as they would postmortem the game and snap irritatedly, each to the other, about the failure of the second baseman in the fifth inning to relay to the center fielder the switch in the catcher's sign for the next pitch. Mays had made the catch when the batter hit the ball, but he had to run all-out, and he and Franks knew where the fault lay. And here was the twenty-four-year-old Johnson, shaking, literally shaking, in this unexpected crush of interviewers, trying to say how and why he happened to get the game-winning hit. The truth was that the master had won the game in the fifth inning, not the twelfth, and had broken his ass to do it. The beautiful touch was that nobody knew it, and in the tenor of that oversight a shivering, almost incoherent rookie would win for himself his own place in the sun. So it must have happened, I think, to some apprentice of Michelangelo's, and what a wonderful world it must have been for him. (What things only baseball could do! When Ed Kranepool first came up to the Mets, they asked him for evidence of his experience, and he listed his Little League team. Sixteen years later he was still with the Mets. I thought too of the old-time Giant catcher who contracted a venereal disease from a lady in Pittsburgh. That winter she sent him a Christmas card: *To the best catcher in either league.*)

What a strange game baseball is, I thought, because of the way it insinuates itself into the lives of individuals and even into the public policy. And within the month this thought would get some backing. It would come in a phone call from Russ Hodges to Willie Mays over the house line at the Marriott Hotel in Atlanta. It was the last week in September. The Giants were still in the 1966 pennant race—they would be in it till the final day of the season, and on that day they would be assembled at the Pittsburgh airport, awaiting the Dodger result from Philadelphia in case a make-up game was needed at Cincinnati the following day, it was that close. But when he phoned Mays, Hodges had something more direct in mind.

"Buck," Hodges said, "I've heard from the mayor."

"What mayor?"

"San Francisco. Hunter's Point is going up."

In the shorthand—Mays needed no translation—a Negro section of San Francisco was on the verge of riot.

"How hot is it?" Mays asked.

Hodges in his turn needed no translation. When Mays asked how hot it was, he was asking for the reading on the thermometer. Riots went hand in hand with heat waves.

"Nineties," Hodges said.

"Then they'll be in the streets," Mays said. "We've got to keep them at home."

"That's the thing of it," Hodges agreed. "And what'll keep them home the most is if we televise the game tonight from Atlanta."

Mays said, "It's not on the schedule. What about the unions?"

"Every union across the board has waived whatever has to be waived," Hodges said. "It's all systems go. Except for the thing you said: it's not on the schedule."

"How much time have we got?"

"None. Seven hours till game time. They can spot-announce it back home, but I told the mayor it'd be five times as valuable coming from you."

Within twenty minutes a feed of Mays's voice, urging San Franciscans to watch the Giants on TV that night, was on its way to California. Within ninety minutes every radio station in the Bay Area was broadcasting the spot, and would for the remainder of the afternoon. The town stayed home that evening to watch the Giants on the tube, and Mayor John Shelley told Horace Stoneham afterward that nothing else could have prevented all-out rioting and looting. "The TV did it," Shelley said. "Just being able to see you play."

"And win," Stoneham murmured.

"My God," the mayor said, "I never thought of that part."

The 1966 season would be the last in which Mays appeared in more than 150 games, and it would be another four years before the Giants were serious pennant contenders once again, though those two facts were not particularly correlated. Injured and flu-ridden during the '67 season, Mays still appeared in 141 games, but his production was noticeably off—22 home runs might be a gladsome total for most; for Willie it was his worst full-season total ever—and at season's end the brightest note the Giant publicity office could find was that he had not been thrown out stealing since May 13, 1966. (Actually, his base-stealing effectiveness improved as he got older, a fact Mays himself attributed in equal measure to greater experience, greater selectivity, and the retirement in 1965 of umpire Jocko Conlan.

(With the coming of the Negro to organized baseball, teams for the first time started having their first basemen guard the bag to hold the runner with two out. Before that, runners did not do much stealing with two out, so the first baseman would take up his normal fielding position. The real *why* of it was not so easily discerned: there were base stealers in the all-white game too. I mentioned it one time to George Halas, the patriarch of the Chicago Bears and himself a former baseball player: "Why didn't you used to hold the man on first with two out?" He answered the question with a question: "Why'd we always used to punt on third down?" But beginning with Jackie Robinson, who won the National League's base-stealing title in his first season of 1947, baserunning would take on a new aspect . . . one dominated utterly by nonwhites. It was not just a matter of the individual stolen-base titlist in any year; it was the works. By 1959, the top five base stealers in the National League were all nonwhites, in 1962 the top *sixteen!* In 1965 the top five in the

National League were all Negroes; the top five in the American were three Cubans and two Venezuelans. And from facts such as those, it was convenient to deduce that in the good old U.S. of A., the minorities run faster. In several cases that come to mind, one could hardly blame them if they did. In a more appropriate analysis, it could be demonstrated that sports were a chief avenue for the upwardly mobile Latin or black, and that, player for player, white club owners likely looked more for speed in a nonwhite prospect than otherwise; and so the situation fed upon one main thing, which was itself. I do recall covering the Penn Relays one year for the old International News Service, and watching one sprinter who came advertised as the world's fastest human. In truth, he was the second fastest. While he was winning his sprint event, the world's fastest human was stealing his street clothes from the locker room at Franklin Field in Philadelphia.

(It is basic of course that base stealers not only steal bases but unsettle the defense. Statistics are not capable of showing this. In the case of Jackie Robinson, it was an exciting thing for fans to watch. In the case of Willie Mays, it took a quantum jump, for he perfected what was called the "Mays play," so named not only for the fact that he performed it regularly, but for its collateral, which was that no one else did it at all. Put Mays on second base and have the batter hit a ground ball to the third baseman or shortstop. Routinely in such circumstances, the fielder "looks" the runner back to second, then throws the hitter out at first. Not with Mays. He simply would go to third base on the play, and there was no way to defend against it. If you "looked" him back, he'd wait till you threw to first, then take off for third and beat the return throw. If you thought you had him trapped off second and threw there, then you were throwing behind him, and à la Dodger Stadium, you didn't throw behind Mays. If [as I think happened twice] you caught him in a rundown, he would hang himself up long enough for the hitter to reach second anyway, so the situation would be no different than if an ordinary runner had held second and you'd thrown the batter out at first. The added fun in all this was not only the way Mays somehow made it to third, but the number of times the hitter, with the defense so discombobulated by the Mays presence, beat the throw to first himself, not only advancing Mays but leaving two men on instead of one and no more outs than there were before. Even when Mays didn't advance, the hitter could wind up safe at first because of him. "He got me three base hits in one season," Dirty Al Gallagher, one of the Giant third basemen, would say. "He's on second base and I hit three ground balls to the left side, and because of him I beat out all three of them.")

At the end of 1967, a doctor in an operating room looked up and, lapsing into the dialect of his childhood, said, *"Dit lyk of dit gaan werk!"* Half an hour later, he was on the telephone to the superintendent of the hospital.

"Dr. Burger?"

"Who's this?"

"Professor Barnard."

"What do you want?"

"We have just done a heart transplant and thought you should know . . . no, it wasn't dogs. It was human beings . . . two human beings."

In New York, Richard Nixon reread a letter he had received from a stranger, a thirty-one-year-old high school English teacher in Pennsylvania:

Run. You can win. Nothing can happen to you, politically speaking, that is worse than what has happened to you. Ortega y

Gasset in his *The Revolt of the Masses* says: "These ideas are the only genuine ideas; the ideas of the shipwrecked. All the rest is rhetoric, posturing, farce. He who does not really feel himself lost, is lost without remission . . ." You, in effect, are "lost"; that is why you are the only political figure with the vision to see things the way they are and not as Leftist or Rightist kooks would have them be. Run. You will win.

At the National League office in Cincinnati, publicist Dave Grote was updating the contents of the Green Book, the league's press manual, in preparation for the 1968 season. It would contain the note that "Willie Mays, Giant outfielder, with 16 years and 131 days service, heads the list of veteran National League players."

PART FIVE

NIXON

His Mama Didn't Have But One

So HIS BIG-LEAGUE PLAYING CAREER would span five Presidents of the United States, four of whom would not live to see the impeachment resolutions against the fifth. The succession was in all ways traumatic—how else would one get from Hiroshima to Watergate by way of Dallas? "Having won a great war," Manchester would write, "Americans . . . had assumed they would spend the future in tranquility." In fact, Americans would die in war under all five postwar Presidents, and for tranquility one had to go back to Calvin Coolidge, the last to complete the office before Willie Mays was born. "Mr. President," a woman tourist said to him, "the most important thing is that my husband bet you wouldn't say three words to me." "You lose," Coolidge told her.

In Washington, Senator McCarthy (R., Wis.) attacked President Truman; at Wrigley Field in Chicago, Willie Mays stole second base. In Washington, Senator McCarthy (D., Minn.) attacked President Nixon; at Wrigley Field in Chicago, Willie Mays stole second base. In between times, Eisenhower was humiliated by Khrushchev, Kennedy by the Bay of Pigs, Johnson by Eartha Kitt; at Wrigley Field in Chicago, Willie Mays stole second base. He hit home runs in the time of Cassius Clay; he hit home runs in the time of Muhammad Ali. In 1951 Richard Nixon said it was akin to treason for anyone to advocate the admission of Red China to the United Nations; in the 1951 World Series Willie Mays played center field for the New York team of the National League. In 1973 Richard Nixon expressed his self-congratulation for getting Red China admitted to the United Nations; in the 1973 World Series Willie Mays played center field for the New York team of the National League.

This speaks to the Mays longevity, and with some purpose. He would wind up playing twenty-two seasons and owning more records in more categories than any other player in history. True, he does not hold the record for seasons played: others had more, including a pitcher named Jack Quinn, who appeared in a profound total of 755 games, though most people never heard of him. True also that at the end of Willie's career, the almost dreary factor of accumulation was at work, so that he would and did set records through the mere act of little more than showing up. In this case, however, he cut the needle early on. One looks at the achievements of the famous outfielders at the outset of their full-time play—the first seasons in which each appeared in 130 games or more—from the Sam Crawford and Ty Cobb of the turn of the century to Carl Yastryzemski and Reggie Jackson of the sixties. The list would be a good one, and would include Aaron, Clemente, DiMaggio, Heilmann, Shoeless Joe Jackson, Kaline, Mantle, Musial, Ruth, Ott, Speaker, Paul Waner, Ted Williams. Check any of them for the three averages—batting, slugging, fielding—in their first full season, and Mays comes out the only one among the top three in all three categories.

These figures come courtesy of *The Baseball Encyclopedia*, a reference source made unique for the way computer technology was used in producing it. Among other things, it made available the record of Shoeless Joe Jackson, which had been expunged by fiat when Jackson was banned from the game because of his role as one of the fixed players who conspired to throw the 1919 World Series. (Because of that fix, the White Sox are remembered as the Black Sox. The real fix belonged to language and image: white was the color of purity, black the color of evil. "Black is beautiful" notwithstanding, that has been the penalty imposed on the Negro for all the ages of time: even in Negro theater, the good guy wears the white hat. Yet one of the most implacable and constant hatreds of this century has been white vs. white in Northern Ireland. The story is told of a man who finds himself seized from behind on a darkened Belfast street. "What are you?" the voice asks. "Catholic or Protestant?" Fast-thinking, the man opts for safe ground: "I'm Jewish." "Oh, boy," chortles his assailant. "I gotta be the luckiest Arab in town.")

What brought *The Baseball Encyclopedia* into being was set forth in the opening two paragraphs to the preface of that 2,337-page book:

> When Bobby Thomson hit his game-winning home run in the last inning to give the Giants a 5–4 victory over the Dodgers and a pennant in 1951, there was a rookie waiting in the on-deck circle. It was Willie Mays. Although he was later to go on to greatness, Mays was then just another player with much promise. The same may be said of the first modern computer, which was also unveiled that year.
>
> There seemed to be no relationship between baseball and computers until 1967, when an information systems company, Information Concepts Incorporated, decided to produce a complete and comprehensive baseball reference work. This was to be accomplished by building a data bank of major league baseball's existing statistics through the findings of a staff of skilled researchers.

Jacques Barzun was right, about what baseball said for America, and here the computer took its rightful place. (Why not? A baseball box score is a data bank in its own right. See how the offensive and defensive facts dissolve from the team to the individual: the ultimate cross-check, for the run scored by the man on offense has to be a run scored against the pitcher on defense.) The flavor of it is there. So Paul Gallico would write:

> The baseball diamond is no diamond at all, but actually a square set up on one of its points, and the bases, home to first, first to second, second to third, and third to home, are each exactly 90 feet apart. The pitcher's box is 60½ feet from home plate. The distance from home plate to second base, which is the line on which the catcher throws in the attempt to catch a man out who is stealing, is a fraction over 127 feet. And the entire science and thrill of the American game of baseball, developed from an old English game called rounders, lies tucked away in those measurements. They are very rarely examined, and still

more rarely thought of, even by the players. Most of the men who play the game haven't the vaguest notion of the miracles of timing and precision that they perform.

The infielders, for instance, have a fraction under three seconds in which to field a batted ball and get it over to first base ahead of the runner, because the batter only has to run a distance of thirty yards to reach first. From a standing start a fast man can do it in three and two tenths seconds. . . . If the fielder can get the ball to first base in just under three seconds, the runner is out. A few tenths of a second over the three seconds and he is safe and a potential run is menacing the defense.

Now, look at the second hand of your watch and note the time it takes for three seconds to tick off—one . . . two . . . three and gone. In this time, the infielder judges the speed and direction of a ball hit with all the weight and force behind the body of a man, moves in to meet it, figuring the hop as he does so, and the number of steps he must take to reach it, catches it and throws it again all in one motion while still moving forward. There is nothing prettier for timing and rhythm in any sport than to watch a shortstop or third baseman (whose problems are greater because, of the infielders, they are the farthest removed from first base and have a greater distance to throw) come in fast for a slow roller, and as he is moving, swoop on the ball like a gull dropping for a fish, and with a continuation of the same movement with which he picked it up, get it away on a line for first base with an underhand throw across his forward-bending body. So precious and vital are those tenths of seconds that if he tries to straighten up, or draw his arm back to gain more speed and accuracy, the play is over. The runner has crossed first base.

How much faster, then, and more beautiful in speed and execution is the double play when three men handle the ball and retire two runners in one play, the man speeding to second (and he has a good head start) and the batter heading for first. Three seconds flat or better, and yet the shortstop fields the batted ball, or rather scoops it over to the second baseman, who sends it on to first. It would take a delicate timing instrument to measure the fraction of a second that the shortstop actually has possession of the ball. Crack! goes the bat. Step, and flip, goes the shortstop! The second baseman in that time has run from his position perhaps five or six yards from the bag as the ball is started toward him by the shortstop. Ball and man meet on the base, and likewise with the same motion, in which there is no check or hesitation, the second baseman whirls and lines the ball down to first. He can whip that ball the ninety feet from second to first in three fifths of a second. And he is lucky to have that much time left.

In this book, *Farewell to Sport*, Gallico would have more to say:

So, too, the crowd as a whole plays the role of Greek chorus to the actors on the field below. It reflects every action, every movement, every changing phase of the game. It keens. It rejoices. It moans. It applauds and gives great swelling murmurs of surprise and appreciation, or finds relief in huge, Gargantuan laughs. I can stand outside of a ball park and listen to the crowd and come close to telling exactly what is happening on the diamond inside. That quick, sharp explosive roar that rises in crescendo and is suddenly shut off sharply as though someone had laid a collective thumb on the windpipe of the crowd, followed by a gentle pattering of applause, tells its own story, of a briskly hit ball, a fielder racing for it, a runner dashing for the base. The throw nips the runner and the noise too. That steady "clap-clap-clap-clap . . ." Tight spot. Men on base, crowd trying to rattle the pitcher. A great roar turning into a groan that dies away to nothing—a potential home run, with too much slice in it, that just went foul. The crowd lives the actions of the players more than in any other game. It is a release and something of a purge. It is the next best thing to participation.

In Philadelphia in 1907, a booklet was published entitled *History of Colored Baseball*. It included advice on "How to Pitch" from a veteran named Andrew Foster:

The real test comes when you are pitching with men on bases. Do not worry. Try to appear jolly and unconcerned. I have smiled often with the bases full with two strikes and three balls on the batter. This seems to unnerve. In other instances, where the batter appears anxious to hit, waste a little time on him and when you think he realizes his position and everybody yelling at him to hit it out, waste a few balls and try his nerve; the majority of times you will win out by drawing him into hitting at a wide one.

Andrew Foster has been called by John Holway, author of *Voices from the Great Black Baseball Leagues*, "the one preeminent figure in black baseball—even ahead of Joe Williams, Satchel

Paige, or Josh Gibson." Foster not only knew how to pitch but, as Holway recounts, "He taught the New York Giants' ace, Christy Mathewson, to throw a screwball. He managed the best black team in the nation in the pre-1925 era, the Chicago American Giants. And he organized the first black league in 1920, a turning point in the development of black baseball."

The Joe Williams referred to by Holway was "a lanky 6-foot 5-inch Texan who beat the best pitchers in baseball—Walter Johnson, Grover Cleveland Alexander, Eddie Plank, Chief Bender, Rube Marquard, Waite Hoyt, Satchel Paige." Holway continues:

> On a mellow autumn afternoon in October 1917, he faced John McGraw's National League champions, the New York Giants, with their World Series lineup intact. For ten innings he showed them smoke, striking out 20 Giants. No one got a hit.
> He lost the game on a tenth-inning error, 1–0. But as the Giants' right fielder, Ross Youngs, trotted past him after the game, he said, "That was a hell of a game, Smokey." And thus was born Joe Williams' nickname.

Andrew Foster also had a nickname—Rube. He gained it by outpitching Philadelphia's ace, Rube Waddell, in 1902. Foster's younger half-brother, a lefthander named Bill Foster, could pitch too. Holway says he "probably won more Black World Series and playoff games than anyone else." During his career, he was 14–13 won-and-lost against Satchel Paige.

In the twenties and thirties, a barnstorming team called the House of David, whose players favored the long hair and longer beards of biblical injunction, would travel from town to town, and it was inevitable that they must meet up more than once with Satchel Paige. This happened, and in Denver, in 1935, an episode occurred which would register Paige not only as a pitcher (by that time he had recorded some two dozen no-hitters with approximately three quarters of his career still ahead of him) but as a philosopher for the ages. As Richard Donovan wrote:

The beards still fascinated him. One unusually lush growth so attracted him, indeed, that he fired a pitch into it, thus raising a technical baseball point so fine that no one has yet been able to settle it.

The argument took place in the seventh inning. Paige had two strikes on the owner of the great beard when he was seized by an overpowering desire to part the man's whiskers with a Long Tom. When he did, the umpire promptly ruled that the man had been hit by a pitched ball and waved him on to first.

According to an impartial witness, Paige then raised an arm to halt the game. Striding up to the struck man, he asked permission to exhibit his beard to the umpire.

"Empire," said Paige, combing the luxuriant growth with long fingers, "if you will kindly observe here, you will see that these whiskers can't rightly be called no part of a man. They is air."

The umpire, seeing the logic, began to hem and haw. After about five minutes, however, he got mad and returned to his former ground. Paige was defeated, but the crowd was with him and the question is still considered wide open.

George Carlin tells how he grew up on a street bordering Harlem, and how it was that the whites on his block inevitably picked up the speech patterns of the adjacent Negro neighborhood, rather than vice versa. Thus Carlin would say "empire" for "umpire," just as Paige; and "Pitchburgh" for "Pittsburgh." Along the way, the black man's speech not only created the more effective imagery—empire and Pitchburgh are the true descriptives of umpire and Pittsburgh—but an uncanny purity of grammar. And by association, à la Carlin, the whites picked it up from the blacks. A few black exclusives remain—"onliest" as the extra-superlative of "only" and a truly beautiful example. But when Willie Mays said "Who do?" he was utilizing the collective, just as Charley Dressen, a white manager, had said, "The Giants is dead." The sports writer will say, "So-and-so flied out to left." The baseball player, in pickup from black speech, will say, correctly, he "flew out to left," which is far more delightful. There were times when I felt ready to swear that Willie Mays was exercising a dazzling put-on with his speech. Acting as guest host for the Dick Cavett show—one of his many such appearances in the seventies following his retirement as an active player—Mays announced a commercial break by saying, "We'll be back in one minute with this message after we return." Dutifully, the audience applauded.

But they applaud bad grammar too, particularly when it comes from one they believe to be a master of language, like a Howard Cosell, who operates on the Alvin Dark principle of enlarging an earthly fault by overpreaching the opposite. "Is Cosell's English really that good?" was asked me at one point in 1970. The short answer would have to be no. The man liked to showcase a large vocabulary, and was gifted enough to do it correctly on most occasions (though "He was accredited with a poor throwing arm" is great prime Cosell). What was utterly fascinating, however, was Cosell's private war with the relative personal pronoun (as opposed to the vertical personal pronoun, with which he had no difficulty): "I asked him, 'Whom do you think are the ones to watch out for?'" "On deck is Darrell Porter, whom as Keith articulated held this team together." As always, the audience would applaud dutifully. They knew Cosell knew his English, because he had told them so, and they took to it under what Fowler's *Modern English Usage* called the "hypnotism of repetition." But, says the Fowler, published pre-Cosell in 1926:

> *Speculation is still rife as to* whom will captain *the English side to Australia./There is quite a keen rivalry between father & son as to* whom is *to secure the greater share of distinction as a cattle-breeder./ There has been some speculation as to* whom *the fifth representative from South Africa* was./ The French-Canadian, who had learned whom the visitors *were, tried to apologize to Prince Albert.* The mistake is a bad one, but fortunately so elementary that it is nearly confined to sports reporters.

Yet what baseball and language have done for each other, in word, phrase, image, and thought, is a thing almost awesome to contemplate. One thinks of the poor-fielding Boston shortstop who was nicknamed the Ancient Mariner (he stoppeth one of three), or the corpulent Chicago first baseman of whom it was said that he still had the first dime he ever played on. Or:

ABBOTT: We have players with strange names on our team. Who's on first, What's on second, I-Don't-Know's on third. . . .
COSTELLO: Wait a minute. What's the name of the first baseman?
ABBOTT: What's the name of the second baseman.
COSTELLO: I'm not asking you who's on second.
ABBOTT: Who's on first.
COSTELLO: I don't know.
ABBOTT: He's on third.

Historian Manchester, describing Douglas MacArthur's escape from Corregidor during World War II, wrote that the rescuing flotilla of PT boats "would sail in a diamond formation, with PT-32, PT-34, and PT-35 at first base, home plate, and third base, and the lieutenant's flagship, PT-41, leading them at second base." One supposes that the foreign reader of Manchester's work will have no difficulty with the imagery. During the outset of a conference in Moscow, President Nixon (who fancied the brand of "hardball" played in his White House) told his Russian translator of the need for some "ground rules." The translator had no problem with that. Even the Englishman who has never seen a baseball game will use *close call, screwball,* and *slump* in everyday conversation. From baseball comes the codified felony *hit-and-run* driving, and from baseball the medical syndrome of *Charley horse.* (Mencken traced an etymology here to Duke Esper, a lefthanded pitcher of the 1890s whose first name was Charles and who walked like a lame horse.) Just as medical—not so polite, perhaps, but commonly heard, and used conversationally, by the most eminent Freudians—is *switch hitter* as the coefficient of bisexual.

This is not to ignore baseball's general service to straights, as in Dear Abby's response to a nubile female teenager: "DEAR WEAK, . . . If, at age 14, you've gone to 'second and third base,' you had better get out of that league or you'll be known as the 'Home Run Queen' by the time you're 15."

Even those phrases taken by baseball from other fields—*doubleheader* (railroading), *grand slam* (bridge), *pinch hitter* (the "pinch" comes from "How much can you raise in a pinch?" which in turn was the bartender's way of getting paid by miners whose money was the gold dust carried in a purse)—rebounded into public use with baseball coloration. ("Pinch hitter" is especially fascinating: like "under par" from golf, it means in general use the opposite of its specialized meaning. Under par in golf is good, in other things bad. The pinch hitter in baseball is a superior substitute; in other walks of life, inferior.) From within the game, meanwhile, has come a feast of expression, to the infinite enrichment of the language. Everybody knows somebody who's a foul ball, or out of his league, or who never got to first base, or is out in left field, or was born with two strikes on him, or never took the bat off his shoulder, or doesn't know his ass from third base. One is confronted in everyday life by people who are caught off base, or who want their last licks; by the fact that the game isn't over till the last man's out in the ninth; by advice to get in there and pitch; by people who got shut out and events that were called on account of. It's a *ballpark guess* that in the past week or so most readers of this book will have used *batting average, here's the pitch,* or *rain check* in routine conversation, not to mention the phrase *ball game,* whatever its nuance. (If your wife wakes you up to say the baby is coming, it's the ball game. If she has triplets, *that's* the ball game.) And the list goes on and on: *warming up, in the bullpen, touched all the bases, put it across, put one over, boner, holdout, bench-warmer, Ladies' Day, squeeze play, curve ball, high hard one, double/triple play, boot* (as a verb), *assist* (as a noun), *circus play, grandstand play, bleachers, home park, extra innings, backstop, utility man, big league, bush league, nothing/something/plenty on the ball, old pro, cleanup man, lead off, on deck, semipro, rhubarb, bobble, go to bat for, play-by-play, three strikes and out, the big time, rookie, right off the bat, play ball, crossed him up, safe at home, right over the plate, keep swinging, pull a fast one,* and so forth. Describing a managing editor he once worked for, Morton Thompson wrote, "He reached puberty but forgot to touch second."

What is remarkable is not just the wealth of phrasing that baseball has contributed to the language but the paucity of it in the case of other sports. Prizefighting, horse racing, golf, and tennis have contributions that are vivid, if not many, but neither the sports nor the words are native American. Football has contributed amazingly little, when you stop to think about it; basketball nothing at all. Impressionist David Frye, in one of his routines, had President Nixon call his son-in-law David Eisenhower a hockey puck, but that about does it for hockey. In contrast, the case can be made that word pictures derived from baseball occupy our speech and thought not only more than from any other sport, but any other activity of any kind. (In offering this assertion, I am *playing the percentages* and *going by the book.* Anyone who disagrees is an *all-American out.*)

The Baseball Encyclopedia was of course a product of the computer age, which, as its preface said, came into being with the coming of Willie Mays to the majors, and without question the computer was the greatest single technological phenomenon of Willie's time. The book as we have said was a printout. Yet it tells us literate and unnumbered things, among them that in the history of organized baseball there were three players named Mays, of whom Willie was the last. The first was a pitcher from the Ohio Valley named Al Mays, who one season (1887, when he pitched for New York of the American Association) started 52 games and gave up 551 hits. No record exists to say if he was righthanded or lefthanded, but he died at the age of thirty-nine. The second was another pitcher, Carl Mays, also a pitcher for the New York Americans (who had become the Yankees), who in August of 1920 accidentally hit Ray Chapman in the head with a pitch and killed him. And Willie's grandfather had been a pitcher, though not in organized ball. But Kitty Kat, Willie's father, told the boy, "I don't want to see you pitching. There's too many other things you can do." (Babe Ruth had made the same discovery—or it had been made for him. He was an extraordinary pitcher. But pitchers don't play every day.)

Perhaps Kitty Kat had fears in another direction. What distinguishes the computer is that it can spit not only numbers but nicknames. One did not wish to go through a baseball lifetime as a pitcher known as Boom Boom Beck or Line Drive Nelson. Strange and wondrous enough are the nicknames that pervade *The Baseball Encyclopedia*. So the computer accounts for Sweetbreads Bailey and One Arm Daily, and for Flame Delhi, a fastball pitcher who lasted three innings in the majors; for Riverboat Smith and Phenomenal Smith; for Cozy Dolan, The Only Nolan, Boardwalk Brown, and Putsy Cabellero; for Slow Joe Doyle, who lasted 433 ⅓ innings longer than Flame Delhi; for Happy Iott and Sad Sam Jones; for Razor Ledbetter, a fastball pitcher who lasted one inning in the majors; for F. F. McCauley (whose real name was F. F. McCauley); for Pussy Tebeau, no relation to White Wings Tebeau, the brother of Patsy Tebeau; for the Dutches and Frenchies, and Irish Meusel, Germany Schaefer, Squanto Wilson, Egyptian Healy, and Superjew Epstein; for Fidgety Phil Collins, Pretzels Pezzullo, Twitchy Dick Porter, Jumping Jack Jones, and Herky Jerky Horton.

Hear it too for Honest John Kelly, Cannonball Titcomb, and Old Hoss Twineham; for Chicken Wolf, Sea Lion Hall, Coot Veal, and Peek-a-Boo Veach; for Blue Moon Odom and Moonlight Graham; for Bunny Fabrique and Bunny Madden, and for Bubbles Hargrave, Buttercup Dickerson, Candy La Chance, Queenie O'Rourke, Cuddles Marshall, Blondie Purcell, Beauty McGowan, Dolly Stark, Tilly Walker, and Lady Baldwin.

Chain-smoking his way through the remotest archives of the

land, historian Lee Allen traced to their source literally hundreds of baseball nicknames. From Allen's book *The Hot Stove League* are chosen two examples:

Pongo Joe Cantillon was a major and minor league player and manager who was in uniform for forty-five years, from 1879 through 1924, and for all those seasons his strange nickname followed him around, though few players or fans were aware of its origin. Early in his career Cantillon played for San Francisco at a time when Charlie Dryden, later more famous as a baseball writer and wit in Chicago and Philadelphia, was with one of that city's papers. A reader wrote to Dryden one day, asking Cantillon's nationality, and the printed reply, written with the Dryden tongue in cheek, stated: "Cantillon's real name is Pelipe Pongo Cantiliono. He is an Italian nobleman who fled to America to escape an idle life of social ease." The Italian residents of the Bay area were delighted and immediately made the Irish Cantillon their favorite. The cry of "Pongo, Pongo," reverberated through the stands each day, but whenever rooters approached Pongo Joe and spoke to him in Italian, he would draw back fiercely and reply in tones so guttural and threatening that his listeners would hurry off in astonishment.

Hollis (Sloppy) Thurston was the most immaculate of players. Thurston inherited his nickname from his father, who ran a high class restaurant at Tombstone, Arizona, that became known as Sloppy Thurston's place because of the proprietor's habit of feeding soup to tramps at the back door. Later, Sloppy, Jr., while a pitcher for the Dodgers, opened a bar and grill on the Pacific Coast that he called First Base. Dropping in one night for a snack and a chat, Earl Sheely, a teammate of Thurston's on the White Sox years before, said to the proprietor, "Why do you call your place First Base, Sloppy? Nobody ever stopped at first when you were pitching!"

And still, as in the fable of how the sea was turned to salt, the computer grinds out the nicknames: Boileryard Clarke and Brickyard Kennedy; Doggie Miller, Hiker Moran, Icebox Chamberlain, and Crazy Schmidt. Dummy Hoy, Dummy Leitner, Dummy Taylor. Noodles Hahn and Piano Legs Hickman. Bad Bill Egan and Bad News Hale, Socks Seibold and Broadway

Aleck Smith, Steamer Flanagan and Showboat Fisher, Spook Jacobs and Still Bill Hill. Soldier Boy Murphy and General Crowder. Yo-yo Davalillo and Kiddo Davis. Trick McSorley. Mysterious Walker. And the Say Hey Kid.

Not even the citizens of Pitchburgh, where the Waner brothers, Paul and Lloyd, starred for the Pirates over so many years, are apt to know the origin of their nicknames, Big Poison and Little Poison. (It was, Lee Allen discovered, a corruption of "person," coming into being "when a baseball writer overheard an Ebbets Field fan continually say, in Brooklynese as the Waners came to bat, 'Here comes that big poison' or 'Here comes that little poison.' ") And over the passage of the years, the corruption of language as a social function: thus the tradition of playing "My Old Kentucky Home" each year to signal the parade to the post in the Kentucky Derby; the playing of it would stay intact, but the verses would become more and more unfit to sing. ("The darkies are gay": first casualty was the noun, then the adjective, which by the late sixties left only the "are," with the baseballian collective threatening to change that to "is" at any point.)

But the end-all example along this line occurred during Richard Nixon's 1968 campaign for the Presidency, and grew out of one of his TV commercials, this one about the war in Vietnam. "The advertising agency working in behalf of Richard Nixon unveiled another unattractive campaign spot announcement," wrote TV critic Jack Gould of *The New York Times*. "Scenes of wounded GIs were the visual complement for Mr. Nixon's view that he is better equipped to handle the agony of the Vietnamese war. Rudimentary good taste in politics apparently is automatically ruled out when Madison Avenue gets into the act." However, Joe McGinniss would write in his book *The Selling of the President 1968*, "The fallen soldiers bothered other people in other ways." And some of the "other people" were Nixon's own:

There was on the Nixon staff an "ethnic specialist" named Kevin Phillips, whose job it was to determine what specific appeals would work with specific nationalities and in specific parts of the country. He watched *Vietnam* and sent a quick and alarmed memo to Len Garment: "This has a decidedly dovish impact as a result of the visual content and it does not seem suitable for use in the South and Southwest."

His reasoning was quite simple. A picture of a wounded soldier was a reminder that the people who fight wars get hurt. This, he felt, might cause resentment among those Americans who got such a big kick out of cheering for wars from their Legion halls and barrooms half a world away. So bury the dead in silence, Kevin Phillips said, before you blow North Carolina.

Another problem arose in the Midwest: annoyance over the word "Love" written on the soldier's helmet. [Such a soldier had appeared in the TV montage.]

"It reminds them of hippies," Harry Treleaven said. "We've gotten several calls already from congressmen complaining. They don't think it's the sort of thing soldiers should be writing on their helmets."

Len Garment ordered the picture taken out of the commercial. Gene Jones inserted another at the end; this time a soldier whose helmet was plain.

This was the first big case of "political" guidance, and for a full week the more sensitive members of the Gene Jones staff mourned the loss of their picture.

"It was such a beautiful touch," one of them said. "And we thought, what an interesting young man it must be who would write 'Love' on his helmet even as he went into combat."

Then E.S.J. Productions received a letter from the mother of the soldier. She told what a thrill it had been to see her son's picture in one of Mr. Nixon's commercials, and she asked if there were some way that she might obtain a copy of the photograph.

The letter was signed: Mrs. William Love.

As McGinniss relates, there was another commercial done by the Gene Jones production outfit that worried Harry Treleaven and his cohorts in the Nixon camp:

"Run it through again, would you please, Gene?" Len Garment said. "There's something there that bothers me."

The film was rewound and played again.

"There, that's it," Garment said. "Yeah, that will have to be changed."

"What will have to be changed?" Jones said.

The film had stopped just as Richard Nixon, reciting his litany to the "forgotten Americans," had said, "They provide most of the soldiers who died to keep us free." The picture that went with those words was a close-up of a young American soldier in Vietnam. A young Negro soldier.

Len Garment was shaking his head.

"We can't show a Negro just as RN's saying 'most of the soldiers who died to keep us free,' " he said. "That's been one of their big claims all along—that the draft is unfair to them—and this could be interpreted in a way that would make us appear to be taking their side."

"Hey, yes, good point, Len," Frank Shakespeare said. "That's a very good point."

Harry Treleaven was nodding.

Gene Jones said okay, he would put a white soldier there instead.

A couple of weeks later, when Treleaven told Gene Jones to shoot a commercial called *Black Capitalism*, he was surprised to hear that Negroes in Harlem were reluctant to pose for the pictures.

Jones had not been able to find any pictures that showed Negroes gainfully employed, so he decided to take his own. He hired his own photographer, a white man, and sent him to Harlem with instructions to take pictures of good Negroes, Negroes who worked and smiled and acted the way white folks thought they ought to. And to take these pictures in front of Negro-owned stores and factories to make the point that this is what honest labor can do for a race.

An hour after he started work, the photographer called Gene Jones and said when he had started lining Negroes up on the street to pose he had been asked by a few young men what he was doing. When he told them he was taking pictures for a Richard Nixon commercial, it was suggested to him that he remove himself and his camera from the vicinity. Fast.

Gene Jones explained to Harry Treleaven.

"Gee, isn't that strange," Treleaven said. "I can't understand an attitude like that."

The candidate himself probably understood it. Of the five Presidents of Willie's time, the argument can be made that each wanted the job less than his successor. Harry Truman had to be cajoled into accepting the Vice-Presidential nomination on the same ticket with an FDR who patently had little chance of surviving another term. Richard Nixon not only wanted the thing so bad he could taste it, he already had tasted it—in 1960, when, his backers insisted, only a fraudulent vote count stood between him and victory over John Kennedy. And now in 1968 Nixon would defeat Hubert Humphrey. The popular vote was close: 31,770,222 to 31,267,744. The electoral vote was not: 301 to 191. But, as in 1960, it had been another long night of waiting, following a harrowing period of erosion, with the embattled Humphrey picking up a net of 11 points over Nixon in the Gallup Poll readings since September. Nixon was to emerge as the first President in over a century to achieve the office with the opposing party still controlling both houses of the Congress.

As the result of the election became final, two men immediately fell to planning their Presidential strategy for 1972. One of them was George Wallace, the governor of Alabama, whose third party had picked up 9,897,141 popular and 45 electoral votes. The other was Nixon himself. The Wallace candidacy in 1968 obviously had drained votes from him, not from Humphrey: Wallace was the anti-black candidate, and if he had stayed out of the race his voters would not have gone to the pro-black Humphrey any more than they had gone to the pro-black LBJ four years earlier. Humphrey in 1968 had been mortally wounded by his own party, with the assassination of Robert Kennedy, the Kennedy-Johnson split over Vietnam, the riot-accompanied Chicago convention, the resultant party split and lack of funding. Nixon could rely on no such factors to squeeze him through in 1972. And for Wallace, meanwhile, '68 seemed only a beginning: his next run would have to be far better organized, far more formidable. And so in his moment of 1968 victory, the newly elected President would put first things first, and first of all was his re-election in 1972. Thus came about Nixon's notorious "southern strategy." Next time around, he would out-Wallace Wallace.

In time this would become apparent to all. Nixon would do blatant things, such as unleashing Spiro Agnew, his Vice-President, to pour abuse upon minority aspirations (in recollection of the 1952 campaign, when Eisenhower held the high road while letting Nixon prowl the gutter, Agnew found himself being called "Nixon's Nixon"). Nixon would nominate Clement Haynsworth to the Supreme Court. (Haynsworth was from South Carolina, a state that Senator Strom Thurmond had won for Nixon, alone against the Wallace bolt in the rest of the deep South, and some saw this as the shabbiest of political payoffs, with Senator Muskie of Maine calling Nixon "a refugee from Uncle Strom's cabin.") Wrote Bill Manchester:

> The AFL-CIO and the NAACP denounced Haynsworth as antilabor and racist. He might have survived that, but Birch Bayh of Indiana turned up evidence that the judge had ruled in favor of firms in which he held stock. The nomination was rejected 55 to 45, with seventeen Republicans, including Minority Leader Hugh Scott, in the majority. Nixon called the attacks on Haynsworth "brutal, vicious, and . . . unfair." Two months later he announced his second choice, federal Judge G. Harrold Carswell of Florida.
>
> Carswell's chief qualification appeared to be that he wasn't rich and thus, unlike Haynsworth, couldn't be charged with conflict of interest in corporate verdicts. Unfortunately he had other

liabilities. A reporter dug out a sentence from a 1948 Carswell speech: "Segregation of the races is proper and the only practical and correct way of life in our states." Confronted with the quotation, the nominee called it "obnoxious and abhorrent," but the NAACP came out against him anyway. Then it was revealed that Carswell had participated actively in a campaign to exclude blacks from a Tallahassee golf club, had insulted civil rights lawyers in his court, and had been often reversed on appeal. This last development inspired a well-meant comment by Senator Roman L. Hruska of Nebraska. He told a television interviewer that "even if he were mediocre, there are a lot of mediocre judges and people and lawyers. Aren't they entitled to a little representation and a little chance? We can't have all Brandeises and Cardozos and Frankfurters and stuff like that. I doubt we can. I doubt we want to."

Richard Harris, in his book *Decision*, said of Hruska's statement, "To some, that there stuff meant Jews. In any case, the remark was to go down as one of the greatest political blunders in the history of the Senate, and, in the opinion of those most intimately involved in the battle over the nomination, it contributed as much as any other factor to Carswell's defeat. Throughout the country, lawyers and laymen, high and low, arose in indignation at the idea that a man whom his own supporters apparently considered mediocre should be elevated to the Supreme Court, while editorial writers and political cartoonists had a field day unequaled since William H. Vanderbilt said, 'The public be damned.' " In this, Manchester's *The Glory and the Dream* would concur:

Later Hruska was asked if he regretted saying it. "Indeed I do," he said, "indeed I do." A GOP floor leader remarked later, "Everywhere I go I hear that word—mediocre. If there was one single thing it was that. You could see the votes deserting in droves." Before Hruska said it, Senator Kennedy had forecast a maximum of 25 votes against Carswell, and Scott had predicted that the most the opposition could muster would be "in the 30s." In fact the ayes were 45 and the nays 51; "the nomination," said the presiding officer, Vice-President Agnew, "is not agreed to."

Two days later an angry President Nixon told newspapermen that as long as the Democrats controlled the Senate "I cannot successfully nominate to the Supreme Court any federal appellate judge from the South who believes as I do in the strict construction of the Constitution."

How anyone with Carswell's reversal record could be deemed a strict constructionist (regardless of geography but particularly so in this case where it was other southern judges doing the reversing), Nixon never managed to explain. But nobody ever asked him to. (Some future historian may develop a box score —baseball phrase—not just on how many points that caused the press to savage Nixon but, to pick up on something that has gone almost totally ignored, how many he got away with. And as General George Armstrong Custer observed at the battle of the Little Big Horn in 1876, you can't win 'em all. That too was a baseball expression, said to have been uttered that same year by Cincinnati manager Charlie Gould, whose 1876 team won 9, lost 56.)

But the Haynsworth and Carswell nominations did not come about until Nixon had been President for more than a year. Nixon's "southern strategy" had set in long before that. It overlooked nothing in its zeal for a repeat in 1972, and the notion is persuasive that it commenced with the very first pitch of the new ball game. Some of it was seamy: perceiving Senator Edward Kennedy as their likeliest foe in 1972, the Nixon forces had a private detective on the scene at Chappaquiddick, site of the death by drowning of Mary Jo Kopechne while riding in Kennedy's car, within hours after her body was recovered. In other ways, as out-Wallacing Wallace, the President could be more couth. He offered cabinet jobs to prominent Negroes in the cynical and totally accurate foreknowledge that they would turn him down. Campaign pledges to promote "black capitalism" somehow went forgotten. In John Mitchell ("Watch what we do, not what we say," he told a group of astounded Negro leaders) Nixon had an anti-busing attorney general, who covered all the bases—baseball phrase—in dismantling, through the subtle means of nonrenewal, nonfunding, or dilution—the legislative gains secured by blacks during the Johnson administration. A favorite Mitchell stunt was to leave it entirely to southern law enforcement to process desegregation cases, which in the common parlance was to have the fox guard the chicken coop. (Americanese had a more basic phrase for this type: the guy with the clap is running the clinic.) Welfare cheats were denounced but not really discouraged—the chief beneficiaries of welfare were after all the vendors, not the recipients: the doctors, pharmacies, and hospitals at the health end, and the supermarkets which somehow raised their prices the same day the welfare checks came in the mail. In Arizona, the great agribusiness conglomerates found ways to smuggle Mexicans across the border and transport them to their farms to pick the crops; once the harvest was over, the employers would turn the workers in as illegal aliens, leaving it up to the government to pay the cost of deporting them back to Mexico. In the cities, minorities were supposed to be helped by the Law Enforcement Assistance Administration. As Richard Harris pointed out, within two months of Nixon's entering the White House, a mysterious siphon process had set in. The cities were the high-crime areas, but of $880,000 initially allotted to Pennsylvania to set up LEAA in that state, only $62,000 went to Philadelphia; in Oklahoma, Tulsa got $12,000 out of the state's total funding of $267,000; in Massachusetts, Boston got $20,000 out of $464,000.

The public at large did not learn things like this, chiefly because it was not interested enough. Neither did the people most affected learn it, and for the same reason. "I recall little discussion and no excitement in 1954, when the Supreme Court supposedly outlawed the segregation of the schools," wrote St. Louis outfielder Curt Flood in his book *The Way It Is*. "By then

I was sixteen. I think that I would have been aware of local reaction, had there been much. Just as the ghetto warps its victims, it also insulates and lulls them." Come the Watergate denouement twenty years later, and Richard Nixon would claim that he too had been insulated and lulled. It is possible he was. It is also possible a bear does not relieve himself in the woods. "There is scarcely a noble principle in the American Constitution that he hasn't defended in theory or defied in practice," James Reston wrote of him.

What did not leave the blacks insulated or lulled in the election year of 1968 was the assassination of Martin Luther King, Jr., in Memphis on April 4. It is a grace note to record that major league baseball canceled the opening-day games of its season the following week, whereas the National Football League played its regular full Sunday of games two days after the assassination of President Kennedy in 1963. In fairness to football, it might be pointed out that the game lacks the amenity of the rain check: postponements under football's structure are the next thing to impossible. (This would be proved for all time on November 27, 1978, when city officials in San Francisco, stumbling and crying incoherently over the assassination that forenoon of Mayor George Moscone and Supervisor Harvey Milk, pleaded for the sake of simple decency to have that night's pro football game at Candlestick Park postponed for 24 hours. The outcome of this request was reported the next day by Frank Blackman in the *Examiner*:

> They played a football game last night at Candlestick Park. The 49ers and the Pittsburgh Steelers. Big deal.
> There are times when watching grown men running around and falling down becomes much, much less than just a silly, pleasant pastime. Sometimes it is just plain stupid. Yesterday,

after the Mayor of San Francisco was gunned down in his office, it felt almost obscene trying to deal with something as meaningless and ephemeral as a football game.

Sports is full of metaphors about life and death struggles, doing or dying. How grotesque these cliches seem in the aftermath of this tragedy. The final gun sounded, the final out recorded, athletes leave the field, take a shower, *and go on living*. There is, almost always, another game, another opportunity to win one for the Gipper.

Real life isn't that tidy or romantic. Real people bleed. Even die. Too soon. Way too soon. . . .

They played the game last night anyway. The Park and Rec Commission wired the 49er owner and National Football League Commissioner Pete Rozelle asking that it be postponed 24 hours. The league said no way. There was no chance because it was a Monday night national TV game and beer and deodorant companies had spent a lot of money on commercials. Big bucks were at stake. Plus, the folks in Toledo and Nashville were ready for fun and games. It was a tough break for that Mayor what's-his-name, but life goes on. The game goes on.

I think I'm going to be sick.

But the slaying of Martin Luther King in 1968 had consequences of another nature: riots in 168 cities, 2,600 fires, 21,000 persons injured. Again, looting was widespread, and this time the police showed restraint, for obvious reasons not dealing totally with philanthropy. Said *Time* magazine, "Heeding the advice of the Kerner riot-commission report, which warned that the 'use of excessive force—even the inappropriate display of weapons—may be inflammatory and lead to worse disorder,' lawmen in most cities refrained from gunplay, and magistrates quickly processed those arrested for rioting, setting low bail as the commission suggested. 'It seems to me a high-policy decision was made to trade goods and appliances for human lives,' remarked Negro Psychologist Kenneth Clark.' "

The knee-jerk liberal view that understood how people with not enough to eat would, if given the chance, loot grocery stores, lost something for the number of groceries that went untouched. Not all the parents of the looters had that many stupid children. Their prime target instead—and it hit black-owned stores as well as white, in spite of hastily written BROTHER signs in the windows—was, as before, television sets: Charles Reich's "riot box." In *The Greening of America,* Reich said:

> When advertising paints a picture of consumer hedonism and freedom, and work is considered only a means to that end, the machinery of the Corporate State begins to work toward its own destruction. Consider the hereditary poor. Advertising intended for an audience that can afford what it offers also works (with perhaps even greater effectiveness) on those who cannot afford it. . . . Perhaps the poor are "better off than they ever were before," but they can hardly be expected to be satisfied after watching television. A continuous display of better living is paraded before them. Rich people know that not every day is filled with sports and glamour; they even know that the person who has everything might not even want all these things. The poor have no way of knowing this; television advertising is far more effective with the unsophisticated. Is there any wonder that we have riots?

And the riot box itself had grown more attractive, and therefore the merchandise it displayed, including, as always, more riot boxes. By the time of King's death, nearly 60 million American households had at least one television set and more than 14 million of the receivers were color sets. All national and more and more local shows and commercials were being beamed in color, with results so effective that commercials advertising color TV sets had, like the NBC peacock, distinctive impact on the majority of viewers who saw them in black and white. (During the July blackout in New York City in 1977, one TV announcer said, "For those of you whose power has not yet been restored, here's what to do"; bewitching evidence of TV's influence even on those who could not watch it at all.) In a way it was sad, because television is a form of photography, and the best photography always has been black and white: cf. Karsh of Ottawa, or the original *Stage Coach, King Kong,* or *Mutiny on the Bounty* (then see the efforts in the sixties and seventies to remake those movies in color). It would have been a desecration to do *Casablanca* or *Citizen Kane* in color. The world watched America's most impressive telecast—the funeral of President Kennedy—in black and white, which were its only appropriate shades.

Meanwhile, the poor continued to watch in black and white: TV was their cheapest form of entertainment, and black and white was cheaper than color. They were aware of color, yes, and it whetted them, but in the end it was too simplistic to set all social unrest at television's doorstep. The liberals had a different (and even more simplistic) idea. This one was that the Negro in America was simply somebody Whose Time Had Come, in the historical mold of other immigrant peoples—the Irish, the Italians, the Jews, et cetera. Thus what was going on now was nothing more than the product of historical necessity. The beauty in this outlook was the implicit exculpation it afforded the bearer at no extra charge. Not everyone, however, agreed with it. Wrote Curt Flood in *The Way It Is:*

> I probably cannot influence those whites who complain that they are tired of feeling guilty about what their grandfathers did to my grandfathers, but I can at least suggest that they stop making idiotic comparisons between my people and European immigrants. I think it is wholesome to bear in mind that American statute and unlegislated custom not only enslaved my people but outlawed their languages, their religions and their expressions of group and individual dignity. Including their desire to form abiding family relationships. They were bred like cattle. It is inspiring that so many survived with their finer feelings intact, after a century of emancipation in which color has been the badge of ineligibility. To hell with your grandfather, baby. Just get out of the way.

Flood had sat out one season—and the $100,000 salary that would have come with it—in an unsuccessful challenge to baseball's free-agency structure, but the action had helped pave the way for others in later years to succeed where he had failed.

When he played center field for the Cardinals at the height of his big league career, the reigning prince of the game was Willie Mays, whose ability to capture the devotion of the fans of rival teams, Flood would relate in his book, reached even the family level:

> Whenever we played in San Francisco, my nephews and nieces would come from Oakland to cheer for me as enthusiastically as they could in rather difficult circumstances. Fate had burdened them with divided loyalties. They worshiped Mays, yet my own claim to family encouragement could not be denied. I sometimes heard them rooting for both heroes at once, their voices shrill as noon whistles.
> "Hit that ball, Willie! Hit that ball!"
> *Crack!*
> "Catch it, Curt! Catch it!"

But his book also took its whack at Willie:

> All but a very few major leaguers share my view of baseball reality. Among those who do not, the most prominent is the great Willie Mays, who reports from the privileged isolation of his huge success that he has absolutely nothing to complain about. The most vociferous champion of the *status quo* is Carl Yastrzemski, a go-getter for whom a bright future is predicted in the upper reaches of baseball administration. Among former stars who differ with me, Stan Musial should be included. We played side by side for eight years, occupied space in the same locker room, negotiated with the same employer and, within those limits, had experiences in common. But he had other things going for him.
> Stan was one of the outstanding players of all time. He was so exceptionally talented, popular and durable that he played for twenty-one seasons, amassed substantial wealth and became a member of the Cardinal management. As an authentic superstar, he lived remote from the difficulties encountered by lesser athletes. Like Mays, he saw the world entirely in terms of his own good fortune. He was convinced that it was the best of all possible worlds. He not only accepted baseball mythology but propounded it. Whereas the typical player all but choked while reciting the traditional gibberish of gratitude to the industry, and

whereas Bob Gibson, superstar of another hue, would simply change the subject, Musial was a true believer. Gibson and I once clocked eight "wunnerfuls" in a Musial speech that could not have been longer than a hundred words.

"My biggest thrill is just wearing this major-league uniform," Stan used to say. "It's wunnerful being here with all these wunnerful fellas."

On such occasions, Gibson would hang his head in embarrassment and mutter, "Shitfuckpiss." We admired Musial as an athlete. We liked him as a man. There was no conscious harm in him. He was just unfathomably naive. After twenty years of baseball, his critical faculties were those of a schoolboy. After twenty years, he was still wagging his tail for the front office—not because he felt it politic to do so, but because he believed every word he spoke.

If that extract says more about Musial than Mays, it does not have to say any more about Mays. Mays was a black and Flood was a black. And Jackie Robinson was a black, and Willie took his whacks from him too. To quote again from Robinson's book *Baseball Has Done It:*

Big-league Negroes are aware. They are eager to help in the struggle. Many more than those in this symposium volunteered to speak for publication. Rarely did anyone decline.

Among those who did were two of the game's greatest stars, Willie Mays and Maury Wills. Both might have contributed revealing facts and offered helpful suggestions. No doubt they did not wish to stir things up.

But there's no escape, not even for Willie or Maury, from being a Negro, which is more than enough to stir things up when bigots are around.

Willie is the highest paid star in baseball. He is a certain future member of the Hall of Fame. . . . I hope Willie hasn't forgotten his shotgun house in Birmingham's slums, wind whistling through its clapboards, as he sits in his $85,000 mansion in San Francisco's fashionable Forest Hills. Or the concentration camp atmosphere of the Shacktown of his boyhood. We would like to have heard how he reacted to his liberation in baseball, and to his elevation to nationwide fame. And about his relations with his managers, coaches, fellow players and his many loyal friends, black and white.

Willie has faced the same problems that confront every Negro. He knows Harlem's good and bad; he met with bitter opposition when he tried to rent a house in a mixed neighborhood in San Francisco. Few athletes have won such acclaim as Willie on his return to New York in 1961 for an exhibition game at Yankee Stadium, where tens of thousands blocked traffic around the ball park.

Willie is the hero of a Negro success story. What has he learned from life? We'd like to know.

Willie didn't exactly refuse to speak. He said he didn't know what to say. I hope that he will think about the Negro inside Willie May's uniform, and tell us one day.

Willie was scouted by the Dodgers when he was seventeen. Wid Mathews reported that he couldn't hit a curve ball and Mr. Rickey passed him up, which is how he happened to become a Giant. I wish that he had been a Dodger, not only because his tremendous play and high spirits would have made us the unbeatable team of all time, but because if he had been a Dodger he would have learned the true meaning of equality from Mr. Rickey.

Maybe it is nothing more than respect for a senior that Rickey comes out "Mr. Rickey" while Mays comes out "Willie," even from Jackie Robinson, but viewed at arm's length it might read like plantation talk. Another Negro star, Roy Campanella, was brought to the Dodgers by Rickey, but Campanella has taken a less ecstatic position about it. In his zeal to integrate not only the majors but the minors, Rickey kept Campanella away from the big leagues for most of the 1948 season, though the need for him was apparent. He would go on to become the National League's Most Valuable Player three times, and when he was looking for ways to put his salary to work to protect his future, he talked to Rickey about his idea to open a liquor store. In his book *It's Good to Be Alive*, Campanella said:

He didn't think that liquor and baseball were a good mix and felt that people might get the wrong idea if a ballplayer sold whiskey.

"Campy," he said, "why don't you invest your money in a sporting goods store or something else where there will be no taint?"

I told him, "Mr. Rickey, you're a white man. Maybe you don't understand the problem a colored man has going into business. How many businesses do you think are open to colored men, outside of entertainment? My people drink. They'll make better customers for whiskey than for sporting goods."

Somewhere in Terence Rattigan's play *Separate Tables,* one of the characters says, "The trouble with being on the right side is that one takes on such questionable allies." Pee Wee Reese, a Kentuckian who played shortstop alongside Robinson and was the first southern white to befriend him, would say in later years that the pioneering done by Robinson in breaking down racial barriers was viable only for the balance provided by less explosive Negro players. It was the old saw—but highly persuasive withal—of the slaughter that must result if a thousand disciples of Dale Carnegie's *How to Win Friends and Influence People* were suddenly to congregate under the same roof. When Willie Mays first reached the big league in 1951, the black players on the Giant team stayed in separate hotels not only in St. Louis, which touched the South, but even in Chicago, where they occupied the Pershing on the South Side while the whites were at the Edgewater Beach. In St. Louis, Robinson was instrumental in desegregating the Chase Hotel, first in its rooms, then its restaurants, finally even its swimming pool. It was Robinson who took a stand. If that was all it had been, the Chase would not have given a damn. But each time he took the stand, the Dodger management backed him up and threatened to move the entire team out of the hotel. It is hardly to Robinson's discredit that he staged the clamor; neither is it to the discredit of the other blacks on the team that they did not join him. Sometimes the individual speaks for principle better than the mob.

None of which augments the position of Willie Mays, which was the position of no position. It was nearly 1960 before the Adams Hotel in Phoenix, where the Giants stayed during spring training, would admit Negroes, and here Mays proved to be the precise opposite of a Robinson: far from asserting his right to stay at the Adams before it integrated, he wouldn't stay at the Adams after it integrated. Instead of the threat of a boycott, here was the enactment of one. Robinson before him having insisted on a welcome, Mays would refuse it when it came. Likely Reese was right: Jackie drummed the lesson from one direction, upon which Willie picked up and drummed it from the other. There is a great deal to be said for the blacks who pressured Governor Lester Maddox of Georgia to desegregate his chicken restaurants. And not just a little to be said for the ones who stayed away after he did.

Mays of course was what Robinson and Flood were not. In 1978, NBC telecaster Tony Kubek, himself a former star ballplayer, voice-overed a shot of No. 24 swinging the bat and connecting by saying, briefly and simply, "That's the best that ever played this game." That was not said of Robinson, let alone Flood. (In 1974, Dave Anderson of *The New York Times* reported a conversation between Joe DiMaggio and a teenage Puerto Rican hopeful. "Always try for perfection," DiMaggio said through an interpreter to the youthful player. "There's never been a perfect ballplayer. Willie Mays came closest to perfection. But always try.") But Mays was something else that Robinson and Flood were not. Robinson was born the son of sharecroppers on a plantation near Cairo, Georgia. Flood was born in Houston, Texas. Mays was born in Westfield, Alabama. But at the age of thirteen months, Robinson went to California; at the age of twenty-three months, Flood went to California. From their times beyond earliest memory, they were northern Negroes. One saying has it that in the South no one cares how close a black gets so long as he doesn't get too high, and in the

North no one cares how high a black gets so long as he doesn't get too close. Read that for oversimplification as one may, it still spells different worlds. Fellow blacks would be among Mays's severest critics, but not those fellow blacks who like him were reared in the South. As quoted in Robinson's book, Monte Irvin says, "I was born in Alabama but my family moved to New Jersey when I was six." And:

> We were housed with the team in the two border cities of St. Louis and Cincinnati. We had been segregated at the Chase Hotel in St. Louis at first but Jackie broke down the ban. Baseball was the first to desegregate many hotels—it's been involved in many firsts long before the present civil rights campaign began. We Negro Giants desegregated the Adams Hotel at our Arizona training base in Phoenix. At first the dining room and swimming pool were closed to us. Phoenix was then an almost completely segregated city. One night Kenny Washington and I went to a movie theater. Kenny had been All-American in football with Jackie at UCLA. He and Bob Waterfield, the most popular football player in Southern California, were intimate friends. Kenny had also played small parts in pictures. He took for granted that he was a full American citizen. But that movie theater wouldn't sell us tickets. It was a disillusioning experience for him. He never quite got over it.
>
> The same thing happened to Willie Mays in Phoenix. I can't for the life of me understand why I and the others, including Willie, didn't protest more than we did. If we had, the situation might have been remedied much sooner.
>
> In '54 the Giants and Indians barnstormed through the South on an exhibition tour. There were five Negroes on the Indians and four on the Giants. The two teams ate together, slept in the same hotels on the first leg of the trip and had a hell of a good time. Then we reached cities in the Deep South. When we arrived at a railroad station there'd be a bus for the white players, while we had to wait around with our bags until a Negro cabdriver came along, which might be half an hour or more. We were tired, then disgusted, then bitter, knowing how much we were contributing to our teams and baseball. "We ought to quit

this team until it hits New York," we'd tell each other. But we never did. We weren't concerned with our civil rights; we were concerned with our comfort. We should have tried to correct injustices as they arose. If you sit around waiting for something to fall into your lap, you're likely to get hit in the head.

This was the same Monte Irvin who had temporized a racial situation when the Giants and Indians were in Las Vegas at the start of that same barnstorming tour of 1954, as seen in Roger Kahn's account of that episode in the second chapter of this book. Now Irvin hit the Deep South and was shocked. But he was of a piece with the Robinsons and Floods who had left the South in early boyhood. Willie Mays, in contrast, grew up there. And so his acoustics would be different.

They were different certainly in 1970 when the Giants made a pre-season tour of Japan. While they were there, a pre-season all-star game would be held at Dodger Stadium in Los Angeles upon the second anniversary of the death of Martin Luther King. It was mandatory not just to the clear interest of the Giants but the Department of State as well that Mays appear throughout the swing through Japan. It was mandatory to Mays that he be in Los Angeles for the King game. The dilemma was total. I asked Mays about it afterward. "It was like an appearance for the President," he said to me. "Nixon was your President. But Martin Luther King was my President."

The story never got out. Another player might have made headlines out of it. Mays, the southern Negro, took it privately to Horace Stoneham. "I know you have a problem," he told Stoneham. The latter nodded. "Yuh," he said, "but there's no choice. What will the game in Los Angeles mean without you? Go there."

It was a time—the end of the sixties—when airplanes were being hijacked to Cuba at the rate of slightly better than one a week. "Up, up and olé!" Johnny Carson advertised as a new airline slogan, and a story told of a passenger on a flight to New York who invaded the flight cabin, pointed a gun at the pilot, and said, "Take this plane to New York!" The pilot protested that this was where they were supposed to go in the first place. "That's what you said the last time," the hijacker said.

Willie Mays would buy a magnificent estate home in Atherton, swankiest of the suburbs south of San Francisco. A glimpse of it could be had from a passing Southern Pacific commuter train—the main house, the guest house, the pool—from between a formidable stand of protective trees and high-standing hedge. "You've come a long way from Birmingham," a friend said to Mays. "Not really," Willie said. "Train still runs out back."

———◆———

But he said that figuratively. No train ever ran behind his boyhood homes in Westfield and Fairfield. The only tracks he ever saw were those of U.S. Steel's private freight line, until he was seventeen and the bus of the Birmingham Black Barons broke down and they had to travel by train while it was being fixed. That bus was a beaut. It was driven by the batman: he was the bat boy for the Black Barons, but he was in his fifties, so he was not bat boy but batman. He drove Piper Davis crazy, because he believed in the bus. Once, in the mountain country of North Carolina, it lost its brakes on a long downgrade outside of Asheville, en route to a night game with the Indianapolis Clowns. "An old player named Bumpers started calling signals," manager Davis recalled. "If we came to a right turn in the road, everybody leaned left and vice versa. One of the players tried to jump off the bus, and he opened the door and put his foot down, but the speed kicked him back into the bus. I'm saying to myself, 'Lawd, get me out of this, I won't ride this bus no more,' and finally the batman used his gears so we stopped. All I can say about that trip down the mountain, it's lucky we didn't meet nobody and didn't catch up with nobody." But

Davis was not faithful to his pledge, and on another trip—this one to New York, where Mays and the Barons would play at Willie's future home, the Polo Grounds, in a game against the New York Cubans—the bus was tooling through the Holland Tunnel when Jersey Joe Walcott, soon to become the heavy-weight champion of the world, drew abreast of the Barons in the fast lane and waved at the batman. The batman waved back. "Hey, Jersey Joe," he caroled, "what's new?" "Your bus is on fire," Walcott caroled back. "That's what's new." The Barons beat a heady retreat from the bus, then piled back into it to rescue Mays, who had returned to salvage his suitcase. The old saying that you could not tell the players without a scorecard applied strangely to the ensuing game against the Cubans, since both teams were wearing the Cubans' uniforms.

Jackie Robinson may have been laying it on a bit when he wrote of the "concentration camp atmosphere of the Shacktown of [Willie's] boyhood." If that was so, Willie was not aware of it. Summertimes, he swam in a magnificent pool almost of Olympic dimension—the Tennessee Coal & Iron industrial cooling reservoir—and he was in the cleaning and dyeing course at Fairfield Industrial High School. He starred in basketball and football, was chased by girls, and worked one day in his life, as a dishwasher at Thompson's restaurant in Birmingham. "It just didn't feel right," Mays has recalled. "I didn't even go back to get my pay. If I wanted to play ball that day, I wouldn't get there till the fourth or fifth inning, with the hours they had at the restaurant." Actually, Mays was being paid for playing baseball by the time he was fourteen. But that hardly made him a role model. "He was an example for youngsters," Garry Schu-macher said, "up to a point: the hero of heroes in the flesh, who could say don't drink, don't smoke, get your tetanus shots, re-spect your parents. But what was he going to say after that? You'll grow up to play baseball like me? *Nobody* was going to grow up to play baseball like him, and the kids knew it. If he even taught them the basket catch he'd be teaching the wrong way to catch a ball, and *he* knew it." Study hard in school? Not even Jackie Robinson would—or should—have expected that. "My brothers, their friends and acquaintances, all older than me, had studied hard and wound up as porters, elevator operators, taxi drivers, bellhops," Robinson wrote. "I came to the conclusion that long hours over books were a waste of time."

Five years after his career had ended, Mays was approached by the ad agency representing Miller beer to make one of their commercials. He refused. Then Schaefer, a New York beer, came to him with the same request. This time Mays said yes. The thrust of the Miller ad was to depict him as a drinker. In the Schaefer, the spot would show him serving the beer to friends at a cookout, much as Kate Smith, a nonsmoker, used to advertise that she offered Philip Morris to her guests. So slender a line of principle could be expressed by Mays, and perhaps in the mix it did no disservice. After his year's holdout, Curt Flood had returned to baseball, and for an estimable reason: he needed the money. If Mays's home in Atherton was luxurious, the house Robinson bought in Stamford was not exactly a walk-up in Watts. It could be trumpeted that Mays never rocked the boat, and the charge was perfectly true. How to measure the difference between a Mays and a Robinson on that account was a more difficult undertaking. At the first Black Athletes' Hall of Fame dinner in New York in 1974, the two celebrities most fondly welcomed were Mays and Rachel Robinson, Jackie's widow. In the adulation of a sophisticated all-black audience that included Congresswoman Shirley Chisholm, spokesperson for civil rights and women's rights, Mr. Mays and Mrs. Robinson were more equal than separate. And the bottom line was what united them, not what divided them. A Puerto Rican player named Vic Power—and there were no Puerto Ricans at that dinner—had expressed it in an interview reprinted in Robinson's book:

We were riding from Fort Myers to West Palm Beach where I used to train with Kansas City. The bus stop so we could go into the men's room at a gas station. The whole club went into the bathroom, and I was the only colored one. I notice the gas attendant, he didn't like it, I could tell by the way he look at me. I come out and I bought a Coca-Cola from a machine. I took the bottle to the bus and I was sitting in the bus, and this man, the attendant, he come and is real nasty. "You not suppose to take this bottle," he say. I say, "Why not? I pay you a quarter for this bottle. Let me finish drinking this Coke." He say, "I don't want your quarter. I want the bottle back." Then the ball players, they all get mad at him, and I got mad, and cursed him. "Here, you take this bottle," I say, and call him a name. He left and we left and around ten minutes after that we were riding and up come the sheriff of the police in a car and stop the bus. This gas guy was with the sheriff. The sheriff, he say, "You are under arrest for using obscene language." And they wanted to put me in jail because of that. The players, they guard me. They say, they want to put up a bond for me. Finally, we collect money from the ball players and I pay five-hundred-dollar bond so I can go later on trial. Then they say, "You better not go back, Vic—they put you in jail for a long time in this part of the country." I say, "What kind of a country is this?" So the club took the money out of my salary to pay back the ball players, and I lose five hundred dollar for buying a bottle of Coke. They told me that it was best that way because if I go back they might kill me down there, you know, how they do. . . .

My trouble was I get married to a light-skinned girl, we been married for six year, we very happy, but in places where they segregate, they don't like it even though she is Puerto Rican. In Puerto Rico we are all the same, white to black, we call each other Puerto Rican. My mother is light complexion, my father was dark. You have like Tité Arroyo, he's white; Cepeda, he's a little darker but not as dark as Clemente—we all mix together. But in Kansas City every time I take my wife to the ball park and they see me with her, they say, "Oh, there's Vic Power with that white girl again." And then the writers go all around the country saying, "Power, he no good, he goes after white girl."

And Curt Flood, in his own book, reporting an added dimension:

Eighteen-year-old players and others of unestablished talent usually started their careers in the Class D leagues, the lowest of the low minors. The Reds assigned me to the High Point–Thomasville club in the Carolina League, which was Class B. Apparently I had made a good impression. I was beginning to feel like myself again. It would be good in North Carolina. I would find a nice apartment. I would establish myself in the community. I would proceed to the fame and riches that awaited me. After only one year of minor-league experience, Frank Robinson had just been promoted to the Reds. I could hope to do as well.

As I rode the bus to my new home, I saw myself returning there in later years, burdened with prominence. Dear friends, including many girls, would wave at me from the curbs. Substantial citizens would slap each other on the back, proud that good old Curt had come to pay them a visit. I would have lunch with the mayor, dedicate the new library, endow an animal hospital and give all the little children rides in my new Rolls-Royce.

I was ready for High Point–Thomasville, but the two peckerwood communities were not ready for me. Or maybe they were. One of my first and most enduring memories is of a large, loud cracker who installed himself and his four little boys in a front-row box and started yelling "black bastard" at me. I noticed that he eyed the boys narrowly, as if to make sure that they were learning the correct intonation. Wherever we played in that league, at home or away, the stadiums resounded with "nigger," "eight-ball," "jigaboo" and other pleasantries.

At Fayetteville, North Carolina, I heard spluttering gasps: "There's a goddamned nigger son-of-a-bitch playing ball with them white boys! I'm leaving."

The few blacks in these audiences included a demoralized handful who seemed to enjoy echoing their oppressors. Some cracker would bawl at me, "Move yo' ass, snowball!" and, sure enough, a boozy voice—separate but briefly equal—would pipe from the Jim Crow section, "Move yo' ass, snowball!"

If one does not find Willie Mays recording moments like that, it is because he didn't record them, not because of any failure to experience them. Because he played only 81 games in the lower minors—with Trenton of the Class B Interstate League in 1950—his exposure was more limited than that of Flood and many other Negro players; but it was concentrated enough, particularly when the Trenton team played at Hagerstown, Maryland, which despite its deceptive location on the map lay in fact below the Mason-Dixon line and was as segregated as any other southern town. In one way Mays was better prepared than a Flood would find himself: the latter, arriving from California for his first year of spring training in Florida, noticed two drinking fountains at the Tampa airport, one marked "White," the other "Colored." For an instant, he writes, he "wondered whether the signs meant club soda and Coke." A Mays, who had grown up in Birmingham and had traveled the segregated pathways of the South in the Black Barons' team bus, would think little if anything of things like that, or of the fact that he would be housed with a black family while the rest of the team put up at a motel: again here an example of how what came as a shock to the northern Negro could come fatalistically to his southern brother. In one respect, though, Mays and Flood had the same novel experience of hearing nigger talk—and from the occasional black as well as whites—from the stands in a Hagerstown or a Fayetteville, for each in his first minor league season was playing on an integrated team before segregated audiences. Mays had it actually worse than Flood in one respect (though things like this are a matter of second-order degree): he came to Class B ball in 1950, six years before Flood's appearance; and in Willie's time the public still was new to the idea of race mixing on the baseball field. This does not mean Mays heard different epithets in Hagerstown than Flood in Fayetteville, but he did hear more of them. (On the other hand, Mays had one southern town in his league; Flood, in the Carolina League, had all eight.) And another point accentuates the difference in the time factor: in 1956, when Curt Flood was in his rookie minor-league year in the Carolina League, his future employer, August A. Busch, Jr., owner of the St. Louis Cardinals, offered Horace Stoneham, the owner of the Giants, one million dollars for the contract of Willie Mays. That was in the days when a million was more than tipping money. Stoneham said no.

The fact is he lucked into Willie. The Dodgers and the Braves were both scouting the young center fielder when a Giant scout, Eddie Montague, wandered into the stands at Rickwood Park in Birmingham to look at a Black Barons first baseman named Alonzo Perry. "I had no inkling of Willie Mays," Montague wrote some years later in a letter to sports editor Tim Cohane of *Look* magazine, "but during batting and fielding practice my eyes almost popped out of my head when I saw a young colored boy swing the bat with great speed and power, and with hands that had the quickness of a young Joe Louis throwing punches. I also saw his great arm during fielding practice, and during the doubleheader his speed and fielding ability showed up. This was the greatest young ballplayer I had ever seen in my life or my scouting career."

The better to believe his eyes, Montague clambered up onto the roof of the grandstand, a vantage point that he noticed was favored by others, one of whom was Thomas Hayes, the Negro entrepreneur who happened to own the Birmingham Black Barons but who, like Montague, was in Birmingham only as a visitor. Hayes's home base—*not* a baseball phrase—was Memphis, where he had an insurance business and also operated a funeral parlor. "He was all right," Piper Davis would say of Hayes, years afterward, "so long as you understood one thing: if he told you the sun was going to rise in the west, you better be facing China."

Montague already had it in his mind to sign Mays, but his meeting with Hayes on the roof was circumspect. "What might you be asking for the boy's contract?" he asked.

Hayes measured him. "Fifteen thousand," he said. "Half now and half when he reports."

"What do you mean, half now and half when he reports?"

"I want him playing with my team for the rest of this season."

"I'll need a little time to think," Montague said.

"Take all the time you like," Hayes told him.

The little time Montague needed lasted till the Barons went

to the clubhouse to shower and dress. Montague met Mays coming out of the shower. Their conversation was brief and, on Montague's part, a trifle guarded. He found Mays likable and promised to see him perform with the Barons at Tuscaloosa the following night. Then he hightailed it back to his hotel and put in a call to New York to Jack Schwarz, the Giants' scouting director.

"I saw Perry," Montague said. "I don't think he's a major league prospect, but he's okay for Class A."

"Fine," Schwarz said. "Anything else?"

"Do we have any reports on Willie Mays?"

"Who?"

"Hold onto your hat," Montague said, and proceeded to relate what he had seen at Rickwood Park that day. He also told Schwarz how much Hayes was asking for Willie's contract. Schwarz said that sounded possible, "if he's as good as you say he is." He did not sound oversold.

They rang off with Montague's plan to watch Mays in action the following night at Tuscaloosa. Overnight, however, the scout began to fret. There was something too amiable, too relaxed in the way Hayes had chatted with him on the grandstand roof. Montague conferred with another Giant scout, Bill Harris, who also had seen Willie play. This was not Mays's first season with the Black Barons, but it was the first since his high school graduation, which made him eligible for signing by organized ball. Visions of sugar plums dancing in Hayes's head danced in Montague's head. The owner's condition for sale—that Mays must play out the remainder of the 1950 season with the Black Barons—presaged a bidding war for Willie's contract which would make the $15,000 behave opposite from the way initial asking prices are supposed to: instead of coming down, this one could only go up, as more and more major league teams picked up on the young center fielder. (Jackie Robinson's subsequent version that the Dodgers had seen Mays and passed on him is subject to some question, for the following night at Tuscaloosa Montague saw a Dodger scout in the stands. The likelier probability is that Hayes with his precondition was playing the big leaguers for time, simply to get the price up.)

The first person to show up at the Tuscaloosa ball park the next night, some three hours before game time, was the groundskeeper. The second was Eddie Montague. He was on hand to meet the Black Barons' bus as the batman wheezed it up to the player entrance, and as Mays debarked, Montague drew him to one side.

"Do you want to play organized ball for the Giants?"

"Sure."

"When?"

"Any time a deal's all right."

"You don't want to play out the rest of the season with the Barons?"

"No law say I have to."

"Well, I'll have to talk to Mr. Hayes about your contract."

"What contract?"

———————◆———————

In the spaniel face of Mr. Montague, the eyes went large. He said, "The contract you signed when you started in playing for the Barons. When was that?"

"More'n two years ago," Mays said, "but there wasn't no contract. Mr. Hayes don't own me."

Montague's hands were fishing frantically for pencil and paper. "Let me have your address and phone number." (Interesting that he would assume Mays had a phone, but he did, and rightfully. Again here, the overkill of Jackie Robinson's reference to Willie's "shotgun house in Birmingham's slums," where such amenities as telephones would be unheard of. But the Mayses of that time occupied an attractive, well-kept home on an attractive, well-kept street in Fairfield. Willie alone was making $300 a month during the baseball season, and his father had returned to full-time work at TC&I. The Giants were to pay him $250 a month for playing later that season at Trenton.) Like every other scout, Montague had assumed automatically that Mays was under contract to Hayes—it would be nothing more or less than standard—and Hayes was letting them assume it. "The other clubs were dealing with Mr. Hayes," Montague would write later in his letter to Cohane at *Look*. "We signed Mays and dealt with Mr. Hayes later, which in my opinion is the reason Willie Mays is playing for the Giants today."

The actual game at Tuscaloosa was almost moot, but Mays had another fine night, hitting line drives to all fields and making a great catch and throw, while a pound of butter failed to melt in the onlooking Montague's mouth. The following morning, he called Mays's home and, according to his account, was told by Willie's Aunt Sarah that he would sign for a $5,000 bonus. Whereupon Montague phoned farm secretary Schwarz in New York, told him the astounding noncontract news and the price Aunt Sarah was asking, and predicted that Mays would be playing center field for the Giants in the Polo Grounds within two years. "Go ahead and sign him," Schwarz said, delighted by the price. "Even if it takes three years." On that count, both men proved wrong: it was one year.

But all hands agree that $5,000 was not the total expenditure. In the first place, both Mays and his father, who signed the contract on behalf of his under-twenty-one son when he returned home from the steel mill that afternoon, recall that the bonus was not $5,000 but $10,000. Willie and Kitty Kat remember too that Aunt Sarah took charge. Kitty Kat received $250. To Willie, she gave around $3,000, with which he bought some clothes and a new green Mercury. The balance went to buy a new house for Sarah, which wound up in the name of her daughter.

Montague and Mays do agree that owner Hayes of the Black Barons received a $10,000 bonus all his own. According to Montague's account, "Jack Schwarz told me that we might have to pay something for Mays after all, as the Giant officials felt it was the right thing to do, so Mr. Hayes was sent a check for $10,000, which made everyone happy and also proves again and again what a grand organization the Giants are." As Kitty Kat has remembered it, "I said to the scout, 'Why should Mr. Hayes get anything? I ain't signed no contract with Mr. Hayes, Willie ain't signed no contract with Mr. Hayes.' He say, 'Well, we don't want no trouble later. He might come back and try to sue us.' " Willie's memory is: "I got ten, and he [Hayes] got seven then and another three when I made the big club."

So one way or another it is recorded that Hayes got $10,000 for Willie's contract—which, since Willie had no contract, was, if not what Hayes had hoped, still a fruitful modern-day rewrite of the fable of the Emperor's New Clothes. In any event, a far more violent clash of memories prevails to this day as to who it was who made sure Willie never signed a contract with Hayes to begin with. From manager Piper Davis to father Kitty Kat to other members of the Black Barons who were senior to Willie —which means all of them: Willie joined the team when he had just turned seventeen, and he was the baby, to be cared for by all concerned; the next-youngest Black Baron, pitcher Bill Greason, was seven years older than Willie, and the club as a whole averaged over thirty—regardless, each takes individual credit for making sure Willie was not indentured to the club owner. Perhaps all deserve the credit. "I haven't got any time to waste with children," Piper Davis said gruffly when he was asked to take a look at Willie. But he took the look. And told him he could play for the Barons.

The middleman here was Jim Canady, a Birmingham figure well known to all associated with Negro baseball in the area. There were semi-pro teams, like the Fairfield Gray Sox, the team on which Willie and Kitty Kat played together. There were the industrial teams. There were the Negro "minor leagues." And there were the major leagues, and the Birmingham Black Barons were major league. They had taken their name from the white Birmingham Barons of the Southern Association, and played their games at Rickwood Park while the white Barons were on the road. Game for game, they outdrew the white Barons in attendance. Game for game, they would have kicked the whey out of the white Barons—had any such interracial booking been possible. A time or two each season, the white Barons, returning from an out-of-town swing, would sidle softly into Rickwood Park to watch the Black Barons play and acclaim with awe. (No less did Mays and other members of the Black Barons go to the ball park upon their arrival in St. Louis to watch Ted Williams hit for the Red Sox.) The best consensus of the reading on the teams of the Negro National and Negro American leagues was that they suffered for lack of pre-season training and depth of pitching and utility men. The white Barons of the Southern Association were Class AA. The worst level of the Black Barons—overtired pitching—was Class AA. In everything else, on the white index, the Black Barons were either AAA or major league or—in fielding—better than major league. In the individual performances, the black leagues had Hilton Smith, Terris McDuffie, Bill Byrd, and Jonas Gaines, any one of whom, in Monte Irvin's estimation, would have won 20 games a season in the white majors. There were Roy Partlow and Raymond Brown and Willie Wells and Ray Dandridge.

And there were the Big Four: Satchel Paige, Josh Gibson, Buck Leonard, and Cool Papa Bell. They all rest today in the Hall of Fame at Cooperstown, and properly so. Paige is beyond question the best pitcher in history. Gibson hit more home runs, and hit them farther, than any other man on record. Leonard's eyesight as a batter was considered on a par with Ted Williams's, at least. And Bell at the age of forty was still scoring from first base on a bunt. (Willie Mays at the age of forty scored from first base on a bunt, but that was later.)

The legends abounded. "Let me tell you about Cool Papa Bell," Paige told Mays during one conversational interlude. "One time he hit a line drive right past my ear. I turned around and saw the ball hit his ass sliding into second." In turn, one of the great Negro league catchers, Biz Mackey of the Baltimore Elite Giants, told Richard Donovan a story about Paige. "A lot of pitchers have a fast fall," Mackey said, "but a very, very few —Feller, Grove, Johnson, a couple of others besides Satchel— have had that little extra juice that makes the difference between the good and the great man. When it's that fast, it will hop a little at the end of the line. Beyond that, it tends to disappear. Yes, disappear. I've heard about Satchel throwing pitches that wasn't hit but that never showed up in the catcher's mitt, nevertheless. They say the catcher, the umpire, and the bat boys looked all over for that ball, but it was gone. Now how do you account for that?" And, again from Donovan's "The Fabulous Satchel Paige," the ageless pitcher recalls another feat of disappearance, this one when he was working for the Pittsburgh Crawfords:

> Paige's battery mate on the Crawfords was the late Josh Gibson, the *aficionado's* choice for the long-ball hitter of all time. Paige has the greatest reverence for Gibson, and it shocks him to run into people who have not heard of the great man.
>
> Not long ago, a sassy young reporter, fuddled with the doings of the Musials, the Mantles and so on, tried Paige severely by yawning while he was recounting some of Gibson's prodigies. To fix him, Paige recalled one game.
>
> "We was playin' the Homestead Grays in the city of Pitchburgh," he said quietly. "Josh comes up in the last of the ninth with a man on and us a run behind. Well, he hit one. The Grays waited around and waited around, but finally the empire rules it ain't comin' down. So we win.
>
> "The next day," Paige went on, eyeing the youth coldly, "we was disputin' the Grays in Philadelphia when here come a ball outta the sky right in the glove of the Grays' center fielder. The empire made the only possible call.

" 'You're out, boy!' he says to Josh. 'Yesterday, in Pitch-burgh.' "

What gives credence to this account is a matter of geography. Historically, with one astounding exception—Abner Double-day Field at Cooperstown, baseball's shrine of shrines—all ball parks were laid out to keep the afternoon summer sun out of the hitter's eyes. This means that the pitcher as he addressed the batter would be facing west (thus a lefthander's throwing arm would compass-align toward the south, thereby bringing the word *southpaw* into the language). To the point here is that Philadelphia lies east of Pittsburgh. If the order of the two cities were reversed in Paige's account, he could be suspected of a tall tale.

(Candlestick Park was faithful to the classic compass align-ment; thus in his most usual habitat Mays was left hitting into the prevailing wind. One can only speculate how many homers he would have hit in a more congenial home park, but there's nothing unique in that: the same speculation can be made for many hitters. In Mays's case, however, a far less speculative case can be made in terms of the playing time lost to military service in his early twenties. Were it not for that hiatus, Willie Mays, not Henry Aaron, would have been the first to eclipse Babe Ruth's record of 714 home runs.)

Where the youthful Willie Mays might be ranked, as the leg-ends are retold, is conjectural. Three times in his career, he threw the ball on one bounce from more than 400 feet away to nail runners at the plate. Three times his impossible catches were even more impossible, being made with the bare hand. Asked on one occasion to confirm that Mays was the greatest all-around ballplayer he had ever seen, Chub Feeney said, "He may be the greatest *athlete* I ever saw." While in high school, Willie received college scholarship offers both in football (where he was a quarterback who ran as well as passed) and basketball; the football team was so good it used to scrimmage college teams, and hold them even; the basketball team won the state title in its division with Mays as its standout performer despite his being the shortest man on the squad. His spring, coordination, peripheral vision, and above all the great spread of his oversize hands more than made up for any lack in height. Through the years, once he reached the majors, the Rawlings and MacGregor sporting goods houses designed a line of fielding mitts for Willie that were huge in themselves, and made more so that he wore them completely off his hand, controlling the glove by the pressure of fingertip grip. His success as a fielder would pioneer the most radical equipment change that baseball has seen in this century. Before Willie's time only first basemen wore the glove off the hand. Now other outfielders, then infielders, finally even pitchers would begin opting for the off-the-hand models whose function was to extend the reach instead of merely to protect the hand. To the question of why there have been no .400 hitters since Ted Williams in 1941, the fact that seven defenders could now reach batted balls with arms in the net eight inches longer than they used to be would supply a strong segment of the answer. In compensation, if not consolation to the individual batsman, the same shortstop who now flagged down ground balls he could never have reached before would overall make fewer double plays: getting to the ball with the extended glove was one thing; fishing it out was another.

(Mays himself may have established his preference for the oversize mitt by accident. The Fairfield Gray Sox were a catch-as-catch-can outfit, and on more than one occasion Willie might find himself playing outfield or second base while wearing a first baseman's mitt that happened to be the spare glove in best repair. When he saw the extent to which he could control it, the longer glove became his trademark. And the encouragement to other players to follow suit came in more ways than one: in 1954, Rip Repulski, a Cardinal left fielder who still wore the old-style finger mitt that simply covered the hand, nabbed a deep line drive off the bat of Mays and later was congratulated for his game-saving catch. "What catch?" Repulski responded. "It nailed me to the wall.")

As soon as school was out in 1948, the year he turned seventeen, Mays turned to baseball full-time. Through the offices of Jim Canady, he secured a post with the Chattanooga Choo-Choos, a Negro "minor league" club whose owner, a man named Becker, had him play first base and shortstop, which was fine with Willie. What was less fine was that if it rained, nobody got paid. "We'd get into a town and it would rain and we wouldn't have any money for maybe three days," Mays has recalled. "We'd eat loaves of stale bread and sardines and crackers and RC Cola, and I remember—we were in Dayton, Ohio, at the time—I said to myself, if this ever get over with, I'm quitting."

He lasted about a month with the Choo-Choos. Then the club returned to Chattanooga, only a $2.50 bus fare north of Birmingham. Mays phoned his father collect to say he was coming home. Then he went to club owner Becker and said, "I need $2.50 to get home. My mama's sick."

Becker fished a trifle sadly for the $2.50. "You be back tomorrow?" he asked.

"Yeah," Willie lied.

In the meantime, both Canady and Kitty Kat had spoken to player-manager Piper Davis of the Black Barons, who had seen Willie play a time or two with the Gray Sox and agreed to give him a try. The deal, which Davis cleared only later with club owner Hayes, was for $250 a month, to go to $300 following any month in which Mays hit .300. Davis did not urge a contract on Willie, and Hayes did not press for one. For one thing, Willie was stunningly under age: the youngest player the Barons ever hired. For another, the need was immediate. The Barons' regular left fielder had just broken his leg. So Mays became a left fielder. Kitty Kat recollects that "soon as the left fielder's leg mended, the center fielder broke *his* leg." And so the "son of Kat," as Willie was locally known, would become by unremarkable accident the most renowned occupant of that particular position in baseball history. "They named him for center field," someone said to Garry Schumacher. "No," Schumacher said. "They named center field for him." (A variation on that observation came from Ted Williams in 1978, when Mays was voted the all-time All-Star in a poll going back to the inception of the All-Star game in 1933. Williams came in second to Mays in that balloting. "They invented the game for him," Ted remarked.)

Willie's deal with the Black Barons was that he would play full-time when school was out, and home dates, nights, and weekends when school was in session, spring and fall. If he was not compared to Paige, Gibson, Leonard, or Bell, neither in one respect were they compared to him. The Black Barons, and all the teams they played against, picked up on it instantly. "Nobody," Piper Davis said, "and I mean *nobody*, ever saw anybody throw a ball from the outfield like him, or get rid of it so fast."

Mays had another trait: it didn't happen often, but once was more than enough to notice it: he would catch a line drive with his bare hand instead of his glove. Obviously, he preferred the glove, but the factors of wind, fade, or misjudgment occasionally made the meat hand the only feasible means for the putout. To say it again, three times in his major league career he would make the bare-hand catch. The crowds and the players stared in disbelief when he did it. As a youngster with the Barons, he did it even more often, but a certain sentiment prevailed that the glove was there for a purpose, so his teammates landed on him for it.

They picked up also on another Mays trademark—the way his cap flew off when he ran. In this there was nothing artificial or contrived: any wind-tunnel test would produce the same dynamic result. It was not just the innate speed of Mays, but the way he turned it on. This would be seen on offense in the way he broke from the plate on a batted ball; on defense in the way he broke for a batted ball even before the ball was hit. (Watching Mays create motion from a standing start in the outfield was an eerie experience, for he seldom broke into action on a foul ball; something in the swing of the bat told him when *not* to move or even lean from the stationary position.) Most of all, however, the ingredient was marked in Mays for the way he could shift gears while running less than all-out—as on a routine fly ball inexplicably mishandled by the fielder while Mays was on the bases—and suddenly turn on like an afterburner. And then the cap really flew off.

And between his ability to reach base—and what he could do once he was there—many baseball men said that were it not for the way it would waste his long-ball power, he would have to be the ideal lead-off man in the batting order. It could even be theorized that it was worth having Mays lead off even if it meant a guaranteed time at bat every game where he would be up with no one on base ahead of him. And one such theorist would decide to put it into practice. Not with the teenage Mays, though. It was an idea that flowered instead when Willie was going on thirty-eight.

The theorist in this case was named Clyde King. When Herman Franks's pre-set four-year term as Giant manager ran out with the conclusion of the 1968 season, King, who had been managing the Giants' Triple-A Pacific Coast League farm club at Phoenix, was named to replace him. He thus became the first Giant manager in history, with the exception of Leo Durocher, who had not served in some previous capacity with the parent club, and in King's case it showed. At least Durocher had managed in the big leagues before, but King had not done this either, and this showed too. His strong point as a minor league manager and big league coach had been the way he worked with pitchers, no mean accomplishment in itself. King himself had been a pitcher. (He had a fine 13-and-6 won-and-lost record as a relief man with the Dodgers in 1951 . . . Willie Mays hit a home run off him that year, but by 1969, when King came to manage the Giants, Mays no longer remembered it. He did remember King striking him out in '51. "He quick-pitched me," Willie said.) But when it came to overall managerial strategy, King with the Giants seemed at times to be ill at ease. He was unaccustomed to having the larger major league complement of 25 players at his disposal (the roster limit at Phoenix was 21; in the lower minors, where King also had managed, even fewer than that), with the result that with the Giants he would carry only two catchers and nine pitchers (of whom at any typical point only eight might be ablebodied), as if he were afraid he would run out of people to play the other positions. Typical too of this phobia was that no one can remember King, while managing the Giants, ever "turning the order"—a common big-league move under which a manager bringing in a relief pitcher also makes a simultaneous personnel change at some other defensive position: this enables him to switch the two new men in the batting order, so the new pitcher will not have to give immediate way to a pinch hitter. (The lesson here was apparent for all but King to see at one early-season point in '69, when in a game against the Mets his best relief pitcher had to be replaced after pitching to only two hitters, because King needed a pinch hitter to get the tying run. He did get the tying run, but the next relief pitcher walked the winning run home for the Mets in the bottom of the ninth. Had King "turned the order" when he brought the first relief man into the game, the latter could have continued to pitch.)

The new manager found himself plagued also by a rash of strange on-the-field happenings. One of these was the strange adventure of Rule 4.09, which states, "A run is not scored if the runner advances to home base during a play in which the third out is made (1) by the batter-runner before he touched first base; (2) by any runner being forced out; or (3) by a preceding runner

who is declared out because he failed to touch one of the bases."
Reducing that to the part that applies to this story, it means that
if a man scores before the final out of an inning-ending double
play, his run will not count if it was a force double play. On any
other kind of double play, if he scores before the final out, his
run does count.

Now comes a 1969 encounter between Pittsburgh and the
Giants at Candlestick Park. The Giants have Ron Hunt on
third, Bobby Bonds on first, one out. The batter sends a long fly
to left-center. Hunt tags up and scores after the catch. Bonds,
either forgetting how many were out or taking the not-always-
unwise risk that on a misplay he could score from first, is running all-out from first and is well past second by the time the
catch is made. The Pirates get the ball back to first before Bonds
has a chance to retrace his steps, and so it becomes a double play
and the inning is over. But it was not a force double play (which
could only happen on a ground ball, not a fly—Bonds was not
forced to leave first base), and so, there being no question that
Hunt had scored well before the Pirates got the ball back to first
to complete the double play, the run had to count.

Except that it didn't.

The home-plate umpire is supposed to signal the press box
on such a play to denote whether the run scored before or
after the third out. Hunt had scored in this case so far ahead
of the third out that none of us in the press box even looked
up to check the signal. It may be that the umpire, in this
case the rookie Satch Davidson, felt similarly that the run
was so apparent, no signal was necessary. Later the scoreboard operator swore he had seen a signal from Davidson
that the run did *not* count. If that was what Davidson ruled,
he was to have plenty of company.

My first intimation of the event came from an eminent Pittsburgh baseball writer named Wrong Feeney (Charles Feeney
was his actual name; he was known as Wrong to distinguish him
from Charles "Chub" Feeney, the Giant vice-president who

within a year became president of the National League). From several seats away from me, he yelled, "What the hell is that?" He was pointing at the scoreboard, which showed a zero for the Giant scoring in the inning just completed. I said, "I'm a sonofabitch if I know," and went to the phone that connected the press box to the Giant dugout. At the other end, Giant coach Ozzie Virgil picked up the phone. I said, "Ozzie, don't you get a run for Hunt scoring?" "You can't score a run on a double play," Virgil responded, and hung up. But to cite this conversation is not to single out Virgil for censure: he just happened to be the one who picked up the phone. The shade that had come over the Giant minds was collective: no one on the team—not Virgil, not any of the other coaches, not any of the players, not manager King nor for that matter captain Mays, had thought to say a word about it.

The next step was delicate. In the press box, Feeney, Garry Schumacher, and I retreated to the rule book, in an attempt to uncover the governing regulation. I don't know how the two of them felt, but I had the unnerving feeling that maybe the umpire and Virgil were right, and I had been laboring in error for a quarter of a century. But Feeney and Schumacher were certain of the ground, and unearthed 4.09, and there it was. With Schumacher it could not have been otherwise. First as a sportswriter in New York, then as publicity chief for the Giants, he had accumulated a feel for the game that inhabited six decades, and a feel for baseball is a feel for its rule book. It was his mission and his pleasure to know the game. Now it would become his mission but not his pleasure to take the rule book down through the stands and hand it as unobtrusively as possible to the bat boy, who would hand it to Clyde King.

All of this took time. We observed Schumacher as he wended his way down through the stands and handed over the evidence. We watched King as he took the book and studied the rule. By now an inning and a half had gone by. And here King came out of the dugout, to address the umpires.

The conference was short and sweet. No one questioned that the run had scored, and the scoreboard operator was signaled to rectify the mistake. On the board, the zero came down for the Giants and a one went up in its place.

Came now a figure from the Pittsburgh dugout—Pirate manager Larry Shepard. The conversation between him and plate umpire Davidson went approximately as follows:

SHEPARD: Do you know of any reason why I shouldn't play the rest of this game under protest?
DAVIDSON: On what grounds?
SHEPARD: I don't know on what grounds. All I know is, I was sitting in my dugout, minding my own business, and I look up at the scoreboard, and there's the other team scoring a run while my team's at bat.

The name of Shepard had a certain *déjà vu* to it, where Willie Mays was concerned. The Pirates won that particular game in 1969, so any protest became moot, happily saving league president Giles from another restroom judgment; but Mays could remember another Shepard with the Pittsburghs, a catcher named Jack Shepard who in 1955 tagged Willie at home plate with an extra degree of enthusiasm. Mays came out of his slide with his hand cocked and fist clenched, but thought the better of it and went on into the dugout. His role as peacemaker in the Marichal-Roseboro affair of 1965 took on overtones of great public sociological significance, and the fact was that no umpire ever kicked him out of a game. But he had his moments of temptation, as with catcher Shepard in 1955, and a time or two besides. Playing winter ball in Puerto Rico in the off-season of 1951–52, he engaged in an on-the-field scuffle with teammate Ruben Gomez; in 1962, he was briefly engaged at second base by a Mets infielder named Elio Chacon who, frustrated at seeing Mays slide around him, started to punch at him. Willie's response was to pick him up, carry him a short way into center field, and drop him. In 1968, Mays himself became frustrated and tried to climb into the stands back of first base at Candlestick to go after two beered-up men who had been taunting him all game.

And in a game at Houston in 1969, Willie went after manager King. It happened in the dugout, in full view of most of the spectators, and it tells its own story to say that Mays, whose conduct on its face was unforgivable, was neither fined, suspended, nor asked to issue an apology. King may have been King in name, but in all of baseball, Mays was the man who was king in title. Even the Reggie Jackson of the late seventies would be suspended for crossing manager Billy Martin, but no one was about to suspend Willie Mays. The Giants of 1967 had finished ten games off the pace; the Giants of 1968 nine games off—no serious contending factor either time. But both those years they led not just the National League but both major leagues in road attendance. Even at home, where the 1968 arrival of the Oakland A's cut mercilessly into an area whose population simply could not support two teams, the Giants counted their crowds in terms of the same factor—Willie Mays who was, beyond dispute, the greatest individual crowd lure in the history of the game.

The why of Willie's going after King sounds petty in retrospect, and was fairly so at the time. The manager had promised Mays a night off in Houston, but Willie found his name posted on the starting lineup in the dugout. His version is that he went back to the clubhouse to get his glove; King's assumption was that the Mays retreat to the clubhouse indicated his refusal to play, so the manager changed the lineup and wrote somebody else in for center field. In either event, Mays now returned to the dugout and found his name scratched out and took it for a King attempt to show him up, posting a Mays-included lineup and then making it Mays-excluded. The outburst that followed was not characteristic, and fellow Giants peeled Willie off King before any damage was done. But the association between the two men was typified by misunderstanding. (One example of this was Mays's new habit of turning a double into a single by daring baserunning-in-reverse. Time and again he would get a two-base hit, then at a point halfway or more to second suddenly put on the brakes and race back to first. His reasoning was that Willie McCovey, who followed him in batting order, had the only other authoritative bat in the Giant lineup, and for Mays to be on second with McCovey up and first base open was to take the bat out of McCovey's hands. The other team would either walk McCovey intentionally or pitch around him. The Mays presence on first base, on the other hand, not only pressured the other team to throw strikes to McCovey but, by virtue of the first baseman's playing on the bag to hold Mays close, opened up the right side of the infield so that even a McCovey grounder could go through for a hit. "I told King time and again why I was doing it," Mays has said. "I just don't know if it ever got through.")

But the misunderstanding arose early—at King's first press conference, when he was named manager months ahead of the start of the 1969 season—and here it was King's own doing. His view was that under Herman Franks, who was not only Mays's baseball manager but his business manager, the center fielder had been pampered to an excessive degree. (Was it true, someone asked Franks at one point, that he had accorded Mays the status almost of co-manager when it came to lineup choices and field strategy? "Yes," Franks replied. Why? "Because he knows more about those things than I do," Franks said. "You got any hard questions?") King in his own turn felt that he had to demonstrate authority. Coming from the Phoenix farm club without any previous experience with the big club, he might be accused of favoring the youngsters he had developed over the established regulars. So at his first press conference he announced an even-handed policy: all Giant players, regardless of duration of service, would be required to practice equally, and in fact would be treated as equals in all ways. No doubt this was properly intentioned, but where Mays was concerned it was like Rudolf Bing taking over the Metropolitan Opera and telling Maria Callas she had to sing scales.

One must not be too hard on King. As mentioned, he did have a gifted way of working with pitchers, and one may not envy him his task of trying to take over the Giants. He had not bargained for the distractions, either, including, as they did in a seriocomic way, a newly formed fan club called the Giant Boosters. Brainchild of a Bay Area insurance man named Allan Murray, the Boosters were something else. They not only supported the Giants, they traveled with them: first on tours to Arizona for spring training, then alongside the team on road trips throughout the season. Male or female regardless, the typical Booster was old enough to remember Repeal as the standout event of a lifetime. "Where'd you get this group?" Jack Kane, manager of the Giants' spring-training installation at Casa Grande, Arizona, asked Horace Stoneham. "They're not only older than you are but they drink more." In fact, the Boosters became the largest and most enthusiastic organized fan club in baseball, and they adored their Giants. "Christ, they never sleep!" one of the pawed-over players said. (In late 1978, Boosters president Murray was contemplating a 1979 junket to Montreal for club members. "Can you get a drink in Montreal?" one of the new members asked him. "Is the Pope Italian?" Murray responded.)

The Boosters were there to cheer mightily, at the start of spring training in 1969, and one of the things they cheered the most was Clyde King's promise, as set forth at the outset of this section in this book, to make Willie Mays the lead-off man in the Giant batting order. "It makes all kinds of sense," King said. "There's nothing more important in baseball than to be the team that scores the first run, and with Willie's speed we're the ones with the best chance to get it."

In its way, this was an astounding tribute to Mays: seventeen years earlier, he and Mickey Mantle had broken into the big leagues simultaneously as speed-merchant rookies. Now going into 1969, Mantle—who was five months younger than Mays— had announced his retirement from the game, while Mays meanwhile was finding himself proclaimed the speediest runner on his team. Which more than likely he was.

The implicit compliment was therefore as accurate as it was extraordinary. (The experiment lasted through spring training and eleven games into the regular season, at which point King saw the light and junked it.) Certainly Mays could bat lead-off, and his baserunning skills could only augment the persuasiveness of the idea. And an established hitter can bat anywhere in the lineup without strain. But where would be the runners on base ahead of him, and could a young rookie like the King-appointed Bobby Bonds handle the pressure of occupying Mays's habitual number-three spot in the batting order? "King is a crazy man," Charley Fox said to Herman Franks, in the stands at Phoenix. "Let him find out on his own," Franks responded. "It won't take him all that long." It didn't.

The Giants under King took a good run at the divisional title in 1969. Though they did not win it, they were in first place as late as the night of September 22. What kept them there was a game-winning pinch-hit home run in the seventh inning by Willie Mays that night at San Diego. It was the 600th home run of Willie's career, and it was almost dreamlike. Mays hit the ball far up into a near-empty bleacher stand in left field. His teammates poured out to greet him as he reached home plate, and the rival manager, Preston Gomez, confessed afterward he had the impulse to join them and was afraid his players would do the same. Instead, Gomez found himself consoling Mike Corkins, the pitcher who had thrown the ball. Corkins was in his first season in the big league. He looked almost pleadingly at his manager. "Why'd it have to be me?" he asked.

"Son," Gomez said gently, "there've been 599 before you."

Technically of course that figure was incorrect, for it did not take into consideration the repeaters. This is a statement of praise for the repeaters: the better they were, the more they pitched; the more they pitched, the more they faced Willie. It is a measure of the lasting career of the great Hall-of-Famer

Warren Spahn that he gave up not just the first home run Mays ever hit in the majors but also numbers 47, 58, 98, 109, 110, 124, 200, 223, 258, 292, 318, 320, 359, 383, 407, and 408. After 1964, Spahn never pitched again against Mays, or it would have been more. Yet by no means would he qualify as Willie's "favorite" pitcher, because—quite strange to tell—Mays never had any favorite pitchers. He could discombobulate a couple of them; leading off first base against Vinegar Bend Mizell, he would reduce Vinegar Bend to a jellied mass. And, as recounted earlier in these pages, he hexed Harvey Haddix. But generally speaking, if Mays ever had one favorite pitcher, it would have been another all-time great, Whitey Ford, and since Ford pitched for the Yankees in the American League, those confrontations came chiefly in the All-Star game. Few as they were, they were so pronounced that Mays's batting average against Ford was .700. When Ford failed to make the American League All-Star team for the 1963 game, he dispatched a telegram to Mays: DEAR WILLIE—SORRY—WHITEY.

It is the converse that strikes me as a high credential for Mays: he performed equally against all comers, this team or that team, lefthander or righthander. Art Santo Domingo, who served as statistician for the Giants in the sixties, got it into his head one time to survey Willie's hit production against opposing teams. He chose as his starter year 1962, when the National League expanded to ten teams, with the Giants meeting each other team eighteen times per season, and charted it over the three seasons of 1962–63–64. The even tenor of Willie's average number of hits per season, against nine other clubs over that three-year period, has to be recorded to be believed. Against Philadelphia and Milwaukee he averaged 19 hits per season; against Cincinnati, Pittsburgh, and Los Angeles, 20; against Chicago and Houston, 21; against New York and St. Louis, 22. Did he do particularly well against the good clubs of those years? No. Did he do particularly badly? No. His overall average production against all clubs was practically identical to his average against the three best other clubs in the league for each of those three years. If it was a shade better against the good clubs, it was because he seldom missed a time at bat against the good clubs.

Mays's 600th home run, in 1969, would not write finis to his landmark list. In January of 1970, he was named Player of the Decade by *The Sporting News*. In July of 1970 he collected the 3,000th hit of his major league career. On September 28 of that year he became the sixth player in history to compile 10,000 official times at bat. And there was the day of May 23, 1970, which was the birthday of manager Clyde King. In celebration, his players went out and scored 16 runs against the San Diego Padres. In that same game the Padres scored 17 runs. Giant president Horace Stoneham summoned the birthday boy and fired him.

King was replaced by Charley Fox, long a member of the Giant organization. The floundering Giants of 1970 continued to flounder, but under Fox they did win 37 of their last 54 games —the hottest end-season rate in the league—and they were something to conjure for 1971. Fox also restored Mays to the most-favored-nation status he had enjoyed under Franks, and Willie began the 1971 season like a frisky colt, slamming four home runs in his first four games, and, with the imminent approach of his fortieth birthday, leading the Giants to first place in the division standings. Not only had Fox renewed Willie's role as closet manager, he had actually named him player-coach, to work with the other outfielders. "Willie is the greatest player I ever saw or heard of," Fox said, going into the 1971 campaign. In training at Phoenix, Fox went out to the ball park one morning to confer with the groundskeepers. It was shortly after eight o'clock—too early for the Boosters—but there was Mays in center field, talking to seven outfielders gathered around him. Fox said to Mays, "What the hell are you doing here so early?" Mays said to Fox, "What the hell are *you* doing here so early?"

"He knows what we're all about," one young Giant left-hander, Ron Bryant, said of Fox, and in one game in late April Fox let two other young lefthanders, Steve Hamilton and John

Cumberland, pitch successively to the great Henry Aaron, who earlier in the game had cracked the 600th home run of his own career. With this defiance of percentages, Aaron popped up both times. Gaylord Perry, who had started the game for the Giants, was less amused. "Perry's sore that you took him out," somebody said to Fox. "Who cares?" Fox replied cheerily. The Giants had won the game, 6–5, in the tenth inning, on Willie Mays's fourth hit of the evening, and afterward, with Mays's fortieth birthday party only a week away and a grand testimonial banquet scheduled to commemorate the event, Fox decided he would serenade Mays at the dinner. He had a plausible tenor, and, to the music of "Sonny Boy," he began rehearsing:

> Climb upon my knee, Willie Boy,
> Though you're only three, Willie Boy;
> When there are gray skies,
> I don't mind those gray skies,
> Long as I have you, Willie Boy!

At the dinner he actually sang it. He was followed by Horace Stoneham, who rambled. Stoneham was followed by his nephew Chub Feeney, now the National League president, who recited a poem. It was an Irish tenor, a drunk, and a poetry reading, but they were part of a singular evening of sentiment and affection. The audience sang "Happy Birthday," and entertainer Teresa Brewer had a version of "Hello, Dolly":

> We hear the band playin'
> And the man sayin'
> It's another circus catch like 'way back when!
> So . . . throw that ball, Gibson,
> It's gonna clear the wall, Gibson,
> Willie'll never go away again!

All in all, it was to become what commissioner Bowie Kuhn, who was also there, called later the warmest such baseball function in his memory. To Kuhn fell the honor of reading a telegram from President Nixon saluting Mays on his fortieth birthday "as proof that people over the age of thirty can be trusted." Having become commissioner over the body of Feeney at the end of 1969, Kuhn met with some mixed reviews when he first assumed the office, and he was responsible for some memorable gaffes, like his failure in 1973 to salute Hank Aaron for his 700th home run. That the commissioner ignored the occasion was a regrettable oversight, but it might have passed, save for the cover-up excuse he offered: "I didn't want to set a precedent," he explained. Oh.

Kuhn did have his detractors, but it could be argued on the other side that anybody who appeared simultaneously on the shit lists of Charlie Finley and Howard Cosell could not be all bad. Certainly he did not pass up the chance to attend Willie Mays's fortieth birthday party, though the extra thrill for the audience on that occasion, I think, must have been the sight of an all-time outfield—Mays, Aaron, DiMaggio—all sitting at the head table. And seated at a front table in the audience was a woman eight years younger than Willie. Her name was Mae Allen, and later that year, in a ceremony at Acapulco, she would become his wife.

It would be Willie's second marriage, Mae's first. In 1956, Mays had married Marghuerite Wendell, a woman older than himself, and twice married before, first to a member of the original Ink Spots, the hit singing group of the forties, whose name was Kennedy; then to a doctor named Wendell. Marghuerite had a daughter by her first marriage, but no child by her second and none with Willie, and when they moved to San Francisco they began to talk to adoption agencies and in 1959 became the adoptive parents of a five-week-old boy whom they named Michael. He would brighten their marriage but not save it. The word got out that all was not well between the parents, and as baseball phrasing has permeated the language, so it would happen here: "He hit her like he owned her" was one encapsuled newspaper account of a domestic spat between the Mayses. It might have been "She hit him like she owned him," but, lacking the correct baseball transfer, and lacking also a quotable eyewitness, it never appeared that way. In conflict, the two of them moved to divorce in 1962; as he grew, Michael would continue to share custody time with one or the other.

But Mae Allen was different. In curious counterpart she too was interested in adoption, but as a trained social worker who was one of the pioneers in the single-parent adoption program. Her direct presentation of this was enough to win the funding endorsement of Governor Ronald Reagan of California. But what brought her to California was a blind date with a man who happened to play baseball for a living. Her home was Pittsburgh (Pitchburgh if you choose). A relative had named a friend, or a friend had named a relative, take it as you may, but either way it was the classic blind date. Mae was in her mid-twenties at the time, and impressionable, but not all that impressionable. The phone rang and she picked it up, and, by her account, "This high squeaky voice said, 'Mae Allen? You don't know me, but my name is Willie Mays.'"

"Fine," she said into the telephone. "You're Willie Mays and I'm Martha Washington." And she hung up.

Remarkably close at hand was the sports section of the morning Pittsburgh paper, and now she gazed at it and saw the headline: MAYS & CO. IN TOWN TO PLAY BUGS. "And I said to myself," she has related, "oh, my good God, what have I done?"

Would the high, squeaky voice ever call back? It did. And so Mae got to meet Willie. "It's a good thing I'm not that much into astrology," she would say, years later. "But I'm into it enough to know that Willie is a Taurus, and people tell me the signs may conflict." But the signs didn't conflict, and Mae knew it. It was something other than that. There was one thing, she came to know, that her husband would not deal with, and that one thing was death. If death has a cold hand figuratively for all of us, it had that cold hand literally for Mays: as a boy in Alabama he had, as said before, awakened one morning literally in the cold clutch-embrace of the Uncle Otis who had died in the bed the two of them shared. Willie went to the funeral. He would attend only a handful of funerals in all the future years to come—his Aunt Sarah's and Jackie Robinson's and the one for Russ Hodges—but then only under pressure, and there were times when he couldn't withstand the pressure. In 1953, Mays went to Birmingham to attend his mother's funeral. But he could not bring himself actually to go to the services. A quarter of a century later, in 1978, he went to Los Angeles for the funeral of Jim Gilliam, his close friend who had played, then coached, for the Dodgers. But he could not bring himself actually to go to the services. It was even worse than that: in 1974, the year after Mays retired from active play, TV producer Lee Mendelson did another hour-long special on him, this one a full review of his career. This was the one that had Jack Klugman as its narrator, and its final scene began with the showing of black-and-white still photographs of the ball parks that were there when Willie first came to the Giants but had long since ceased to be: Shibe Park in Philadelphia . . . Forbes Field in Pittsburgh . . . Braves Field in Boston . . . Sportsman's Park in St. Louis . . . Crosley Field in Cincinnati . . . Ebbets Field in Brooklyn . . . the Polo Grounds in New York. Then the screen went to color again, and the viewer saw an empty Candlestick Park in San Francisco, watching the shadows of late afternoon as the camera captured them in stop-action and transformed the scene gradually from day to night, over which Klugman read the words of the Rolfe Humphries poem "Polo Grounds":

> Time is of the essence. The shadow moves
> From the plate to the box, from the box to second base,
> From second to the outfield, to the bleachers.
> Time is of the essence. The crowd and players
> Are the same age always, but the man in the crowd
> Is older every season. Come on, play ball!

Mays enjoyed the show and asked Mendelson for a tape of it that he could play at home, and some time later Mendelson and his wife found themselves among the guests for an evening at Willie's place in Atherton, and Mae turned the tape machine on and replayed the program. "Willie sat through the whole thing," Mendelson told me later. I asked what was so strange about that. "The whole thing," Mendelson repeated, as if he had not heard me, "till it got to that business at the end, with the ball parks and the shadows. Then I looked around and he was gone." Some four years later, I asked Mae about it. "It's true," she said. "We've run the show any number of times. But when it gets to that part at the end, Willie won't stay in the room." So in the end truth, he *was* Peter Pan: if he could not stand final services for others, neither could he stand them for himself.

There were dozens of TV tapes at the Mays residence in Atherton, scores of record albums. Crowded in among the latter was a George Carlin album someone had given Willie and Mae shortly after their marriage. The album is called *Take-Offs & Put-Ons*, and on one of its bands Carlin takes the role of Biff Burns the sportscaster. "In the sportlight spotlight tonight," Biff reports, "first a baseball trade: The San Francisco Giants today traded outfielder Willie Mays to the New York Mets in exchange for the entire New York Mets team." On the record, the audience howled with laughter. So, listening to it, did Willie and Mae. "The Giants," adds the Burns/Carlin of the record, "will also receive $500,000 in cash, two eskimos and a kangaroo." Again, the audience and the Mayses break up laughing.

At the age of forty in 1971, the old man had led the Giants to the National League's western division title. Among other things, he had more stolen bases than in any year since he was twenty-nine. In one doubleheader against the Mets he played center field the first game; then, to rest not only Willie

McCovey's legs but his own, first base the second . . . and made sensational plays in both games. "I can't very well tell my batters don't hit it to him," Mets manager Gil Hodges said thoughtfully. "Wherever they hit it, he's there anyway."

There is already recorded, earlier in this book, the account of how Nevada bookmakers would not even accept bets on the Giants' final game of the regular '71 season, so sure was the San Francisco victory. But Mays had no zest for the celebration that followed. He was bone-weary from this season-without-end— even with manager Fox resting him whenever he asked, the demands were there and he had appeared in 139 games. And even with the Giants winning the first game of the pennant playoff against the Pirates, there was a perceptible lack of optimism in the San Francisco camp: the other old Giant warriors were tired too. Pittsburgh won the next three games (in the first of those Mays hit one of the most meaningless home runs of his career—it meant that instead of losing 9–3 the Giants would lose 9–4) to wrap it up. Some people—Mays included—would quarrel with Charley Fox's managing strategy, which was to go by the book, which says you never let the other team's best hitter beat you if you can help it. So he had his pitchers throw nothing but balls to Pittsburgh's Willie Stargell. "Shit, pitch his ass!" Mays stormed. "He ain't hit the ball good in a month!"

But then Willie returned home to rest, and to play golf—his favorite avocation, and he had become so good at it he was a scratch player—and to await the coming of the 1972 season. In the pages of *Life*, Hugh Sidey wrote of President Nixon and Vietnam, "He remains convinced that the rate of withdrawal he set is essentially correct, and resents the fact that he gets so little credit for judgment. . . . A few days ago the corridor outside his Oval Office was filled with people who had just been to see him. As they sauntered away together, they mingled with other visitors. Suddenly, one man noticed that Nixon was in their midst, yet nothing was said, no head turned, there was no ripple in his wake. The President moved almost unnoticed through the crowd, ducked down a stair and out of view, a lonely man in a world of his own." And: *TCP/2/ is the latest improvement in Shell gasolines. Less than half a teaspoon per gallon is enough to help your engine stay in tune.* And: *Sure you could get a perfectly good suntan in your own back yard. Sure you can do without the best things in life. But why? Why not treat yourself to a smoother, lighter whisky—Canadian Lord Calvert. STAZE: The original SECURITY CREAM for FALSE TEETH. HAWK INTO VIOLENT DOVE: The conversion of Dan Ellsberg, the man at the center of the top-secret storm of the Pentagon papers. Sirs: I am 15 years old and adopted. Your article made me see how fortunate I am to have grown up with a good family. I would never give up my family for my real mother. Sirs: What we have with the draft is a mere extension of the basic Communist principle that the nation-state is everything and the individual is nothing. Karl Hess once wrote: "Given a nation that not enough citizens can be attracted to defend voluntarily, you probably also have a nation that, by definition, isn't really worth defending." The need for the all-volunteer army is plain. I think it's about time we return to our heritage of rugged individualism and isolationism and institute a volunteer army by July 1971. Sirs: It appears when publisher Lyle Stuart has a hot streak in Las Vegas, it is a very hot streak indeed. The probability against calling the dice as Stuart called them (5,2; hot six; 11; 4; 9) is 1,259,712 to 1.*

Montage of the early seventies, this too from the pages of *Life*, under the by-line of Derek Wright, a senior lecturer in psychology at Leicester University in England:

The much-vaunted sexual freedom that the sex researchers and their disciples insist we share is turning out to be a new bondage. We have escaped from one trap to be ensnared by another; for freedom from ignorance and fear is being bought at the price of submission to the tyranny of social norms and the authority of the "experts."

On the face of it the new ideology looks innocent enough. Like fresh air, exercise and wholesome food, sex does you good, and within certain broad and tolerant limits the more you have the better. Since knowledge emancipates, we cannot know too much about such things as the physiological possibilities for pleasure our bodies offer, the cultural relativity of sexual mores and, of course, how everyone else behaves.

However, complacently aware of its benefits, we have failed to pay enough attention to the fact that this kind of knowledge generates not freedom but social pressures. We begin to grade our sexual partners, as they us, though we do not talk about it. And standards are rising. Too often for the sex experts, the merely possible is instantly the optimal, and tomorrow, for the rest of us, the normal. How we pity or scorn the impotent and frigid! While, absurdly, some people use sex to exorcise their insecurities, others who find it difficult, distasteful or merely dull conclude that they are odd, outcast and, most desolating of all, inadequate. It is so easy to build a prison around a man by convincing him he is a prisoner.

The beginning of the 1972 season was no beginning. It was taken up instead by, in the words of Roger Angell, a "bitter, unprecedented strike called by the Players Association at the end of March, which wiped out the first two weeks of the season and did away with most of the anticipation and good cheer of baseball's spring." In charge of Willie Mays's financial affairs (this was never a permanent post: before Herman Franks there had been a congenial and effective San Francisco banker named Jake Shemano, and in coming years Franks would be replaced by an accountant), ex-manager Franks was dealing with Horace Stoneham for Willie's future security. Salary meant nothing: Stoneham had already put Mays in the $150,000 bracket. The factors instead were those of time and dependability. For the first time in his life, Mays became a holdout, and the misunderstanding San Francisco sport pages landed on him for his "ego trip," as one writer called it. In truth, the dealing was between two close friends, Franks and Stoneham, and the problem was that Stoneham was running out of money. He had been done in by the presence of the Oakland A's across the bay, and ultimately the toll would force him out of the game: in 1975, the National League acted in receivership to take over the club; in

1976, the Giants were sold. The 1972 impasse with Mays was resolved temporarily by a two-year contract with the Giants calling for $165,000 in salary in '72 and the same amount again in '73. Neither Mays nor Stoneham took delight in the deal: Mays would have settled for far less in exchange for the security of a multi-year contract; knowing he couldn't do that, Stoneham wasn't even that sure he could make the short-term agreement. He was marking time so he could seek out someone else to guarantee Willie's future. That someone was two someones—chairman M. Donald Grant and president Joan W. Payson of the New York Mets. And so on May 11, 1972, George Carlin's belly laugh came true—and nobody laughed. Mays in fact was truly angered, if not by the news itself then by the way it was handled. His first inkling of it reached him via a newspaper rumor, four days before the deal was officially announced, and at no point did Stoneham consult with him or even try to reach him. Nor did the terms of the deal seem anything other than demeaning. In return for Mays, the Mets would give the Giants a pitcher named Charlie Williams, then playing with their Tidewater farm club in the International League; the Giants, in their immediate turn, would farm him out to their Phoenix club in the Pacific Coast League. And by all media accounts, the Mets also paid an "unannounced" sum of cash. The San Francisco *Chronicle*, reflecting similar guesses everywhere, estimated the amount at "between $50,000 and $500,000." As the rumors mounted before the sale was announced, Stoneham became incommunicado, and not just to Mays. To Mays it was a case that without warning, ceremony, or even decent recompense, the only major league club he had ever played for was dumping him because its owner needed some extra cash. Willie saw himself as a castoff, and if his pride was hurt, he had a pretty good case.

But hear now the case for Horace Stoneham. In the first place, he was doing the one thing Mays had wanted the most: ensuring Willie's financial future in baseball over the long term. What Stoneham lacked the resources to do, the Mets could do: they guaranteed Mays a ten-year contract, under which they would pay him his existing salary as long as he continued as an active player, then for the balance of the ten years keep him as a coach at $50,000 per year—the highest coaching salary in baseball history. In the second place, Stoneham would do this only with the Mets, for it would preserve the New York in Mays just as Stoneham himself preserved it in the Giants. It was not a question of opening up a bidding war to see who would offer the most. Maybe there was money in Houston, but Willie Mays in a Houston uniform? No. It had to be New York or nothing. In the third place, the most widely publicized terms of the deal— the player and the money the Giants got from the Mets—had no bearing on the negotiation. The hardball—baseball phrase—of Mr. Stoneham's negotiation with Mr. Grant and Mrs. Payson dealt solely with the details of the spread-out to protect Mr. Mays's future. If the offer did not satisfy on that score, then there would be no deal. Thus there was negotiating time in between Stoneham's first signal to the Mets and the honing of a deal that could be okayed. Here most of all lay the reason why Stoneham did not get in touch with Mays. Was he going to tell Willie he had put out a feeler? What if the feeler fell through? But meanwhile, perhaps inevitably, the press got wind of the ongoing negotiation. If it had been a deal Stoneham knew in advance he could wrap up in ten minutes, he would have had no reason not to alert Mays. But it wasn't that kind of a deal.

In 1978, I phoned Stoneham two or three times at his home in Scottsdale, Arizona, where by now he lived in retirement, to go over some points in connection with this book, and in the course of one such conversation we reviewed the trade of Mays to the Mets. He was cheerful that Williams in the later seventies contributed usefully to the pitching staff of the big Giants, but he confirmed that Williams had been a negligible factor in the Mets deal. It was a balancing of system rosters, he said: give up one, get one, so as not in the net to change the roster limits on any clubs in either the Giant or Met organizations. Then, more or less routinely, I asked Stoneham something else. How much money did he actually get from the Mets for Mays?

I'm not wholly sure why, but his answer stunned me.

He said, "There was no money."

"None?"

"None. Do you think I was going to give him up for money?"

The only element involving money, he said, was what the Mets could pay Mays over the next ten years that Stoneham couldn't.

<hr/>

Not to be eliminated from the account of the deal that sent Mays from the Giants to the Mets is the fact that one member of the New York organization literally gave the shirt off his back. That would have been infielder Jim Beauchamp, who reached a decision, upon Mays's arrival, to wear the number 5 on his uniform. The decision was, rather, reached for him. Up until then he had worn 24, but 24 was Willie's number, and that was that. No one else on the Giants, following his departure, would ever wear that number again, and there was some talk that the Mets would follow suit, making him the only man ever to have his number retired by two different teams. That this didn't happen didn't keep 24 from the scaling of cultish heights nonetheless. Rick Barry, for a time the only white player on the Golden State Warriors basketball team, insisted on 24 because he worshiped Willie. Traded to Houston, and discovering another resident worshiper not so ready as Beauchamp to give up the number, Barry improvised brilliantly: he would wear the number 2 on his home uniform and 4 away.

Meanwhile, for Willie with the Mets it was Habitat '72. The same Roger Angell who in the pages of *The New Yorker*, as quoted earlier in these pages, marked the delightful resurgence of youth in the forty-year-old Mays with the Giants, would now mark it again when he was forty-one years old with the Mets:

> Scorecard: early June. July and midseason creeping up, yet baseball year still at loose ends. Distracting sort of campaign, suggesting no-score ball game in which 15 base runners stranded in first 4 innings; eventful yet forgettable. To date: Hank Aaron wafts 1 dozen homers, passing W. Mays and running maybe 1½ seasons short of the Babe's 714. Willie probably relieved. Willie also rejuvenated & rejoicing as a new Met, out from under heavy 20-yr. burden as Giants' deity & leader, plays occasional 1B or OF for Metsies, signs autogs., runs bases like a 10-speed bike, wins games. Maysless Giants (also McCoveyless, thanks to broken McC. wing) plummet to NL West cellar.

Mays in his first game as a Met won it with a home run against the Giants, his old team, and the first time he returned to San Francisco as a Met he beat the Giants again with another home run, with the crowd going wild for him, not against him. There was game-winning hit after game-winning hit. Elected—not appointed, elected—to his twenty-third All-Star game appearance, he started one more time in that game (his game: he had the records; as Ted Williams said, the game was invented for Willie) for the National League. No pennant contender in 1972, the Mets nevertheless led the league in road attendance. This book has referred more than once to road attendance, but let the picture complete itself: No pennant contender in 1972, the Mets also led the league in home attendance.

Willie was doing this.

He was also doing it from memory.

His lifetime batting average in the National League would go down as .302, and so it would be recorded in the books and at the Hall of Fame in Cooperstown. It was a good average. It was more than a good average. Others who made the Hall would include a broad group that never batted .300—Mantle at .298, Wilbert Robinson at .273, Ralph Kiner at .279, Joe Tinker at .262, Yogi Berra (who was managing the Mets when Willie joined them) at .285. The great Rabbit Maranville is in the Hall, and most deservedly so, with a lifetime batting average of .258. The near-incredible statistic where Mays is concerned is that given his career average of .302, the last eight seasons of that career he batted .288, .263, .289, .283, .291, .271, .250, .211. Yet you showed those figures to one baseball man after another, and every one of them would simply shrug and say the same thing: "So what? He's there to beat you. If he doesn't beat you one way, he'll beat you another."

Willie and Mae had a highrise apartment overlooking the Hudson River, in Riverdale, and when he got home from the ball park she had the hot tub ready for him, and then the burning liniment and the soothing oil, and for two hours at a time she would rub his legs and right arm. If it was bad in 1972, it became worse in 1973. He had hurt his left knee; so, cortisone to fix it, except that that's not the way it works when you're forty-one; at forty-one, you hurt your left knee and automatically favor your right knee, then the right knee goes too. And early in 1973, for the third time in his life, he misjudged a fielding leap against the wall. The first time, in 1959, it produced a broken bone, but the rest of the Mays body was so vitalized he went on playing despite it and let it mend on its own; the second time, in 1961, it rattled his bones generally, though breaking none of them: the only mortifying ingredient was that he had missed the catch. ("I thought he was hurt, the way he carried on," said Harvey Kuenn, playing right field alongside Mays. "Turned out he was just swearing at himself. It wasn't an easy catch, and I told him so. I said: 'I miss those balls every day for breakfast.' He said, 'I don't.' ") But the third time, in 1973, Mays hit against the wall with his right shoulder, and it was hurt, and there was nothing of the boy's body left in him to make it come better. And so, writing of those 1973 Mets in general and Mays in particular, Roger Angell would—understandably—say:

Their injury list, this year as last year, encompasses almost the entire club roster, and the current absence of Bud Harrelson, out with a broken wrist, has finally extinguished the last, low fires of 1969. [1969 was the Mets' world championship year.] No team can be blamed for injuries, but the Mets are suffering just as much from a plain dearth of talent; when compared with other clubs in their league—not just the Dodgers and Giants but also the likes of the new Phillies—they are a team truly without prospects. One of their problems, it must be admitted, is Willie Mays, who is now, at forty-two, the oldest player in the National League and has so far resisted the clear evidence that he should retire. He plays sporadically, whenever he is well and rested, and gives his best, but his batting reflexes are gone, and so is his arm. In that opening game against the Giants, the first San Francisco run came in on a long double to the left-center-field fence struck by young Ed Goodson, the Giants' third baseman. Mays chased the ball down at the fence, picked it up, and unexpectedly flipped it to his left fielder, George Theodore, an innocent spectator of the action. Theodore was so surprised that he bobbled the ball for an instant before making the throw, far too late, to third. I had never seen such a thing. Theodore was given an error, but the horrible truth of the matter was that Mays was simply incapable of making the play. In the bottom of the same inning, Mays grounded out to short, and his batting average for the year slipped below .100. He has subsequently done a little better— .202, with three homers, at this writing—but his failings are now so cruel to watch that I am relieved when he is not in the lineup. It is hard for the rest of us to fall apart quite on our own; heroes should depart.

Before Angell's conclusion saw print, it had been arrived at separately by Mays himself. He had spoken to Mets chairman Grant about it, and it was arranged that a ceremony would be held for him at Shea Stadium the night of September 25, before the game with the Montreal Expos. By then, Mays would have announced his retirement; the ceremony, just before the Mets' last night game in New York that year, simply formalized it. One might have an extraordinary feeling for Angell's "heroes should depart" (though not everyone did—Bill Bradley, the

Princeton/New York Knicks basketball star who later became a U.S. Senator from New Jersey, snapped, "You quit when you quit: what law says you have to leave when you're on top? How do you even know?"). But there was something not Angell, and not Mays, and not Grant had figured on: the fact that the Mets, who were not even playing .500 baseball, were going to win their division!

Babe Ruth announced his departure from the game by not announcing it. He didn't even know it. It was May of 1935, and he was fat and tired and hurt and forty-one, but in one appearance at Pittsburgh he hit three home runs and a single, batting in all but one of the Boston Braves' seven runs—they lost the game, 11–7. The last of the hits came in the seventh inning off Guy Bush, who later said, "I never saw a ball hit so hard before or since. He was fat and old, but he still had that great swing. I can't forget that last one he hit off me. It's probably still going."

Maybe it still is. Robert Creamer wrote of it:

> It was unbelievably long, completely over the roof of the double-decked stands in right field and out of the park. Nobody had ever hit a ball over the roof in Forbes Field before. Gus Miller, the head usher, went to investigate and was told the ball landed on the roof of one house, bounced onto another and then into a lot, where a boy picked it up and ran off with it. [Shades of Josh Gibson: "You're out! Yesterday, in Pitchburgh!"] Miller measured the distance from the first house back to home plate and said it was 600 feet. His measurement may have been imprecise, but it was still the longest home run ever hit in Pittsburgh. . . .
>
> Duffy Lewis, Ruth's old Red Sox teammate, was the Braves' traveling secretary, and he told the Babe after the game that if he was going to quit, he ought to quit then, on top. Claire [Mrs. Ruth] told Babe the same thing. "I can't," he cried. "I promised that son of a bitch [the owner of the Braves] I'd play in all the towns on this trip." And there was still Cincinnati and Philadelphia to go. . . .
>
> On Thursday, May 30, in Philadelphia, he was in the starting

lineup in the first game of a Memorial Day doubleheader. He struck out in the first inning. In the field in the bottom of the first he hurt his knee going after a fly ball and left the game. He never played again. His career ended not with a bang in Pittsburgh but a whimper in Philadelphia.

Mays would not go that way. He would not go the way Di-Maggio did, giving way to a pinch runner and trotting to a dugout from which he would never reappear again as an active player. The way he went was with appropriate ceremony. And so it came time for his night, and before 50,000 roaring fans at Big Shea, with his wife beside him, and his father, Kitty Kat, and the boy Michael, now fourteen and looking properly stiff and uncomfortable in the dress gray of his military school, Willie took the microphone and said, "I hope that with my farewell tonight, you'll understand what I'm going through right now. Something that I never feared: that I were ever to quit baseball. But, as you know, there always come a time for someone to get out. And I look at the kids over here, the way they are playing and the way they are fighting for themselves, and it tells me one thing . . . Willie, say good-bye to America. Thank you very much."

He stepped away from the microphone and put a hand to his eyes and wept as the night sky rocked with the love of New York for Willie. So many of the crowd had been born in New York, lived all their lives there. So many of those lives had not even begun when Willie played his first game in New York. It was a Valkyrian farewell in every way—including the touch that most suited Willie and his dread of farewells. The ceremony over, the game began, and in the dugout manager Berra strolled past Willie and said, "I may need you to play tomorrow. Okay?" "Fine with me," Mays said.

Five of the six teams in the NL East were still in contention for the division title that final week in September. Mays and I had talked on the phone at the end of August when the Mets were in fifth place with a won-and-lost record of 62-and-71—but only 5½ games off the pace. "It's coming true," I said. "First place is there and nobody wants it." "I know," he said. "We've got a chance." On the night of September 21, the Mets reached a percentage of .500 in the standings—they had now won as many games as they had lost—and took over first place in their division! It took a win in the first game of what would have been a make-up doubleheader at Chicago, the day after the final Sunday of the regular season, to clinch the division for them, at won 82, lost 79. Mae flew to Chicago and, with Maxie Lanier's help, poured Willie out of the clubhouse and took him to the hotel. He had had two glasses of champagne and was zonkered.

Now all the Mets had to do was beat the Cincinnati Reds in the National League playoff, which they did, in five games. It was a memorable series, featured by the throwing of garbage at Pete Rose, who had been involved in a contact play with Met shortstop Bud Harrelson. The New York fans became so unruly that the ancient peacemaker, Willie Mays, had to come out of the dugout, along with the likes of Berra, Seaver, and Staub, to wave pleadingly at the stands to let the game go on. Which the stands did. (The Mets were ahead.)

That was the third game of the playoff, and the Mets by winning it took a 2–1 lead, but next day the Reds came back to tie it, so it would come down to the fifth and final playoff game. Going into the last of the fifth, the score was tied, but the Mets untied it for keeps in their half. ("The bases were loaded," wrote Angell, "and Willie Mays—yes, of course, *that* kind of day— batted for Kranepool. Over-swinging, fooled by the pitch, Willie hammered the ball straight into the dirt (or perhaps off the plate itself), so that it bounded high up in the air and came down, thirty feet up the third-base line, far too late for Clay Carroll, the unhappy pitcher, to make a play anywhere, and another run was in. It was the shortest heroic blow in memory, but, as Mays suggested after the game, box scores and record books do not show the distance of hits, or their luck. Two more runs ensued, and in the sixth Tom Seaver hit a double that Pete Rose ran and dived in the dirt for, all in vain, and then Tom came around and scored, of course—7–2 now—and grins and cheers and smiles and hugs and handshakes broke out everywhere, and all of us believed.")

So there was Mays in the final game of the playoff, just as he had been in the final game of the playoff eleven years before, just as he had been in the final game of the playoff eleven years before that. Was any added touch of history needed? Probably not, but perhaps fifty million television viewers got it anyway: As Willie's name was announced, the words of a news bulletin tracked silently across the bottom of the TV screen: SPIRO AGNEW RESIGNS AS VICE PRESIDENT. ("We can't both be innocent," Johnny Carson had quoted Nixon as saying to Agnew. "How would it look?" But if, as was widely thought at the time, the departure of Agnew would take the pressure off the Watergate-belea- guered Nixon, in fact the very reverse was true: many of the same people who wanted most to see Nixon impeached feared more the consequence of seeing Agnew replace him as Presi- dent. With Agnew gone, the final barrier was gone, and it would be open season from there on in.)

Mays started the first game of the World Series against the Oakland A's, a snarling, sharp group of professionals united in one thing: their dislike of club owner Finley. "Mr. Jackson," an autograph-seeking little old lady said to Reggie Jackson as the A's pulled up to the stadium in Detroit one afternoon, "are there any more of your friends on that bus?" "Ain't no friends on that bus," Jackson replied.

Mays started the first game of the Series in center field. It was his last start. His first time at bat, he singled on a line to left field . . . and turned first base, stumbled, and had to scramble back. Outside a television booth upstairs, Joe Garagiola said to me, "It's got so you pray they won't hit a fly ball to him." "Leave him alone," I said. "He's retired." Garagiola nodded heavily. "I know," he said. "So who was that who just got the base hit to left?"

In the second game, Mays entered midway through the contest, which went twelve innings. With the score tied, two out and two on in the top of the twelfth, he came to bat, in the last light of an Oakland day that spelled prime TV time in the east, and in the gloom Rollie Fingers, the Oakland relief ace, fired an outside slider past him. Mays seemed not even to see the pitch. Defensively, he stepped out of the batter's box, held a hand up between his eyes and the sky, and the calliope voice shrieked in despair, "I can't *see.*"

Ray Fosse, the Oakland catcher, said nothing. But down between his legs went the hand against the thigh, one slap for a fast ball. Fingers nodded, wound, threw, and here it came.

In the action of releasing the ball—in other words, too late—he wanted it back. Who had ordered that fast ball? Who had signaled for it? Fosse? Uh-uh. Fosse was just doing what Mays had snookered him into doing. The old man knew in advance what the pitch would be. He'd checked the A's into a cinch.

There went a ripped single back through the middle, on one bounce over Fingers's head, here came the winning run, and there went the ball game. It was, in truth, not precisely the most authoritative base hit of Willie's career, and the embellishment this time was not that he stumbled rounding first but that he stumbled getting away from the plate. In each of two previous innings he had wound up playing safe—a euphemism, particularly in his case, for misplaying—long fly balls to center field, which thereby fell safely for extra bases. But the post-game interview in the clubhouse of the winning Mets went:

NBC Reporter Dick Schaap: Did you think Willie was going to get that hit in the twelfth inning?
Mets Pitcher Tom Seaver: Well, he had a good shot at it . . . I think he decoyed the catcher into thinking he couldn't see.
Schaap: How'd he do that?
Seaver: He said (*imitation of Willie's high voice*), "I can't see, man. I can't see. I can't see! That background is terrible!" So they threw the ball right down the pike and base hit. (*Cheerful peal of Seaver laughter.*)

The series went now to New York, where Mays had one pinch-hitting appearance and grounded out, then returned to Oakland with the Mets leading in games, 3 to 2. But the A's won the sixth game 3–1, and then the seventh, 5–2. Met manager Berra had a chance to use Mays as a pinch hitter with two out and two on and the Mets trailing by three in the last of the ninth, in that final game. The setting was dramatic for such a move, and Mays expected it, but it never came. Some fans would find relief in this, some chagrin. In the Bobby Thomson playoff moment in 1951, Mays had been on deck, expecting to hit. Now, in the final game of his last season, in 1973, he was in the dugout, expecting to hit. Big moment for big moment, the man who fulfilled more big moments than any other player in history would go out the same way he came in: by not coming to bat. In the 1951 instance, he didn't even want to come to bat. In the 1973, he did, and that made it more complicated. If he had come to bat, and had hit a home run, the score would be tied and people would talk about him forever. But people were going to talk about him forever anyway, so that was not the issue. Berra's reasoning instead was more doctrinaire: away from home, you played for the winning run, not the tying run. You hoped to prolong the inning, get closer in the score, and then—*then*—call on Willie. But the hitter of the moment, Wayne Garrett, made the final out, so there went that scenario. Mays went into the clubhouse, dressed, drove home from Oakland to Atherton via the Hayward–San Mateo Bridge across the shallow southern reach of San Francisco Bay, entered the house via the kitchen access to the three-car garage, and kicked over a wastebasket in a small burst of fury. Going thereby not quite gentle into that good night.

More than five months into his forty-third year, he was, with the exception of a couple of pitchers, the oldest man ever to appear in a World Series.

Five full seasons must by fiat expire between the end of a man's last season as an active player and the point where he becomes eligible for election to the Hall of Fame. Accordingly, it was late in 1978 that Jack Lang, the secretary of the Baseball Writers' Association of America, mailed out the ballots that first candidated Mays to a prescribed electorate—those writers who had covered the game for at least ten years—and would announce the results in the latter half of January '79.

In 1978, the advice-to-the-moneylorn column in the *Wall Street Journal* carried the headline: SHOULD YOU DISINTERMEDIATE? I did not read the column itself, not so much for the proper fear that I wouldn't understand it as for the outlandish fear that I would. In the Washington *Post*, newsmen William Greider and David DePree did a piece on football coach Bear Bryant at the University of Alabama, and the greener fields. Some extracts:

> Last year's All-American Ozzie Newsome describes the new reality in Alabama sports:
> "Bryant doesn't give a damn what color you are or anything like that. He just wants a winner. You go into the cafeteria and the cooks want you to win. If we don't win, it's not the blacks didn't win or the whites didn't win. It's Alabama didn't win and we're all in trouble." . . .
> This is the place where George Wallace made his stand in the "schoolhouse door" 15 years ago and said: "Never." Everyone smiled in 1976 when Governor Wallace kissed the Homecoming Queen. She was a black named Billie Faye Scott.

(Everyone had smiled in 1973 when it became known that President Nixon had bugged his own offices and telephones. There was a surprisingly minimum amount of outrage that he would record a visitor's words without the visitor's knowledge; it was somewhat muted even that similar things had been done by others before him, even if not to the same degree. The overriding factor instead was the public appetite to learn what was on the tapes.)

In Tupelo, Mississippi, in 1978, former National League publicist Irv Kase noted a graffito on the wall of the men's room in a gas station:

> Black is beautiful,
> Tan is grand,
> But white's still the color
> Of the big boss man.

From the September 1, 1978, San Francisco *Examiner*: "What do unemployed major league baseball managers do to while away the time? Alvin Dark, a five-time loser fired by San Francisco, Kansas City, Oakland, Cleveland and San Diego, will be in Maine shortly to campaign for gubernatorial candidate Rev. Herman C. (Buddy) Frankland, a Baptist minister." Frankland would run a distant third in a field of three. ABC's election-night anchorman Frank Reynolds said he was "not really a serious candidate."

The Greider/DePree piece in the Washington *Post* said:

> Today, there is a genuine amiability among the athletes of both races who eat and live together at Bryant Hall, the jock dorm. In the early years, the black players clustered together, though Bryant made each of them room with a white player. As the numbers increased, the teammates got beyond self-conscious joking. . . .
>
> Ralph Stokes, a high-school All-American from Montgomery's Robert E. Lee High, now an insurance agent, remembers it well:
>
> "When Coach Bryant came to recruit me, the first thing my mother addressed him with was this question: She said, 'I recall vividly seeing you on television saying you don't want any black boys on your teams and now you say you do. Why are you here now? Why do you want my son?' "
>
> Stokes was deeply impressed by Bryant's answer. So was his mother. As Stokes recalls:
>
> "Bryant told her, 'At that time, that was the way I felt. But times have changed and I've matured and changed. I've grown too. My thinking has changed completely and now I don't see any white players or black players anymore—it's just ball players. People are people and they can't be treated by the color of their skin.' "

(The acerb Abe Kemp had expressed his scorn for statistics; the gentle Roger Angell would express his own misgivings: "So many people come up and ask, What is, or was, Willie Mays really like? I don't think that's the right question. What Willie Mays was really like was that he was an extraordinary athlete. He was beautiful to watch—it lifted your imagination. That's what we should remember and pay attention to—watching what these people do. That's why we go to the ball park. The significant thing is not what the ballplayers say about their managers or what they think about the SALT talks. . . . In fact, this sort of reporting tends to diminish the athlete. It's a form of patronizing an athlete to pay less attention to his performance, and more to his success as a TV personality, or how colorful he is, or how well he does on a game show.") Again from the Washington *Post* piece:

Campus social life is restricted for all athletes, but the blacks have found it reasonably free of hassles. Alabama has 2,000 black students now, so there is no shortage of dates. Alabama has had two black Homecoming queens in the last four years and one black student council president.

Joe L. Reed of the Alabama Education Association, a black educator who has pushed for racial equality in the schools, believes that "sports has had a tremendous positive impact. They said never. Now they're cheering."

But in many parts of the state, the black communities paid a heavy price for these changes—the loss of leadership when black principals and coaches were phased out or fired by local school boards. Read said Alabama had 206 black principals before integration, only 53 now. Black coaches suffered a similar attrition.

From a Herb Caen column in the San Francisco *Chronicle* in November of 1978: "The Ku Klux Klan, big in the San Joaquin Valley, had a 'White Power' rally and cross burning in the Stockton area Sat. night, with no objections from city officials. In fact, Quote of the Week honors to Fire Marshall James Kaiser, who told the Stockton Record: 'No fire permit is required for burning a cross since it is classified as a ceremonial or recreational type fire. If it were something like a college or high school bonfire, a permit would be required.' "

As at the first page of this account in 1951, the train called the San Diegan still operated in 1978, and Jack Smith of the Los Angeles *Times* decided on an impulse to take the train from L.A. to San Diego. "The train was moving," he wrote. "It had begun to move so smoothly that I was unaware of movement until a very subtle sense of vibration and momentum told me that it was we who were moving, not the train on the parallel track. I felt the excitement of departure, but without the anxiety of an airplane takeoff. It is a wonderful feeling, remembered from childhood, from our first train ride, stored away in our gray cells and our muscles."

But when the train met the ocean at Dana Point, there was no mail to be picked up, or any railway post office car on the train. It didn't even have a dining car. "But the ads say breakfast is served on the 10:30 train," Smith reported a fellow passenger saying. " 'We tell the management,' the conductor said. 'And . . .' He rolled his eyes and shrugged. 'Tickets?' he said, moving on."

In New York, they named a candy bar REGGIE, for Reggie Jackson, now a Yankee. "Chocolaty covered caramel and peanuts" said a legend in small print on the wrapper. It had to say "Chocolaty" instead of "Chocolate" because there was no chocolate in it. In even smaller print were the ingredients: sugar, peanuts, corn syrup, hydrogenated vegetable oil (contains one or more of the following: palm kernel, coconut, soy bean or cottonseed oil), non-fat dry milk, soy flour, dairy whey, cocoa (processed with alkali), brown sugar, artificial flavors, salt, lecithin (an emulsifier).

The *New Republic* came out in April and contained an article by former Senator McCarthy—not the Republican Joe from the early pages of this book but the Democratic Gene, who had played baseball and written poetry:

Another baseball season is about to begin. It will be a good season. Every baseball season is a good one. The strength of the game is proved year after year, despite expansion teams (which in recent years have done no worse than the old St. Louis Browns used to do season after season) and changes in rules and record-keeping. The designated hitter experiment seems to have done no lasting harm.

The livelier ball has been introduced, but the relative strength of hitters and pitchers seems to be in reasonable balance. The cowhide cover, proposed as a substitute for horsehide, has been rejected. The hardwood bat has survived the onslaught of aluminum and plastic substitutes.

Team loyalty is adequate. Team spirit and loyalty have never been as important in baseball as in other sports, in any case. Baseball teams do not carry chaplains, as do some football teams. They do not gather, kneeling or standing, in a group to pray or hold hands before the game, as basketball teams do, but proceed decently from locker room to dugout to playing field.

Baseball, forever resilient, has adjusted to night games, to artificial turf, to the Astrodome and to Charley Finley. . . . The game is the same, whether played in the Astrodome, in Yankee Stadium or as described by Robert Fitzgerald in his poem called "Cobb Would Have Caught It":

> In sunburnt parks where Sundays lie,
> Or the wide wastes beyond the cities,
> Teams in grey deploy through sunlight.
>
> Talk it up, boys, a little practice,
> Coming in stubby and fast, the baseman
> Gathers a grounder in fat green grass.
> Picks it up stinging and clipped as wit
> Into the leather: a swinging step
> Wings it deadeye down to first.
> Smack. Oh, atta boy, atta old boy.
>
> Catcher reverses his cap, pulls down
> Sweaty casque, and squats in the dust;
> Pitcher rubs new ball on his pants,
> Chewing, puts a jet behind him;
> Nods past batter, taking his time.

Batter settles, tugs at his cap:
A spinning ball: step and swing to it,
Caught like a cheek before it ducks
By shivery hickory: socko, baby:
Cleats dig into dust. Outfielder,
On his way, looking over shoulder,
Makes it a triple; A long peg home.

Innings and afternoons. Fly lost in sunset.
Throwing arm gone bad. There's your ball game.
Cool reek of the field. Reek of companions.

The announcement in January 1979 was *pro forma:* Willie Mays had been elected to the Hall of Fame at Cooperstown. To put it that way is to trivialize it, for he received more votes than any other candidate in the history of Hall of Fame balloting, and the highest percentage in forty-three years, to rank with Cobb, Ruth, and Honus Wagner as the most nearly unanimous selectees of all time. (That "nearly" part got to a lot of people. "If Jesus Christ were to show up with his old baseball glove," Dick Young wrote in the next morning's New York *Daily News,* "some guys wouldn't vote for him. He dropped the cross three times, didn't he?")

In defiance of precedent, the news of Willie's election came not just as an announcement but as a Happening. He was flown cross-country to New York to appear in person at a media-crammed ceremony, flanked by commissioner Kuhn and the Mets' brass. (The absence of Horace Stoneham went poignantly unnoticed: Mays had played 96 percent of his major league career as a Giant, but he joined the Hall of Fame as a Met.)

The lights were hot and the cameras rolled and you knew Willie was there because you heard that laugh. Came The Automatic Question: "Who was the greatest player you ever saw?" His answer was prompt enough: "I thought I was." There was merriment in his eyes as he looked around the room. "I hope I didn't say that wrong." Nobody appeared to think he had said it wrong.

There were the home runs, the other hits, the baserunning, the throwing. All of them Hall of Fame class. But the questions he got were about the way he caught the ball. No mystery there: hitting and running and throwing are things the onlooker sees from the outset. But nobody ever is looking at the outfielder at the moment the ball is hit. You look up, and a thousand different times on a hundred different ball fields, from New York to Tokyo, from Puerto Rico to San Francisco, from Birmingham to Cooperstown, 24 is going to get there before you. They asked him about the catches off Nelson, Bridges, Clemente, Morgan, Wertz, Bouchee, Musial. But Mays shook his head. "I didn't have a best play," he said. "If the ball went up, I know I must catch it. This was for the enjoyment of the people who came out to see me play." They asked him what sort of salary deal he could command if he were a thirty-year-old free agent in the economy of 1979. "Eight million dollars," Mays said. Nobody thought that was strange either. It was philosophy talking, not bitterness. And the figure might have been a tad on the low side.

"Thomas Carlyle wrote that all greatness is unconscious. Nothing could better describe the genius which Mays brought to the baseball diamond. His was the purest form of athletic beauty, a rare and magnificent talent tempered by nothing and excited by a love for the game matched by no man before or since." So wrote a thirty-year-old sports editor in San Rafael, California. In St. Louis, another writer, more than twice that age, said, "To watch Mays play was to watch Rembrandt paint or hear Caruso sing." Two generations in coalescence, but Mays, like baseball itself, had suspended time. There may have been the quality of rebirth in his election to the Hall, but that is baseball's quality as well. A headline in *The Sporting News* said simply, MAYS WAS THE SOUL OF SPRINGTIME.

In Birmingham a black man in his mid-sixties named Ed Steele had a white man on the massage table in the health club where he worked. Steele had played alongside Mays in the out-field with the Black Barons in the late forties. Steele had had a bad first marriage, a luckless tryout in Class AAA ball, some physical problems. By now he had a bad heart. The man on the table grunted and said, "Why don't you get smart and make yourself some extra money?"

"Like how?"

"Do some baseball scouting around here. With your back-ground, you're a natural for it. Find a couple more like Willie Mays."

"Ain't no more like him. His mama didn't have but one."

In fact, Willie's mother had ten other children—her death in 1953 resulted from the birthing of the last of them—in the course of her second marriage. That did not modify Steele's observation a quarter of a century later. In the massage room, the television set was on, giving off a Buick commercial by actor Glenn Ford: "After all," Ford said, "life is to enjoy." A few months later, Steele himself was dead. It happened, in turn, a few months before the election of Mays to the Hall of Fame. Willie himself did not learn immediately of the death of Steele, whose funeral services were performed by the same Rev. William Greason who had been a righthanded pitcher on those same Black Baron teams Steele and Willie played for. Like a couple of other Barons, Greason had had a brief turn in the majors—four innings, in three different games, for the Cardi-nals in 1954. Then he went home to Birmingham and dedicated himself to the church.

Nearly a continent away, in San Francisco, another black man in his mid-sixties tried to adjust the picture on the TV set in the apartment his son rented for him. The problem wasn't with the set; his eyes were going bad. But still Kitty Kat messed with the knobs of the TV set for better focus. *Fly lost in sunset . . . There's your ball game.*

I fell in love with him that afternoon. And watching him then, I realized unconsciously that it was about time he arrived on my horizon. . . . He was what it was all about. He was the reason. In my head, there was a notion of the way things ought to happen, but never do. Not until Willie came along. And then I could finally sit there and say to myself, Oh, sure, *that's it.*

2,992 games . . . 10,881 at-bats . . . 2,062 runs . . . 3,283 hits . . . 140 triples . . . 523 doubles . . . 1,903 runs batted in . . . 7,095 putouts, 7,290 outfield chances accepted . . . 6,066 total bases . . . 338 stolen bases . . . 660 home runs.

I was at it by myself, and I had a lot of hardship that no one knows about. I don't like to speak about it because I was very ashamed of it. I've been told, "Willie, you don't care about your people." But that's a lie.

Thank God for center field! Doctor, you can't imagine how truly glorious it is out there, so alone in all that space. . . .

Harvey Kuenn gave it an honest pursuit, but the only center fielder in baseball who could have caught it hit it.

Kitty Kat had done all he could to adjust the picture. He sat back in his chair. Down the coast 418 miles, the southbound San Diegan hit the bend at Dana Point at 58 miles per hour.

A Note as to Sources

This book reflects reference to, and frequent quotation from, an unconfined variety of source materials. Even to attempt to list them all in a formal bibliography would be a pointless exercise: the research goes back so far in time as to be, in Tom Meany's phrase, *prima facie* evidence of a misspent youth. Though attribution appears elsewhere in these pages, I want here to list particular acknowledgment for extracts from *Portnoy's Complaint* by Philip Roth (Random House, 1967); *Where Have You Gone, Joe DiMaggio?* by Maury Allen (E. P. Dutton, 1975); *The American Diamond* by Branch Rickey with Robert Riger (Simon and Schuster, 1965); *The Summer Game* by Roger Angell (Viking, 1972) and *Five Seasons* by Roger Angell (Simon and Schuster, 1977), specifically in both cases for those pieces by Angell appearing originally in *The New Yorker* in the decade beginning with the mid-1960s; *How the Weather Was* by Roger Kahn (Harper & Row, 1973); *My Twenty-One Years in the White House* by Alonzo Fields (Coward McCann, 1960); column by Red Smith, New York *Herald Tribune*, October 4, 1951; *Memoirs*, Vol. II, by Harry S Truman (Doubleday, 1956); *The Ordeal of Power* by Emmet John Hughes (Atheneum, 1962); *Plain Speaking* by Merle Miller (Berkley, 1973); *The Glory and the Dream* by William Manchester (Little, Brown, 1974); *A Day in the Bleachers* by Arnold Hano (Crowell, 1955); article by Jack Orr, *Sport*, 1953; *Babe* by Robert W. Creamer (Simon and Schuster, 1974); *No Cheering in the Press Box*, recorded and edited by Jerome Holtzman (Holt, Rinehart & Winston, 1974); *The Making of the President 1960* by Theodore H. White (Atheneum, 1961); serialized article by Richard Donovan, *Collier's*, 1953; *A Thousand Days* by Arthur M. Schlesinger, Jr. (Houghton Mifflin, 1965); *The Final Days* by Bob Woodward and Carl Bernstein (Simon and Schuster, 1976); *Base-

ball Has Done It by Jackie Robinson, edited by Charles Dexter (Lippincott, 1964); column by Charles McCabe, San Francisco *Chronicle*, September 13, 1965; column by Milton Gross, New York *Post*, September 11, 1965; article by Shana Alexander, *Life*, July 16, 1965; article by Derek Wright, *Life*, April 16, 1971; *The Vantage Point* by Lyndon Baines Johnson (Holt, Rinehart & Winston, 1971); *Farewell to Sport* by Paul Gallico (Knopf, 1938); *The Hot Stove League* by Lee Allen (Barnes, 1955); *The Selling of the President 1968* by Joe McGinniss (Trident, 1969); *The Greening of America* by Charles A. Reich (Random House, 1970); *The Way It Is* by Curt Flood with Richard Carter (Trident, 1971); serialized article by William Greider and David DePree, Washington *Post*, September 3–4, 1978; article by Eugene J. McCarthy, *The New Republic*, April 22, 1978.

Brief sections of this book appeared in slightly different version in the author's preface to *The Fireside Book of Baseball* (Simon and Schuster, 1956) and *A Flag for San Francisco* (Simon and Schuster, 1962). Quotations appear here also from my news reports in the San Francisco *Examiner* in 1961 and from scripts and interview transcripts for Lee Mendelson Productions in 1963, 1974, and 1977. Chief among the many record books consulted were *The Baseball Register*, *The Baseball Encyclopedia*, *National League Green Book*, *The Book of Baseball Records* (formerly *The Little Red Book of Major League Baseball*), and the annual media guides of the New York/San Francisco Giants and New York Mets. Other paramount baseball sources, over and above the personal friends and colleagues over the years who both fondly and literally are beyond counting, have been the files of *The Sporting News*, the A. G. Spalding Collection of the New York Public Library, and the National Baseball Museum and Hall of Fame at Cooperstown, New York.

And special grateful mention is owing to my literary agent Eleanor Wood, to Al Silverman of Viking Penguin, and to the production talents of Dolores Reilly, Jeff Kozera, and Wilma Jane Weichselbaum for all they did to bring this 1992 Penguin re-issue of *Willie's Time* into being.   C.E.